PENGUIN BOOKS

THE ACTOR'S BOOK
OF CLASSICAL SCENES

STEFAN RUDNICKI was born in Kraków, Poland, and lived in Stockholm, Sweden, and Montreal, Canada, before arriving in the United States—where he was educated principally at Columbia University and the Yale School of Drama.

In addition to having directed over one hundred thirty theatrical productions in New York, regional theatre, and abroad (more than a quarter of them classics and fifteen by Shakespeare), he is also an actor, producer, award-winning playwright, photographer, and film and video director.

He has taught at the University of Rochester, the Eastman School of Music, New York University, Dartmouth College, the State University of New York at Old Westbury, and Long Island University's C. W. Post campus, where for six years he chaired the Department of Theatre and Film.

He has been artistic director of Skyboat Road Company since 1979, and with his wife, Judith, resides alternately in New York City and Los Angeles, teaching, coaching, developing new film and television projects, and continuing to evolve his Interactive Matrix Process for performers. He is the author of *The Actor's Book of Classical Monologues* and *The Actor's Book of Monologues for Women,* both published by Penguin USA.

THE ACTOR'S BOOK OF

Classical Scenes

COLLECTED AND INTRODUCED BY

Stefan Rudnicki

PENGUIN BOOKS

PENGUIN BOOKS
Published by the Penguin Group
Viking Penguin, a division of Penguin Books USA Inc.,
375 Hudson Street, New York, New York 10014, U.S.A.
Penguin Books Ltd, 27 Wrights Lane, London W8 5TZ, England
Penguin Books Australia Ltd, Ringwood, Victoria, Australia
Penguin Books Canada Ltd, 10 Alcorn Avenue, Suite 300, Toronto, Ontario, Canada M4V 3B2
Penguin Books (N.Z.) Ltd, 182–190 Wairau Road, Auckland 10, New Zealand

Penguin Books Ltd, Registered Offices:
Harmondsworth, Middlesex, England

First published in Penguin Books 1992

1 3 5 7 9 10 8 6 4 2

Grateful acknowledgment is made for permission to reprint excerpts from the following copyrighted works:

Agamemnon by Aeschylus and *Electra* by Sophocles, translated by Kenneth Cavander, from *The Greeks* by John Barton and Kenneth Cavander. Reprinted by permission of the Agency for the Performing Arts, Inc.

Antigone by Sophocles and *Hippolytus* by Euripides, translated by Kenneth Cavander. By permission of the Agency for the Performing Arts, Inc.

The Bacchae by Euripides, translated by William Arrowsmith, from *The Complete Greek Tragedies,* edited by David Grene and Richmond Lattimore. By permission of The University of Chicago Press.

Medea from *Medea and Other Plays* by Euripides, translated by Philip Vellacott (Penguin Classics, 1963). Copyright © Philip Vellacott, 1963.

Lysistrata from *Lysistrata and Other Plays* by Aristophanes, translated by Alan H. Somerstein (Penguin Classics, 1973). Copyright © Alan H. Somerstein, 1973.

CAUTION: Professionals and amateurs are hereby warned that the translations of the plays cited above are subject to a royalty. They are fully protected under the copyright laws of the United States of America, and of all countries covered by the International Copyright Union (including the Dominion of Canada and the rest of the British Commonwealth), and of all countries covered by the Pan-American Copyright Convention and the Universal Copyright Convention, and of all countries with which the United States has reciprocal copyright relations. All rights, including professional, amateur, motion picture, recitation, lecturing, public reading, radio broadcasting, television, video or sound taping, all other forms of mechanical or electronic reproduction, such as information storage and retrieval systems and photocopying, and the rights of translation into foreign languages, are strictly reserved. Particular emphasis is laid upon the question of readings, permission for which must be secured from the authors' agent in writing.

LIBRARY OF CONGRESS CATALOGING-IN-PUBLICATION DATA
Actor's book of classical scenes / collected and introduced by Stefan Rudnicki.
p.   cm.
Includes bibliographical references.
ISBN 0 14 01.5716 6
1. Acting.   2. Drama.   I. Rudnicki, Stefan.
PN2080.A2833   1992
792'.028—dc20   91-46831

Printed in the United States of America
Set in Garamond #3
Designed by Kathryn Parise

PREFACE

When I began to teach acting classes in Hollywood, a friend suggested to me that I downplay my classical background and inclinations, believing that a classical bias would scare away actors who were in the business mostly to work in films and become stars. I found, on the contrary, that actors very soon began bringing me classical scenes they wanted to work on. And indeed it seems to me that any actor serious enough to pursue training on a regular basis will immediately recognize the value of working with classical themes and language. Most of the scenes included in this volume were extensively and repeatedly explored by members of first The Shakespeare Project and then Classical Matrix Lab, both of which I developed so that professionals could study classical theatre with a view to applying the resulting techniques and discoveries to other, more modern material. That work, performed over a period of nearly two years, was successful enough to generate a recognizable and particularly lucid style of performance, a style that could be easily adapted to virtually any material or performance medium. One student insisted to me that he had booked a major national commercial by directly applying to the commercial copy handed him those techniques that we had developed working on Shake-speare. In fact, I have been pleased to find repeatedly that experience with classical theatre helps an actor prepare for on-camera work by enhancing vocal variety, reinforcing clarity and specificity of focus, and, by emphasizing narrative rather than emotional work, making it easier for the actor to perform small segments of script out of sequence.

The "matrix" work, as I call it, is simply defined as a series of techniques intended to ground or center the actor by placing him in relationship to as many things—the space, other actors, props, history, the text itself—as possible. This grounding is reinforced by work on scale, which I define as an association with issues and circumstances beyond those that are merely personal. This sense of scale, not related to size or volume necessarily, helps the actor to raise the stakes, to make everything he does more important, but without overacting or relying on self-indulgent emotional acrobatics. Add to this an awareness of narrative—storytelling, that is—and a reverence for language as a tool for telling that story, and the picture is pretty much complete. I have already presented certain details of these techniques in the introductory material to *The Actor's Book of Classical Monologues* and *The Actor's Book of Monologues for Women.* As the present volume is intended to be an actor's source book and not a textbook, I shall limit my discussion of the techniques to the chapter introductions, trusting the actor to make his own applications. To help the actor in the kind of research that is necessary when facing material from other times and cultures, I am including a bibliography of resource works.

The Shakespeare section is the largest because Shakespeare is still the most accessible ancient to the modern actor, and because in my teaching I have found Shakespeare's plays to be the most comprehensive and viable access point to all other classical material. Although the specific language guidelines I have indicated in my introduction to that section will not necessarily work at all times and with all other playwrights, they represent principles that are sufficiently universal that they should at least be tried whenever possible.

Except for my editorial slant in the Shakespeare selections, I have kept the scenes for the most part intact, direct from my sources, so the material in the other three sections of the book represents a fairly wide variety of editorial styles. I have also usually not cut out the occasional minor character who might serve to suggest the public dimension so often present in these scenes. In my choice of scenes I have not, as with my previous books, placed a great premium on obscurity. Instead, I have allowed famous scenes from well-known plays to rest beside less familiar works, insisting that every selection provide the actors with a new problem to solve and new skills to achieve.

CONTENTS

II   The Age of Shakespeare: Scenes by Shakespeare

INTRODUCTION
75

III The Age of Shakespeare: Scenes by Shakespeare's Contemporaries

INTRODUCTION
267

IV The Age of Style:
Restoration and Eighteenth-Century Scenes

INTRODUCTION
355

PART I

The Golden Age:

SCENES FROM GREEK ANTIQUITY

INTRODUCTION

Work on Greek scenes is the perfect antidote to the smallness and overpersonalization of so much of today's acting. More so than any of the other material in this book, each of these selections is an exercise in public scale and cosmic dimension.

An Exercise in Scale

I suggest that the term "exercise" be taken seriously here. Not only are the language, culture, and theatrical conventions that gave rise to this drama alien to us, but we are also unfamiliar with the extended level of commitment required to even begin to make dramatic sense of each situation. It is not that the characters and relationships are somehow superhuman. Indeed, very often these scenes are enlivened by bits of funny, very human, even domestic detail. It is rather that there is a constant awareness of larger presences that renders every action, every word much more important than we are used to making them.

These presences may be best identified and kept distinct by constructing a time line. In the past is all the history leading up to this very moment. It is populated principally by ancestors, but also by those ancestors' enemies. These are specific characters, with names, personalities, and functions. The actor refers to them, defers to them, and often speaks directly to them. Frequently he even speaks *for* them, finding in the acts of a predecessor the motivation for his current actions. In the present are the masses of people that are being affected by the action of the scene. These are usually represented by the ever-present Chorus, necessarily less individuated than the ancestors, but providing essential social and political contexts for the actor, so that everything he does may be seen in the light of their usually conservative perspective. There is no privacy possible here, no respite from the Chorus's scrutiny and comment. The Chorus, ranging in size from nine to fifteen members, also provides a bridge to the future by representing an onstage audience, a link to the real audience out there in the amphitheatre. For the Greeks a principal function of the drama was to educate, and so to both playwright and actor that audience of citizens would represent the future: the students who were to be taught and who were later to judge for all posterity the historical validity and aesthetic worth of words, ideas, and performance values.

The point of the exercise, then, is for each actor to maintain an awareness of each of these populations—past, present, and future— while performing as fully as possible the actions called for in the scene. I am, by the way, purposely not using the word "character" here. I believe that for the Greeks, as with most classical theatre, there was an acceptance of the actor as speaker that did not depend on those elements which we today consider character values. The actor was narrator and spokesman, sometimes doubling and tripling personas by a simple exchange of masks. In the manner of a story-teller, the actor would emphasize rather than hide the mechanics of his craft, being always very much present himself.

Scenes of the Atreides

The first four scenes take place in the wake of the Trojan War and present several stages in the history of the House of Atreus. Beginning with Agamemnon's triumphant return, the story traces his death at the hands of his wife, Clytemnestra, and her lover, Aegisthus, and the subsequent effect of the murder on the children Electra, Orestes, and, to perhaps a lesser degree, Chrysothemis. It is a classic story of revenge, with every violent act motivated by some real or perceived injustice in the past and with each principal acting in the interest of ending the cycle of violence forever. That the cycle actually ends has more to do, at least in the Aeschylus version, with the intervention of the gods on behalf of the future of Athens than with the efficacy of any individual act.

When Agamemnon first arrives home, he is greeted by Clytemnestra and the Chorus. Their scene is a model of miscommunication and nuance. They have been apart for so long and their agendas are so different that indeed any genuine understanding seems doomed from the start. Clytemnestra lays a trap for her husband by encouraging a public show of pride. Agamemnon, albeit reluctantly, agrees to walk on the tapestries laid at his feet. Far from being an innocent victim, though, he flaunts, quite publicly, his special war prize and concubine, the prophetess Cassandra. The scene at one level is among the simplest ever written, with only a couple of overt actions. Its richness comes from the complexity of its public dimension, where every small detail is to be examined and judged not only by those present, but also by all posterity and, of course, the gods themselves. For Aeschylus, the author of this first scene, that public dimension always takes precedence. It is this that makes his plays seem most distant and difficult to us, appearing static and terribly formal. By fully acknowledging that public, however, a scene like this one can take on a special liveliness, an energy not unlike that of a talk show or a political rally.

After Agamemnon is killed, Electra confronts her mother. This scene, from Sophocles' *Electra,* is less formal, suggesting a more personal involvement between two persons who know each other well enough to place their verbal arrows with keen precision. The public dimension, although not as obvious as in Aeschylus, is still very present, as Clytemnestra confesses to Agamemnon's murder and calls "Justice" to her side in an attempt to justify her actions while trying at the same time to discredit Electra. There is no reconciliation possible; there is only the suggestion that everything that has led these two women to this place and time has been somehow fated. For both mother and daughter, Agamemnon's presence is very strong, and the scene can work only if that presence is physically located in space. Because Clytemnestra recalls Agamemnon with loathing, while Electra remembers her father as a hero, the location should not be the same for both.

When Chrysothemis comes to Electra to tell her that she has

seen evidence of their brother Orestes' presence, the action seems to become even more personal, but it is hardly private. As with every Sophoclean scene both persons argue from a powerful sense of commitment to their own truth, and neither will be deflected from her course. Electra herself says, "I speak for Justice," while Chrysothemis takes a more common-sense stand with "Justice can be lethal." Both invoke history and precedent. And if in spite of all this we still get wrapped up in the family drama, we are reminded of the public dimension by the intrusion of the Chorus: judging, giving advice, taking sides, always present and active.

Even Orestes' homecoming scene is virtually engineered by the Chorus, and only the slightest moment of personal joy is allowed before all is business and murder again. The public sense is heightened here in a particularly interesting way by reference being made in the dialogue to the danger of being overheard by the enemy, Clytemnestra and Aegisthus, in the palace.

The presences of which I have spoken are a much more intrinsic part of this story than they might seem at first glance. I have had the opportunity in workshop to apply the sense of public awareness to scenes from Eugene O'Neill's psychologized updating of the story, *Mourning Becomes Electra,* and have found these principles to operate with considerable success. With O'Neill in particular, there is an exciting melodramatic dimension that is denied by informal, internalized, and unenunciated performance. By placing his retelling in a world populated by public ethical and moral issues, wars, and the ghosts of family history, the stakes are significantly heightened.

Scenes of the Thebans

The story of Antigone is at least as much the story of Creon, Oedipus's brother-in-law/uncle, who must take over Thebes and try to create order out of chaos. Here, in Sophocles' telling, the emphasis is on impassioned, unswerving commitment to a task, an ideal, a moral or civic duty. History, of course, weighs heavily, and it seems that all the future of mankind may in some respect be little more than the playing out of the consequences of these people's actions.

The pivotal scene between Antigone and Creon has been retold by modern dramatists more than possibly any other classical scene. The original, although without Brecht's political emphasis or Anouilh's sentimentality, plays more powerfully than any more recent version. Called to account for having buried her civil-war-slain brother Polineices, Antigone cites "divine law" and her belief in the unexpressed support of the community, while Creon calls upon civil law, his own authority as king, and rational thought. The key to this scene is that they are both right, both justified by their own traditions, and yet each is destined to defend a position that the other cannot comprehend, let alone support.

By the time Creon is visited by his son and Antigone's betrothed, Haimon, matters have gone much further, and Antigone has been condemned. In the speech that precedes their scene, Haimon pleads for her, arguing the need for flexibility, especially in the volatile political climate the situation has caused. Haimon is the rational one this time, while Creon, enraged by his son's apparent betrayal and the apparently unnatural phenomenon of child lecturing parent, completely loses perspective. There is a gentle persuasiveness to much of Haimon's argument that contrasts severely with Creon's explosive anger. Even more than in the scene with Antigone, who argues more completely on Creon's turf, we are seeing the emergence of what today we would call character by means of contrasting styles of presentation.

Scenes by Euripides

The writings of both Aeschylus and Sophocles are remarkable for their clarity: the structural integrity of the stories, the rhetorical precision of the dialogue, and the comprehensive moral and religious world view that is espoused. The plays of Euripides, by contrast, are characterized by ambiguities at every level. Many of his plays end vaguely or are broken-backed, with at least two stylistically unrelated sections. His language is lyrical, more expressive of emotional than rational reality. And instead of placing a premium on justice, fate, or civic pride, Euripides dives into deeper caverns where perception and reality have little in common, where there are secrets lurking behind every door, and where even the gods cannot be trusted. These qualities make Euripides a favorite among modern theatre practitioners, who are happy to interpret his plays in narrow psychological contexts, but remain blind to the massive scale of his awareness and the associated overwhelming religious and cosmic doubts that the plays suggest.

In *The Bacchae,* the first meeting between Pentheus and Dionysus seems at first glance to build in a manner similar to a Sophoclean argument. But it does not. Dionysus does not answer a single question directly; he admits to nothing. He plays an oblique game, to which Pentheus does not know the rules. Pentheus's arrogance, and perhaps his fear, blind him to Dionysus's power, but we know that Dionysus could destroy Pentheus in a flash and that he himself has literally nothing to lose by the encounter. The resulting scene is almost comic in tone, as Dionysus toys with his would-be captor. The Chorus of Asian Bacchae, followers of Dionysus, stays in the background, but they are in on the game, and one can imagine the sly looks, the smirks that they surreptitiously share at Pentheus's expense. The scene is just as public as any in Aeschylus or Sophocles, but each principal is playing to a different audience. There is even a geographical scale that Dionysus brings with him which transcends most other drama of *any* period.

When Pentheus emerges in his woman's getup, he is actually beginning to share Dionysus's reality in some fundamental way. But there is still no contest, as he is completely under the god's control, seeing in his hallucinatory state only what Dionysus wants him to. The scene is perverse, as askew as Pentheus's vision. It is a kind of love scene, a lyrical interlude in which Dionysus seduces Pentheus by way of images of Pentheus's mother, Agave. Here Pentheus achieves the scale of vision that Dionysus offers, but only by losing what power he might still have left. The result here too is at least partly comic, tempered with the horror of what we suspect or know will come. In both scenes, the dialogue is tightly written and needs to be cued, even topped, to maximize the effect.

Although no god herself, Medea also has powers that her spouse and adversary, Jason, has only the slightest inkling of until the end of the play. Her source of power is the earth goddess, Hecate, associated with the night, witchcraft, and blood sacrifices. When hearing of Jason's impending marriage to the Corinthian princess Glauce, Medea is subject to no law but her jealousy. Aided by the dark power of Hecate, she fashions a poisoned garment that burns Glauce to death, and then she kills her own and Jason's children. This last scene, before she flies off in a dragon-pulled chariot, is a mutual public condemnation, in the eyes of audience, history, the gods, and the dead children.

Irrational impulses drive the story of Phaedra and Hippolytus as well, in this case helped along by feuding deities. Innocent Hippolytus, son of the Athenian hero Theseus, is devoted to Artemis, the virgin moon-goddess of the hunt. Aphrodite, the goddess of love, feels slighted and infects Phaedra, his stepmother, with a passion for Hippolytus, which he rejects. Scorned, Phaedra tells Theseus that his son has made improper advances. Hippolytus is banished, then killed by a sea monster, while Phaedra kills herself, and so the story goes.

In the first scene, the Nurse wheedles a confession from Phaedra. The Nurse can be any sort of private servant, not necessarily older than Phaedra. The scene plays in a breathless manner, building to the revelation of Phaedra's love, after which she becomes quiet while the Nurse reacts violently to information she now wishes she did not have. In my experience working this scene, it is useful for the Nurse to physically hound Phaedra, literally following her around, until Phaedra's story begins to emerge and the Nurse begins to back away.

When Theseus banishes Hippolytus, he too is driven by a passion, in this instance irrational jealousy. Hippolytus's defense is a model of reasonable argument, but Theseus will not listen. Nowhere does Euripides' style contrast more strongly with Sophocles', for not only is Theseus patently wrong, but both men, not to mention Phaedra herself, are victims of an uncaring, vicious goddess in a universe that bears no real justice. In fact, most of Euripides' plays center around victims or their powerful torturers.

Greek Comedy

It is difficult to work on scenes from Aristophanes' comedies away from the context of a full production, as they were meant to be performed with extensive music, masks, and costume elements, and therein lies a great deal of their humor. Also, while the political and religious overtones of the tragedies often have at least a resonance of universality, burlesques on the same issues just do not have the comic impact they obviously had twenty-four hundred years ago.

Lysistrata is therefore Aristophanes' most popular play, because it deals primarily with sex, or the lack of it, as the women of Athens go on a sex strike to prevent their men from going to war. The scene I have included probably carries the most universal appeal. Myrrhine, coached by Lysistrata, teases her husband, Cinesias, trying to make him promise to vote for peace. The scene, like most of Aristophanes' writing, is verbally bawdy and overtly physical.

Agamemnon
by Aeschylus

CLYTEMNESTRA, AGAMEMNON

CLYTEMNESTRA

Now my sufferings are over
And I greet you here with joy,
The watchdog of our house,
The forestay of our ship
And the pillar of our roof.
You are like a bubbling spring
To a traveller who is thirsty.

O my love, my darling,
Do not let your foot
Which has crushed the Trojans
Step now upon the earth.
Women, all of you,
Help me to strew the ground
With tapestries and silk.
Come, all of you, strew his way
And lead him as is just
Into this house, the home
He never hoped to see.

(They lay down rich cloths)

AGAMEMNON

Daughter of Leda,
What you have just said
Was much like my absence,

Too long. Do not try
To pamper me like a woman
Or treat me like a Trojan
By bowing to me and fawning.
You've thrown down pretty cloths
For me to tread on: perfect
If I were a god
But I am a human being,
A mortal man; I cannot
Walk upon these things.
If you must honour me
Then treat me as a man
And not as a god. My fame
Doesn't need these frills.
The greatest gift of the gods
Is a mind that is modest.
You know you should never praise
A man for his own good fortune
Till you see how things are with him
On the day he dies.

CLYTEMNESTRA ·

But our house is full
Of lovely things like this.
You are a king not a beggar
And you have come home.
You are like a tree
Whose leaves spread out and shade us
Against the sun. You are
A miracle, a warmth
That comes to us in winter.
And when Zeus comes and ripens
The green grapes into wine
It will be cool and lovely
Because the master's back
And walks about the house.

AGAMEMNON

I've told you what I think:
I'd feel uneasy, false.

CLYTEMNESTRA

Uneasy here at home?
But why? The war is over.

AGAMEMNON

I have said it: I'm a man.
You must treat me as a man.

CLYTEMNESTRA

O give in to me in this:
Let me have my will.

AGAMEMNON

You know my will and I
Do not intend to change it.

CLYTEMNESTRA

But why do you say that?
Are you superstitious?

AGAMEMNON

No, I'm sensible.
I know what I am doing.

CLYTEMNESTRA

You speak as if you'd never
Changed your mind before.

AGAMEMNON

I change it when I'm wrong,
Not when I'm in the right.

CLYTEMNESTRA

If Priam had won the war
What would he have done?

AGAMEMNON

O I am quite certain
He would have marched on silk.

CLYTEMNESTRA

Then you should not fear
What men will say of you.

AGAMEMNON

Why not? I respect
The opinion of the people.

CLYTEMNESTRA

Come, no one admires
The man that is not envied.

AGAMEMNON

I have been honoured enough:
I do not need it here.

CLYTEMNESTRA

No honour is too great
For the conqueror of Troy.

AGAMEMNON

I know you love to argue
But it does not suit a woman.

CLYTEMNESTRA

It sometimes suits great men
To yield a point with grace.

AGAMEMNON

I say this love of battle
Is unwomanly. Give in!

CLYTEMNESTRA

No, it becomes the victor
To yield the victory.

AGAMEMNON

Victory in this argument?
Is it so important?

CLYTEMNESTRA

You are all-powerful:
Let me have some power.
If you will yield in this
Then you will *be* the victor.

AGAMEMNON

If that is what you wish,
You, untie my shoes.
May no god catch sight of me
If I trample underfoot
Such delicate, precious things.
O, I am ashamed
To spoil such workmanship
With my tired, dirty feet.
(CLYTEMNESTRA *takes off his shoes which she gives to the* SOLDIERS
and then embraces him lovingly)
Come, enough of this.
Take in this girl, Cassandra.
You must be good to her.
I think the gods look kindly
On a gentle conqueror.
No one wants to be a slave.
This woman, a princess,
Came to me as the gift
Of the whole Greek army.
Of all Troy's riches
She's the jewel, the flower . . .
(*He unveils and kisses her*)

And now, I am ready.
My will is yours:
I will make my way along
This cascade of pretty things
And go into the house.

Electra
by Sophocles

CLYTEMNESTRA, ELECTRA

CLYTEMNESTRA

You would not still love him
If you really had known him.
He was a self-deceiver
Who always blamed the gods
For his own mistakes. He talked
Of doing what is right
But he never did it. No,
He always did the wrong things,
The selfish, the mean, the easy.
He thought he could steal from Apollo
His so-called "Virgin Priestess";
He thought he could bring her home
And be sweet with her in front of me.

O can't you understand?
Nothing in the world
Hurts a woman more
Than to love and to be hurt.
When a husband looks for love
Outside his marriage
Shall we not do as he does?
Why are we women blamed for it
But never our guilty husbands?

I have no regrets,
And if you think me evil
Look into your own hearts
Before you judge another.

ELECTRA

Well, for once you cannot say
That it's me who provokes you.
Now will you let me reply?

CLYTEMNESTRA

Of course. If you were always
As reasonable as that
I'd be glad to listen to you.

ELECTRA

In spite of all you say
My father was a fine man:
I remember. It is vile
That you try to blot that out.
You admit you murdered him
But what could be worse than that
Even if it was justified?
Love was your real motive,
Love for the man you now live with.
For Iphigenia's death,
It was sacrifice, not murder.
The blame belongs to Artemis
But even if it did not,
Would that excuse you?
By what law did you kill him?
If life for life's your law
Then you yourself must die:
That would be Justice.
Argue yourself out of that.
But I must not rebuke you:
You are my mother.

O no, you're not:
You are Aegisthus' mistress.

What else should I be?
The wife of a husband
Who leaves his bed empty
For ten long years?
Ask any woman.
It is sad but it is natural
But you don't understand that.
You prefer to sleep alone.

Yes I do, but you prefer
To be like your sister Helen:
You both live for lust.
She wasn't raped: she wanted it.
And I remember you
Before you went to Aulis:
You sat before your mirror—
O yes, I saw you—
Setting your pretty curls
And smoothing out your hair.
The wife who takes such pains
To enhance her own beauty
In her husband's absence
Is bad, bad, bad.
You didn't want him back,
No, nor Orestes neither.
Why, when you murdered my father,
Did you not make over to us
Our father's house to rule in?

You know that we hold it
In your father's brother's name.
We hold it for Menelaus

Who was lost in the storm
Seven years ago.
It is said that he still lives
And will come back some day.

ELECTRA

And then you will give it to him?

CLYTEMNESTRA

We will decide that
As and when he comes.

ELECTRA

"As and when he comes":
No, you like your riches
Your Trojan rugs and slave-girls.
O you may call me evil
But if that is what I am
I am only showing the nature
Of the mother who conceived me.

CLYTEMNESTRA

O my child, my child,
It has always been your nature
To love your father most.
That is quite natural.
Some love their fathers best
And some love their mothers:
I understand and I forgive you.
Why can't you do the same?
I am not so happy
With what I've done or am.
Somewhere, at some time
I have lost my way . . .
You, you look dreadful,
All dirty and unwashed.
O it has all turned out
So wretchedly. Perhaps

I let my fury swamp me
More than I should have done.

ELECTRA

If you are so contrite
Bring Orestes home.

CLYTEMNESTRA

I am afraid of him.
They say that he is angry
And this news disturbs me
Just as you disturb me.

ELECTRA

Why do you let Aegisthus
Be so brutal to me?

CLYTEMNESTRA

Because that is his nature.
You are just as stubborn:
You have no shame at all.

ELECTRA

Yes, I do have shame.
I cringe to hear myself,
I cringe at my vicious temper.
This is not the true Electra,
Nor the woman I really am.
You make me what I am
By your hatred of me.
Ugliness is taught,
You see, by ugliness.

CLYTEMNESTRA

It is true that you look ugly.
You do not seem to mind.

ELECTRA

What should I do? Look beautiful
Like you . . . all stench inside?

CLYTEMNESTRA

You are your father's daughter,
Quarrelsome and violent.

ELECTRA

No, I am like these slaves,
Homeless and in your power.

CLYTEMNESTRA

Me, always me.
It's always what I do.

ELECTRA

It's you who does the talking.
Your deeds speak for you, mother.

CLYTEMNESTRA

Why blame me for your misery?
Blame my sister, Helen.

ELECTRA

I do. You are both alike:
Both murderers, both evil.

CLYTEMNESTRA

O what is the point of talking?
You turn it all against me.

ELECTRA

Everything you say
Cries out against you!

CLYTEMNESTRA

Well, you will pay for this
When Aegisthus comes home.

ELECTRA

There. You let me speak,
And then you lose your temper.

CLYTEMNESTRA

I have heard you out.

ELECTRA

No, you've never learned to listen.

CLYTEMNESTRA

Now will you please be quiet
And let me pray to the Gods
As I came here to do?

ELECTRA

O please, Go on. Pray:
I shall not say a word.

CLYTEMNESTRA

(*To her* WOMEN)
Bring the offerings,
The fruits of the earth
So that I may pray
For relief from all my fears.
(*At the altar*)
Great Apollo, hear me:
I whisper to you because
I am not among friends.
Yet hear what I do say:
The dream I dreamed last night,
The dream with the doubtful meaning,
Grant that it may come true

In so far as it was good
But if it was ill-omened
Then let that ill descend
On my enemies, not me.
Let me go on living
Unthreatened and unharmed,
Ruling the house of Atreus,
Living with my loved ones,
And also, if it may be,
With children who do not hate me
Or make me feel ashamed.
O Apollo, hear me,
And give to each of us
What each of us is praying for . . .

ELECTRA

Goddess of Vengeance, hear me.
And speak now for the dead!

CLYTEMNESTRA

She has heard and she has spoken.

Electra
by Sophocles

CHRYSOTHEMIS, ELECTRA

CHRYSOTHEMIS

O my darling, I'm so happy.
Orestes is here. He's home.

ELECTRA

You're mad or you're mocking me.

CHRYSOTHEMIS

I swear to you he's here.

ELECTRA

Who told you?

CHRYSOTHEMIS

I saw the proof.

ELECTRA

What did you see? Tell me.

CHRYSOTHEMIS

Apollo has sent us a sign.
When I got to our father's grave
I saw fresh milk and flowers
And a new-cut strand of hair.
I took it in my hands
And I started to weep for joy.
I knew he must have brought it.
We didn't put it there
And it couldn't be our mother.
She doesn't do such things,
Or if she does
She'd do it publicly.
They are Orestes' offerings.
O my darling, have courage.

ELECTRA

I pity you. What a fool.

CHRYSOTHEMIS

It's true. Why aren't you happy?

ELECTRA

It's a fantasy of yours.

CHRYSOTHEMIS

No, I saw with my own eyes.

ELECTRA

He is dead.

CHRYSOTHEMIS

Who says so?

ELECTRA

A man who saw it happen.

CHRYSOTHEMIS

Where is this man?

ELECTRA

Inside,
Talking to our mother.

CHRYSOTHEMIS

But the offerings at the grave?

ELECTRA

Someone must have left them
In memory of Orestes.

(*Pause*)

CHRYSOTHEMIS

I see that nothing has changed:
Our sorrows are the same
Except that there are more of them.

ELECTRA

Listen, Chrysothemis,
Now that our brother's dead,
I depend on you to help me.
Well, are you strong enough?
Do you dare to help me kill them?

25

Everyone loves courage.
If we do as I say
People will marvel at us:
"Look at those two sisters,"
That's what they will say,
"They rescued their father's house
And risked their lives to do it.
O how we should love them,
Admire them and respect them
For their courage." You must help me.

CHORUS

—Be careful now, think.
—These words are dangerous.
—Before you decide that
Ask if it is safe.

CHRYSOTHEMIS

That is good advice.
O Electra, you forget
You are only a woman.
If you kill Aegisthus
His guards will cut you down.
Fame and respect and monuments
Won't do us any good
If both of us die for it.
Think what you are doing,
Before you destroy us both
And our family as well.
They are stronger than we are.

CHORUS

—Electra, she is right.
—You must be sensible.

ELECTRA

I knew it would go like this.
I must do it alone.

CHRYSOTHEMIS

It's hopeless. They will kill you.

ELECTRA

Go away. You're useless.

CHRYSOTHEMIS

You only see your own way.

ELECTRA

Why don't you run and tell mother?

CHRYSOTHEMIS

I don't want to hurt you.

ELECTRA

You're hurting me now.

CHRYSOTHEMIS

But I want to save you.

ELECTRA

Must I see through your eyes?

CHRYSOTHEMIS

Yes, when yours deceive you.

ELECTRA

I speak for Justice.

CHRYSOTHEMIS

Justice can be lethal.

ELECTRA

You do not frighten me.

CHRYSOTHEMIS

I'll leave you. We have nothing
To say to one another.

ELECTRA

Yes, go away. Leave me.
I won't ask you again
Even if you begged me.

CHRYSOTHEMIS

No, if you are so sure
That your way is right
Then you must pursue it
But when you start to pay for it
You'll wish you'd followed mine.

Electra
by Sophocles

ORESTES, ELECTRA

ORESTES

Is this Aegisthus' palace?

CHORUS

Yes, what do you want?

ORESTES

I am a man from Phocis:
I bring news of Orestes.

ELECTRA

What is it? I am frightened.

ORESTES

I've brought all that remains of him.

ELECTRA

O Gods, give it to me.
Here is all that's left of him . . .
Of Orestes, who lived once
And died far off in exile,
A handful of nothing,
A little jar of dust:
Once I used to nurse you.
I loved you even more
Than your own mother did.
Now you are dead
And I am dead in you.
O brother, take me with you:
I want to end the pain.

ORESTES

You are Electra?

ELECTRA

Yes.

ORESTES

Who makes you live like this?

ELECTRA

The creature called my mother.

ORESTES

Are these women loyal to you?

ELECTRA

Yes, they are loyal.

ORESTES

Give me the urn.

ELECTRA

O no.

ORESTES

Yes. You must not mourn him.

ELECTRA

Not mourn? My brother's dead.

ORESTES

No, don't weep for him.

ELECTRA

I must, he was my brother.

ORESTES

That is not your brother.

ELECTRA

Then where is he? Did you bury him?

ORESTES

No, there is no grave.

ELECTRA

What are you trying to say?

ORESTES

The truth.

ELECTRA

He is alive?

ORESTES

Yes, if I am alive.

ELECTRA

Are you . . . is it you?

ORESTES

Look, here is my father's ring.
Now will you believe me?

ELECTRA

O light of day!
O . . . happiness.

ORESTES

Yes . . . happiness.

ELECTRA

O you have come
And I am holding you.

CHORUS

—You have come to us like the dawn light.
—You are shining like a beacon.

ELECTRA

O women, women, yes,
He has come back to life.
O you have come home again . . .

ORESTES

Yes, but you must be quiet.

ELECTRA

Why? Why? Why?

ORESTES

No one inside must hear you.

ELECTRA

I'm not afraid of them.

ORESTES

You might give us both away.

ELECTRA

You'll never leave me, will you?

ORESTES

No, I'll never leave you.

ELECTRA

I did not weep at the bad news
But now that you are here . . .
A man came and told us
That you had been killed.

ORESTES

We were sent here by Apollo.
His oracle told me to kill
My father's murderers.
Listen now. I quote him:
"Go by yourself and be crafty.
Kill with stealth yet with justice.
Go there with Pylades,
Your friend, and one old man.
Lull their suspicions by saying
Orestes is dead."
So he made all things
Clear and plain and simple.
I must do Justice here.
(To ELECTRA)
Careful. When we go in
Your mother must not see
The joy in your face. No, No,
When it is done you can smile:
Then we will laugh
And both can say "I love you."

ELECTRA

I will do whatever you say.
Aegisthus is not here
But our mother is at home.

Don't fear she'll see me smiling.
Our hatred is too deep.
O you are a miracle.
If you hadn't come
I would have done it for you
Or died trying to.

Antigone
by Sophocles

CREON, ANTIGONE

CREON

Do you deny any of this?
(*To* ANTIGONE)
You! Say something.

ANTIGONE

No. I did it. I confess.
I confess everything.

CREON

(*To* GUARD)
You can go.
(*To* ANTIGONE)
Now, be brief. You know
I issued an order
Prohibiting what you did?

ANTIGONE

Yes. We all heard it.

CREON

Why did you not go back
To your useless dying father?

Why did you take it upon yourself
To defy the law?

ANTIGONE

Zeus did not make this law.
Justice did not make this law.
I did not think your pronouncement
Carried so much weight
That it could override
Everlasting and unwritten statutes
That govern our whole lives.
These laws were not created
Today, or yesterday.
They have existed since before time.
No one knows when or how
They came to be.
I was not about to convict myself
For transgressing
Those laws, simply out of fear
Of yours. Who are you?
One man.
I am sentenced to death.
Well, I would die, no matter what,
Some day. If you hasten my end
A little by your decree, I say
Good. I am happy. I win.
When you live as I do, in misery,
How can death not be a victory?
If I had left my brother to rot
Unburied—*that* would have hurt me.
This does not. It cannot.

CHORUS

Like her father—fierce.
You can see it. She does not bend.

CREON

Yes, but iron that does not bend,
Breaks. I have seen the wildest horses

Curbed by a small piece of leather.
This girl knowingly breached
The limits of what is permitted here.
She shows no remorse,
Not a hint.
If authority can be mocked like this
I am not a man, *she*
Is a man.
She will get no mercy, though,
Nor will her sister.
I suspect they planned this together,
And together they will suffer
The extreme penalty. Fetch Ismene!
If she is on her way to Athens
Stop her!

(A GUARD *obeys*)

                              ANTIGONE
You have caught me. Kill me.
What more do you want?

                              CREON
Nothing. With that, I have all
I desire.

                              ANTIGONE
Then why wait? . . .
But I will tell you this,
And I know you do not want to hear it,
Everybody here is secretly applauding
What I did. They are afraid
To speak their thoughts,
But in their hearts they side with me.

                              CREON
You have no friends here.

ANTIGONE

Yes I do. But they are silent,
Because they are afraid of you.

CREON

You stand alone. Aren't you ashamed?

ANTIGONE

I am ashamed of nothing.
I sacrificed
Everything for those I love.

CREON

He came to tear his country apart.
His brother fought to defend it.

ANTIGONE

Death makes no distinctions.
Death asks us to show
The same respect
To everyone.

CREON

To the criminal as well as the hero?

ANTIGONE

Who knows how right and wrong
Are measured in that other world?

CREON

Death does not make your enemy
A friend.

ANTIGONE

You want me to hate him,
Like you.
It is not in my nature, Creon.
Ask me to love him, and I will.

36

Love heals, and it will heal
This curse.

CREON

Then show your love in person,
Go and be with them, if you must.
So long as I have breath in my body,
No woman will govern here.

Antigone
by Sophocles

HAIMON, CREON

HAIMON

I am your son. I make it my duty
To observe, for your sake,
Everything that people say or do
Or find to criticize,
And I must tell you
That many of your citizens
Are terrified of you,
Terrified to utter a word
Of which you might disapprove.
I hear what is kept from your ears,
I hear what they are saying in private.
Our whole country is grieving for Antigone.
They consider it wicked and unjust
That she should be condemned to death
For something they all feel
Was a brave and noble act.
Father, why be so stubborn?
Why insist that you, and you alone
Possess the truth?
If you can say, "I was wrong,

I made a mistake,"
People will respect you . . .
The tree that bends with the current
Of a river in flood, remains standing.
The one that resists is uprooted.
Think again, be merciful.
Forgive her.

CREON

I am to be lectured by a boy?
At my age?

HAIMON

Only for your own good.
Judge my actions, not my years.

CREON

Your actions! They scream out
"Rebellion," they sanctify it.
She is a criminal.

HAIMON

Not in the eyes of most people.

CREON

And what most people think
I must do?

HAIMON

Father, now it is you who talk
Like a child.

CREON

How am I to run this country—
By my own convictions
Or by asking everyone what they think?

HAIMON

A country that exists
For one man's will
Is not a country at all.

CREON

The people must follow where their leader
Directs. That is the way things are.

HAIMON

You would be an ideal king
For a nation of one.

CREON

I see. Now he turns and sides
With women.

HAIMON

Yes, if you are a woman.
It is your side I take.

CREON

You quarrelsome brat!
You dare take issue with me,
Your father!

HAIMON

You are wrong. You trample
The rights of ancient and eternal powers.

CREON

You spineless creature, skulking
Behind a woman's skirts.
She will never be your wife.

HAIMON

Who else will you murder?
Me? These people? All Thebes?

CREON

Is that a threat?

HAIMON

You seem to think we must all
Stand by while you go on
Killing, and never say a word.

CREON

This is beyond belief.
Get out of my sight!
I will deal with you later.
(*To* GUARDS)
You heard my order.
Let her die, let her lover watch
Let him stand by *her*.

HAIMON

Kill! Kill! That is all
Your senseless brain can comprehend.

(*He runs off*)

CREON

Let him go, let him explode,
He can do what he likes.
His head is full of nonsense
He cannot prevent the law
From taking its course . . .

The Bacchae
by Euripides

PENTHEUS, DIONYSUS

PENTHEUS

So,
You *are* attractive, stranger, at least to women—
which explains, I think, your presence here in Thebes.
Your curls are long. You do not wrestle, I take it.
And what fair skin you have—you must take care of it—
no daylight complexion; no, it comes from the night
when you hunt Aphrodite with your beauty.
Now then,
who are you and from where?

DIONYSUS

It is nothing
to boast of and easily told. You have heard, I suppose,
of Mount Tmolus and her flowers?

PENTHEUS

I know the place.
It rings the city of Sardis.

DIONYSUS

I come from there.
My country is Lydia.

PENTHEUS

Who is this god whose worship
you have imported into Hellas?

DIONYSUS

Dionysus, the son of Zeus.
He initiated me.

PENTHEUS

You have some local Zeus
who spawns new gods?

DIONYSUS

He is the same as yours—
the Zeus who married Semele.

PENTHEUS

How did you see him?
In a dream or face to face?

DIONYSUS

Face to face.
He gave me his rites.

PENTHEUS

What form do they take,
these mysteries of yours?

DIONYSUS

It is forbidden
to tell the uninitiate.

PENTHEUS

Tell me the benefits
that those who know your mysteries enjoy.

DIONYSUS

I am forbidden to say. But they are worth knowing.

PENTHEUS

Your answers are designed to make me curious.

DIONYSUS

No:
our mysteries abhor an unbelieving man.

PENTHEUS

You say you saw the god. What form did he assume?

DIONYSUS

Whatever form he wished. The choice was his,
not mine.

PENTHEUS

You evade the question.

DIONYSUS

Talk sense to a fool
and he calls you foolish.

PENTHEUS

Have you introduced your rites
in other cities too? Or is Thebes the first?

DIONYSUS

Foreigners everywhere now dance for Dionysus.

PENTHEUS

They are more ignorant than Greeks.

DIONYSUS

In this matter
they are not. Customs differ.

PENTHEUS

Do you hold your rites
during the day or night?

DIONYSUS

Mostly by night.
The darkness is well suited to devotion.

PENTHEUS

Better suited to lechery and seducing women.

DIONYSUS

You can find debauchery by daylight too.

PENTHEUS

You shall regret these clever answers.

DIONYSUS

And you,
your stupid blasphemies.

PENTHEUS

What a bold bacchant!
You wrestle well—when it comes to words.

DIONYSUS

Tell me,
what punishment do you propose?

PENTHEUS

First of all,
I shall cut off your girlish curls.

DIONYSUS

My hair is holy.
My curls belong to god.

(PENTHEUS *shears away the god's curls*)

PENTHEUS

Second, you will surrender
your wand.

DIONYSUS

You take it. It belongs to Dionysus.

(PENTHEUS *takes the thyrsus*)

PENTHEUS

Last, I shall place you under guard and confine you
in the palace.

DIONYSUS

The god himself will set me free
whenever I wish.

PENTHEUS

You will be with your women in prison
when you call on him for help.

DIONYSUS

He is here now
and sees what I endure from you.

PENTHEUS

Where is he?
I cannot see him.

DIONYSUS

With me. Your blasphemies
have made you blind.

PENTHEUS

(*To* ATTENDANTS)
Seize him. He is mocking me
and Thebes.

DIONYSUS

I give you sober warning, fools:
place no chains on *me*.

PENTHEUS

But *I* say: chain him.
And I am the stronger here.

DIONYSUS

You do not know
the limits of your strength. You do not know
what you do. You do not know who you are.

PENTHEUS

I am Pentheus, the son of Echion and Agave.

DIONYSUS

Pentheus: you shall repent that name.

PENTHEUS

Off with him.
Chain his hands; lock him in the stables by the palace.
Since he desires the darkness, give him what he wants.
Let him dance down there in the dark.
(*As the attendants bind* DIONYSUS' *hands, the* CHORUS *beats on the
drums with increasing agitation as though to emphasize the sacrilege*)
As for these women,
your accomplices in making trouble here,
I shall have them sold as slaves or put to work
at my looms. That will silence their drums.

(*Exit* PENTHEUS)

DIONYSUS

I go,
though not to suffer, since that cannot be.
But Dionysus whom you outrage by your acts,
who you deny is god, will call you to account.
When you set chains on me, you manacle the god.

The Bacchae
by Euripides
DIONYSUS, PENTHEUS

DIONYSUS

Pentheus if you are still so curious to see
forbidden sights, so bent on evil still,
come out. Let us see you in your woman's dress,
disguised in Maenad clothes so you may go and spy
upon your mother and her company.
(*Enter* PENTHEUS *from the palace. He wears a long linen dress which
partially conceals his fawn-skin. He carries a thyrsus in his hand; on
his head he wears a wig with long blond curls bound by a snood. He is
dazed and completely in the power of the god who has now possessed him*)
Why,
you look exactly like one of the daughters of Cadmus.

PENTHEUS

I seem to see two suns blazing in the heavens.
And now two Thebes, two cities, and each
with seven gates. And you—you are a bull
who walked before me there. Horns have sprouted
from your head. Have you always been a beast?
But now I see a bull.

DIONYSUS

It is the god you see.
Though hostile formerly, he now declares a truce
and goes with us. You see what you could not
when you were blind.

PENTHEUS

(*Coyly primping*)
Do I look like anyone?
Like Ino or my mother Agave?

DIONYSUS

So much alike
I almost might be seeing one of them. But look:
one of your curls has come loose from under the snood
where I tucked it.

PENTHEUS

It must have worked loose
when I was dancing for joy and shaking my head.

DIONYSUS

Then let me be your maid and tuck it back.
Hold still.

PENTHEUS

Arrange it. I am in your hands
completely.

(DIONYSUS *tucks the curl back under the snood*)

DIONYSUS

And now your strap has slipped. Yes,
and your robe hangs askew at the ankles.

PENTHEUS

(*Bending backward to look*)
I think so.
At least on my right leg. But on the left the hem
lies straight.

DIONYSUS

You will think me the best of friends
when you see to your surprise how chaste the Bacchae
are.

PENTHEUS

But to be a real Bacchante, should I hold
the wand in my right hand? Or this way?

DIONYSUS

No.
In your right hand. And raise it as you raise
your right foot. I commend your change of heart.

PENTHEUS

Could I lift Cithaeron up, do you think?
Shoulder the cliffs, Bacchae and all?

DIONYSUS

If you wanted.
Your mind was once unsound, but now you think
as sane men do.

PENTHEUS

Should we take crowbars with us?
Or should I put my shoulder to the cliffs
and heave them up?

DIONYSUS

What? And destroy the haunts
of the nymphs, the holy groves where Pan plays
his woodland pipe?

PENTHEUS

You are right. In any case,
women should not be mastered by brute strength.
I will hide myself beneath the firs instead.

DIONYSUS

You will find all the ambush you deserve,
creeping up to spy on the Maenads.

PENTHEUS

Think.
I can see them already, there among the bushes,
mating like birds, caught in the toils of love.

DIONYSUS

Exactly. This is your mission: you go to watch.
You may surprise them—or they may surprise you.

PENTHEUS

Then lead me through the very heart of Thebes,
since I, alone of all this city, dare to go.

DIONYSUS

You and you alone will suffer for your city.
A great ordeal awaits you. But you are worthy
of your fate. I shall lead you safely there;
someone else shall bring you back.

PENTHEUS

Yes, my mother.

DIONYSUS

An example to all men.

PENTHEUS

It is for that I go.

DIONYSUS

You will be carried home—

PENTHEUS

O luxury!

DIONYSUS

cradled in your mother's arms.

PENTHEUS

You will spoil me.

DIONYSUS

I *mean* to spoil you.

PENTHEUS

I go to my reward.

DIONYSUS

You are an extraordinary young man, and you go
to an extraordinary experience. You shall win
a glory towering to heaven and usurping god's.
(*Exit* PENTHEUS)
Agave and you daughters of Cadmus,
reach out your hands! I bring this young man
to a great ordeal. The victor? Bromius.
Bromius—and I. The rest the event shall show.

Medea
by Euripides

JASON, MEDEA

JASON

You abomination! Of all women most detested
By every god, by me, by the whole human race!
You could endure—a mother!—to lift sword against
Your own little ones; to leave me childless, my life wrecked.
After such murder do you outface both Sun and Earth—
Guilty of gross pollution? May the gods blast your life!
I am sane now; but I was mad before, when I
Brought you from your palace in a land of savages
Into a Greek home—you, a living curse, already
A traitor both to your father and your native land.
The vengeance due for your sins the gods have cast on me.
You had already murdered your brother at his own hearth
When first you stepped on board my lovely Argo's hull.

That was your beginning. Then you became my wife, and bore
My children; now, out of mere sexual jealousy,
You murder them! In all Hellas there is not one woman
Who could have done it; yet in preference to them
I married you, chose hatred and murder for my wife—
No woman, but a tiger; a Tuscan Scylla—but more savage.
Ah, what's the use? If I cursed you all day, no remorse
Would touch you, for your heart's proof against feeling. Go!
Out of my sight, polluted fiend, child-murderer!
Leave me to mourn over my destiny: I have lost
My young bride; I have lost the two sons I begot
And brought up; I shall never see them alive again.

MEDEA

I would if necessary have answered at full length
Everything you have said; but Zeus the father of all
Knows well what service I once rendered you, and how
You have repaid me. You were mistaken if you thought
You could dishonour my bed and live a pleasant life
And laugh at me. The princess was wrong too, and so
Was Creon, when he took you for his son-in-law
And thought he could exile me with impunity.
So now, am I a tiger, Scylla?—Hurl at me
What names you please! I've reached your heart; and that is right.

JASON

You suffer too; my loss is yours no less.

MEDEA

It is true;
But my pain's a fair price, to take away your smile.

JASON

O children, what a wicked mother Fate gave you!

MEDEA

O sons, your father's treachery cost you your lives.

52

JASON

It was not my hand that killed my sons.

MEDEA

No, not your hand;
But your insult to me, and your new-wedded wife.

JASON

You thought *that* reason enough to murder them, that I
No longer slept with you?

MEDEA

And is that injury
A slight one, do you imagine, to a woman?

JASON

Yes,
To a modest woman; but to you—the whole world lost.

MEDEA

I can stab too: your sons are dead!

JASON

Dead? No! They live—
To haunt your life with vengeance.

MEDEA

Who began this feud?
The gods know.

JASON

Yes—they know the vileness of your heart.

MEDEA

Loathe on! Your bitter voice—how I abhor the sound!

JASON

As I loathe yours. Let us make terms and part at once.

53

MEDEA

Most willingly. What terms? What do you bid me do?

JASON

Give me my sons for burial and mourning rites.

MEDEA

Oh, no! I will myself convey them to the temple
Of Hera Acraea; there in the holy precinct I
Will bury them with my own hand, to ensure that none
Of my enemies shall violate or insult their graves.
And I will ordain an annual feast and sacrifice
To be solemnized for ever by the people of Corinth,
To expiate this impious murder. I myself
Will go to Athens, city of Erechtheus, to make my home
With Aegeus son of Pandion. You, as you deserve,
Shall die an unheroic death, your head shattered
By a timber from the Argo's hull. Thus wretchedly
Your fate shall end the story of your love for me.

JASON

The curse of children's blood be on you!
Avenging Justice blast your being!

MEDEA

What god will hear your imprecation,
Oath-breaker, guest-deceiver, liar?

JASON

Unclean, abhorrent child-destroyer!

MEDEA

Go home: your wife waits to be buried.

JASON

I go—a father once; now childless.

MEDEA

You grieve too soon. Old age is coming.

JASON

Children, how dear you were!

MEDEA

To their mother; not to you.

JASON

Dear—and you murdered them?

MEDEA

Yes, Jason, to break your heart.

JASON

I long to fold them in my arms;
To kiss their lips would comfort me.

MEDEA

Now you have loving words, now kisses for them:
Then you disowned them, sent them into exile.

JASON

For God's sake, let me touch their gentle flesh.

MEDEA

You shall not. It is waste of breath to ask.

JASON

Zeus, do you hear how I am mocked,
Rejected, by this savage beast
Polluted with her children's blood?

But now, as time and strength permit,
I will lament this grievous day,
And call the gods to witness, how
You killed my sons, and now refuse
To let me touch or bury them.
Would God I had not bred them,

Or ever lived to see
Them dead, you their destroyer!

(*During this speech Medea's chariot has moved out of sight*)

Many are the Fates which Zeus in Olympus dispenses;
Many matters the gods bring to surprising ends.
The things we thought would happen do not happen.
The unexpected God makes possible;
And such is the conclusion of this story.

Hippolytus
by Euripides

NURSE, PHAEDRA

I have tried everything, the truth is no nearer.
But I will not give up; I will not be discouraged.
Ladies, stay beside me, watch, and remember.
You will see how I serve her, slave for her, even in her sickness. . . .
(*To* PHAEDRA)
Listen, my darling, we'll forget all you said
Just now, shall we? Smile; unravel the frown
That tangles up your brow. Tell me what
You are thinking. I was wrong to let you lead me.
Now I've changed my mind; I mean to be sensible.
Look, if you are ill, and it is something hard to speak of,
There are women here to help you treat it. But if
You can explain to a man what is wrong, say so,
And we can tell a doctor. . . .
See! She refuses to speak.
Secrets, my dear, are sinful, Am I talking nonsense?
Well, prove that I am. Or am I right? Then admit it!

Look at me. Say something. . . . Oh, you frighten me!
Ladies, this is words wasted. I can do nothing—nothing
We are as far away from her as ever. She is hard.
Listen to me, Phaedra—and only the solemn
Ocean could hear this unmoved—if you die,
And leave your children alone in the world,
Perhaps to lose their inheritance . . . your children
Have an elder brother, a brother given them by the Amazon
(Blessed be her name and her power),
Not pure in blood, though he acts as if he were,
Your stepson, Hippolytus. . . .
(PHAEDRA *gives a cry*)
Ah, that is where it hurts.

PHAEDRA

Nurse, that was cruel of you. I ask only silence.
I beg of you not to speak his name again.

NURSE

You see, you have your sanity, and will not use it
To see what is best for your children and your own life's sake.

PHAEDRA

I do love my children. This raging winter
Has nothing to do with them.

NURSE

Child, your hands have not dipped their innocence
In blood?

PHAEDRA

My hands? No, they are clean. The stain
Lies in my soul

NURSE

Someone hates you; it preys on your mind?

PHAEDRA

He is dear to me. It is not his will, it is not mine;
Yet he destroys me.

NURSE

Theseus has wronged you . . . ?

PHAEDRA

May a sin of mine never come to his eyes.

NURSE

But something evil is plucking at your life. What is it?

PHAEDRA

Leave me to my wickedness; it does you no harm.

NURSE

You mean no harm. But why do you keep yourself
Alone?

PHAEDRA

Let me go! You don't know what you are forcing from me.

NURSE

I will know, I will, if I have to stay beside you
For ever.

PHAEDRA

You silly woman, the truth is ugly.

NURSE

Uglier than the pain of not hearing it from you?

PHAEDRA

Do you want to kill me? . . . yet death would be an honest
End.

NURSE

I only ask you because I want to help.
You can't hide it; you must not.

PHAEDRA

It is a sick desire. I try all the time
To make it natural and good.

NURSE

And all the more credit if you tell me what it is.

PHAEDRA

Go away, for God's sake, and let go my hand!

NURSE

No, you have a duty to me. I demand that duty!

PHAEDRA

Oh, duty. If you insist on duty, I must yield.

NURSE

I shall not say a word. . . . Tell the story as you will.

PHAEDRA

It was my mother, poor woman, whose love was the first tragedy.

NURSE

You mean her love for the bull? Is it that?

PHAEDRA

Then my sister, the wife of Dionysus,
Lived through her own horror.

NURSE

Be careful, my dear. You call them unhappy,
But they were your family.

PHAEDRA

And I am the third wretch to fall beneath the curse.

NURSE

I am lost in your story, Phaedra, where are you leading me?

PHAEDRA

The evil runs in my blood; it is nothing new.

NURSE

I have not heard yet what I must know.

PHAEDRA

Oh, nurse, you could not bear to say to me
What you are forcing me to say.

NURSE

I have no second sight, my dear; I cannot read
Your hidden thoughts.

PHAEDRA

Tell me, what is it like to be—what they call—in love?

NURSE

As, sweet, my darling, as . . . and yet in the same
Sweetness there is a sting.

PHAEDRA

Then I know only the second form.

NURSE

Do you mean . . . are you in love, my dear? With whom?

PHAEDRA

Someone who . . . his mother was an Amazon. . . .

NURSE

Not Hippolytus?

PHAEDRA

You spoke his name, not I.

NURSE

No! You must not say these things to frighten me.
Oh, I have been fingered by death!
It is too horrible, this life is too horrible!
And the day, yes, you, the day,
And the sunlight I live through—I hate you, hate you both!
My body—waste! Nothing! Not mine! Get away!
Die, die! Lovely reason smiles
And kisses the beast it hates, and cannot help itself.
Love—you a goddess! Never!
You are a monster, a growth destroying
All of us—myself, Phaedra, the whole house!

Hippolytus
by Euripides
THESEUS, HIPPOLYTUS

THESEUS

We have a wizard here, a perfect sorcerer!
After that act of scorn and violence, he thinks
His magic blandness will conjure me to be meek.

HIPPOLYTUS

But, Father, it is just that which amazes me
In you—your meekness. If you were my son, and I
Your father, your punishment would not have been exile.
If I really thought you had made advances to my wife
I would have murdered you!

THESEUS

Good, how acute! But that is not the death
I intend for you. It is easy to die quickly,
Too easy when life is hard. But in exile, disowned
By your country and your home . . . well you yourself
Have dictated the terms. . . .

HIPPOLYTUS

Father! No, you can't! You must wait
For time to give its evidence. Will you drive me
From my country?

THESEUS

Into another hemisphere! Beyond the Pontus,
Past the Atlantic! Yes, if I had the power!
How the sight of you repels me!

HIPPOLYTUS

But my oath, my word, the omens you can read in the flight
Of birds, you must weigh and probe what they tell you before
You banish me. This is no trial!

THESEUS

You are tried and condemned by this letter. Its proof
Is final. We need nothing supernatural.
Birds flying above our heads may stay there,
For all I care.

HIPPOLYTUS

Oh you powers in heaven, why do I not tell him
Now? I worship you, yet you destroy me. . . .
No, I cannot tell him. I swore I would not
And I would simply break that oath, without convincing
The only person I must convince.

THESEUS

You and your pompous piety make me gasp
For air. This is my country. Get out of it.

HIPPOLYTUS

But where can I go? I have no friends, and who
Will take me in, when they know the reason for my exile?

THESEUS

You have raped women—you would help in any
Low act—whoever likes that sort
Of guest will be delighted to have you.

HIPPOLYTUS

That was foul and cruel! . . . This touches the springs of tears
If I can look evil, and you believe me so.

THESEUS

You should have looked ahead and spent your sorrow
When you forced your way into your father's bed.

HIPPOLYTUS

If only the palace could find a tongue and speak . . .
Then you would have a witness to tell you whether
I have sinned.

THESEUS

The witnesses you appeal to are always dumb; clever,
Yes, but the facts are dumb as well, and they
Pronounce you guilty.

HIPPOLYTUS

Oh, if I could stand apart, and see myself,
Then I would weep for pity at the sorrow of it.

THESEUS

Yes, your feelings are refined and solemn for yourself;
For your parents, for decency, for honor, they do not exist.

HIPPOLYTUS

Oh my poor mother, what bitter blood flowed
From you to me. I would not have anyone
I loved cursed with a mixed descent.

THESEUS

Drag him away, you men! I gave orders
For him to be banished. Or were you deaf?

HIPPOLYTUS

The first to touch me is the first to die. You must
Use your own hands to drive me out, Father,
If your temper is fixed like that.

THESEUS

I will indeed, unless you obey me. I feel
Not a moment of pity for your exile!

(*Exit* THESEUS)

HIPPOLYTUS

I see, it is all decided, and I must suffer.
So much is clear, but I cannot give it sense.
(*To the statue of* ARTEMIS)
Oh Artemis, you are the power I love best,
You are beside me when I hunt, near me when I rest. . . .
I shall never see the glory of Athens again;
I must leave the city that Erechtheus built, the land
He conquered . . . Troezen, your fields were good to be
A child in; I was happy with you. Be happy when I
Am gone. For this is the last time I shall ever see you
Or speak to you. . . .
(*To the* HUNTSMEN)
Well, my friends, you are young, and Troezen is yours.
Wish me luck and escort me to the frontier.
You will never see a man in whom reason
And goodness are more at harmony. It is the truth,
Though my father does not believe it.

Lysistrata
by Aristophanes
CINESIAS, MYRRHINE

· CINESIAS

I've no joy in life any longer since she left home. It pains me to enter the place, it all seems so empty—and my food doesn't agree with me. I'm permanently rigid!

MYRRHINE
(*Appearing on the battlements, pretending to talk to somebody within*)
I love him, I love him! But he won't love me. Don't ask me to go out to him.

CINESIAS

Myrrie darling, why on earth not? Come down here.

MYRRHINE

No, I won't.

CINESIAS

Aren't you going to come down when I call you, Myrrhine?

MYRRHINE

You don't really want me.

CINESIAS

What! I'm dying for love of you.

MYRRHINE

I'm going.

(*Turns to go back inside*)

CINESIAS

No—don't—listen to your child!
(*The* SLAVE *caresses the* BABY *without result*)
Come on, damn you—say "mama"!
(*Strikes the* BABY)

BABY

Mama, mama, mama!

CINESIAS

What's wrong with you? Surely you can't harden your heart against your baby! It's five days now since he had a bath or a feed.

MYRRHINE

I pity him all right. His father hasn't looked after him very well.

CINESIAS

For heaven's sake, won't you come down to your own child?

MYRRHINE

How powerful motherhood is! My feelings compel me. I will come down.

(*She leaves the battlements*)

CINESIAS

I think she looks much younger and more beautiful than she was! And all this spurning and coquetting—why, it just inflames my desire even more!

MYRRHINE

(*Coming out and taking the* BABY *in her arms*)
Come on there, darling, you've got a bad daddy, haven't you? Come on, do you want a little drink, then?

(*She feeds him*)

CINESIAS

Tell me, darling, why do you behave like this and shut yourself up in there with the other women? Why do you give me pain—and yourself too?

(Attempts to caress her breast)

MYRRHINE

Keep your hands off me!

CINESIAS

And our things at home—they belong to you as well as me—they're going to ruin!

MYRRHINE

(Playing with the BABY)
I don't care!

CINESIAS

What, you don't care if the chickens are pulling all your wool to pieces?

MYRRHINE

No, I don't.

CINESIAS

And what about the rites of Aphrodite? How long is it since you performed them?
(Puts his arm around her)
Come along home.

MYRRHINE

(Wriggling free)
No, I won't. Not until you stop the war and make peace.

CINESIAS

Then, if you want, we'll do that.

MYRRHINE

Then, if you want, I'll go home. Till then, I've sworn not to.

CINESIAS

But won't you let me make love to you? It's been such a long time!

MYRRHINE

Nò. Mind you, I'm not saying I don't love you . . .

CINESIAS

You do, Myrrie love? Why won't you let me, then?

MYRRHINE

What, you idiot, in front of the baby?

CINESIAS

No—er—Manes, take it home.
(*The* SLAVE *departs with the* BABY)
All right, darling, it's out of the way. Let's get on with it.

MYRRHINE

Don't be silly, there's nowhere we can do it here.

CINESIAS

What's wrong with Pan's Grotto?

MYRRHINE

And how am I supposed to purify myself before going back into
the Acropolis? It's sacred ground, you know.

CINESIAS

Why, there's a perfectly good spring next to it.

MYRRHINE

You're not asking me to break my oath!

CINESIAS

On my own head be it. Don't worry about that, darling.

MYRRHINE

All right, I'll go and get a camp bed.

CINESIAS

Why not on the ground?

MYRRHINE

By Apollo—I love you very much—but not on the ground!

(*She goes into the Acropolis*)

CINESIAS

Well, at least she does love me, that I can be sure of.

MYRRHINE

(*Returning with a bare camp bed*)
Here you are. You just lie down, while I take off my—Blast it!
We need a—what do you call it?—a mattress.

CINESIAS

Mattress? I certainly don't!

MYRRHINE

In the name of Artemis, you're not proposing we should do it on
the cords!

CINESIAS

At least give us a kiss first.

MYRRHINE

(*Doing so*)
There.
(*She goes*)

CINESIAS

Mmmm! Come back quickly!

MYRRHINE

(*Returning with a mattress*)
There. Now just lie down, and I'll—But look, you haven't got a
pillow!

CINESIAS

I don't want one.

(*He lies down on the mattress*)

MYRRHINE

But I do!

(*She goes in*)

CINESIAS

This is a Heracles' supper and no mistake!

MYRRHINE

(*Returning with a pillow*)
Lift up your head. So.

CINESIAS

That's everything.

MYRRHINE

Everything?

CINESIAS

Yes. Come to me now, precious.

MYRRHINE

(*Her back to him*)
I'm just undoing my bra. Remember, don't let me down on what
you said about making peace.

CINESIAS

May Zeus strike me dead if I do!

MYRRHINE

But look now, you haven't got a blanket!

CINESIAS

But I don't want one! All I want is you, darling!

70

MYRRHINE

In a moment, love. I'll just pop in for the blanket.

(*Goes into the Acropolis*)

CINESIAS

These bedclothes will be the end of me!

MYRRHINE
(*Returning with a blanket and a box of ointment*)
Lift yourself up.

CINESIAS

You can see very well I did that long ago.

MYRRHINE

Do you want me to anoint you?

CINESIAS

No, dammit, I don't!

MYRRHINE

Too bad, then, because I'm going to anyway.

CINESIAS

(*Aside*)
Zeus, make her spill the stuff!

MYRRHINE

Hold out your hand and you can rub it on.

CINESIAS

(*Smelling the ointment*)
I don't care for it. I only like sexy ones, and besides, this positively
reeks of prevarication!

MYRRHINE

(*Pretending to sniff it in her turn*)
Why, silly me, I brought the wrong one!

CINESIAS

Well, never mind, darling, let it be.

MYRRHINE

Don't talk such nonsense.

(*She goes in with the box*)

CINESIAS

Curse whoever invented these ointments!

MYRRHINE

(*Returning with another unguent in a bottle*)
Here you are, take this bottle.

CINESIAS

I've got one already and it's fit to burst!
(*Indicating what he is referring to*)
Come here and lie down, damn you, and stop this stupid game.

MYRRHINE

I will, I swear it by Artemis. I've got both my shoes off now. But darling, don't forget about making peace.

CINESIAS

I'll—
(MYRRHINE *runs off into the Acropolis and the gates slam behind her*)
She's gone! She's been having me on! Just when I was all ripe for her, she ran away!
(*Bursts into sorrowful song*)
Oh what, tell me what, can this woeful laddie do?
And who, tell me who, can this woeful laddie screw?

PART II

The Age of Shakespeare:

SCENES BY SHAKESPEARE

INTRODUCTION

I have arranged these scenes in approximate chronological order, as there are patterns of usage and narrative structure which show some consistency within particular periods of Shakespeare's creative output without necessarily being identified with genres like comedy, tragedy, and so forth that are commonly used to categorize the plays. In fact Shakespeare's plays tend generally to defy such characterization by type anyway, each seeming to encompass a world unique and whole unto itself, with its own special rules of speech and behavior.

Narrative Conventions

As with the Greeks, Shakespeare's actors and audiences were very much aware of the storytelling dimension of theatrical performance. The relationship between actor and audience, however, was much more intimate, performances occurring as they did in a much smaller space, accommodating perhaps a couple of hundred persons at most, and without the intrusion of masks and other elaborate theatrical paraphernalia. Only through an awareness of the narrative conventions underlying Shakespeare's voice as storyteller can to-day's actor begin to suggest the kind of vitality that the original performances must have sustained. And only by studying the textual clues Shakespeare provided for his own actors can we achieve the wide range of expression implicit in the words.

The Texts

For over two years I have tied all my production and workshop activity to a close analysis of the First Folio, working on the assumption, as it was first presented to me fully by the Royal Shakespeare Company's Patrick Tucker, that this text represents the fullest and most accurate *acting* edition of Shakespeare's plays, culled from actual actors' cue scripts and published before editors and academicians had a chance to decide what it was they wanted to see instead. This work has proven to be revelatory.

In my editing of these scenes, I have chosen to concentrate on a few key aspects: original punctuation as it applies to stage business and breath; capitalization of important and proper nouns; variations in spelling that often suggest greater flexibility and ambiguity; patterns of rhythm, alliteration, and assonance, and places where those patterns are purposely broken. In all cases it is my intention to retain as many of Shakespeare's directions to his actors as can be included without seriously confusing the modern reader.

Technique

For the actor beginning work on one of these scenes, I offer a few general techniques that seem to apply to virtually every scene. In fact, these guidelines should also be applied to the Elizabethan, Jacobean, and Restoration scenes in the last two chapters of this book. Although the playwrights' voices differ and the editorial styles vary significantly, there is sufficient common ground in the English theatre to make these exercises useful even when dealing with contemporary playwrights like Harold Pinter, Tom Stoppard, or Caryl Churchill.

The breath and the voice must be fully used. This does not mean that one always speaks at a high volume, but it does mean that the sounds of the words demand full exploration, often most usefully attempted outdoors. In the early stages of rehearsal in particular the sounds need to be savored—the vowels elongated, stretched well past what we are used to; the consonants fully articulated, explosively if necessary. Any repetitions of sounds, words, or phrases need to be emphasized, as if it is the actor who is choosing these repetitions. Double consonants, or places where one word ends in a particular consonant and the next begins with the same or a similiar sound, are best separated. These separations provide important halts in the rhythm of a speech as well as a method of pointing or emphasizing specific key words.

Shakespeare's actors were no doubt used to speaking at a much faster clip than we are. I do not recommend great speed, particularly for actors unused to serious language work, but I do suggest a steady pace of speech, with few if any pauses and essentially un-hindered by most punctuation, i.e., commas, periods, and line end-ings. The actor will then tend to stop at natural breaks like the double consonants, or at those moments when he has to take a breath. The less those breaths are tied to the punctuation of a line, the more the actor will be able to achieve his own unique reading without losing the pace, sense, and logic of the speech.

What I am really suggesting here is a pattern of consistent cueing. This means punching with significant emphasis the first word or syllable of a line or sentence, both between speakers and internally within a single person's lines. Cueing is critical not only to maintain the pace of the action but often to carry the very sense of the scene. Breaths and pauses are rarely taken at the top of a thought, and so the scene is driven to its logical and emotional conclusion. Modern actors are used to taking pauses to think, to reflect, and to allow an emotional response; Shakespeare's actors thought while they spoke. I posit that the appropriate emotional reality can be accomplished in Shakespeare most easily by pushing the scene forward and allowing it to take over, without reflection and without silent deliberation. When lines are cued from one actor to another, look for the cue word, the word in the other person's line that motivates a response. Depending on the degree of topping or overlap Shakespeare wanted, the key word will usually appear three or more words before the end of the previous line, giving the responding actor a chance to think and take a breath, but without a modern pause. Where it is obviously the final word that generates a response, the beginning of that response is often a cover, an exclamation or a repetition that allows the responding actor time to think of a fuller reply while he is talking. In a few instances, a line will clearly *not* be written to be cued. On those rare occasions, the line will begin with a word that will not allow the first syllable to be emphasized, a word like "Alas" or a name like Titania or Orsino, where it is definitely a later syllable that must be stressed. A line beginning with "A" also cannot be cued, and a brief pause for consideration or recovery is usually called for.

Two exceptions to consistent cueing that seem to work most of the time are short lines and colons. A short line, or a verse line that is missing several syllables, is often a sign that some stage business needs to happen at its beginning or end. A colon can sometimes also indicate an action or, more often, a shift in focus. I have found it very useful in early rehearsals to categorize all colons as full stops, demanding that the actor take a lengthy pause and an actual move on each colon. Such an exercise is valuable in exploring the structure of a scene. Later, only those pauses or moves that are most useful are kept in the scene, while the rest of the colons become shifts in focus that do not interfere with the flow of speech.

Prose has fewer significant characteristics than verse, fewer clues to the actor, fewer stops in fact, and is generally written to be spoken even faster, with still fewer pauses.

It must be remembered that not all words are equally important. In addition to the guidelines above, in a verse scene watch for words that fall oddly because of rhythmic changes. Scan every line early in the process, so that these exceptions to regular meter can be spotted. Most of Shakespeare's verse is written in iambic pentameter, the meter that still most closely resembles the rhythm patterns of normal English speech. The most common line consists of ten syllables divided into five "feet," units of one unstressed syllable followed by a stressed syllable. Every exception, even an extra syllable at the end of a line, is in some way significant, but as there are no hard-and-fast rules, it is up to the actor to determine what that significance is.

The last word of a verse line, whether it is the end of a thought or not, usually has special importance. In both verse and prose, watch for parenthetical words or phrases, as they need to be emphasized, hit especially hard, and not swallowed as is common in modern usage. Nouns are generally important for telling the story, setting the scene, and placing the actor; try not to prejudge which nouns are more important than others until you are well into the process of preparing the scene. Ordinary words may become important by means of repetition or arrhythmia, but extraordinary words are, quite simply, extraordinary, and should be treated appropriately.

Movement and Gesture

Because of the narrative conventions at the foundation of Shakespeare's theatre, the actor's work begins nearly always from stillness, with gesture or action added when it is necessary to tell the story. In other words, the more activity in the text, the less the actor has to do. When action is called for, it is usually indicated in the text as spoken stage directions or as gaps in language, silences. If an actor is inclined to move, that move should be simple and direct. It is hard to go wrong, for example, when moving directly toward the person to whom you are speaking, even when that person is the audience. Awareness of audience is critical. There are *no* private moments.

Emotion, like movement, happens when little or nothing is being said. If you can say it, you are probably describing something that has been felt in the past, has already been processed, and may now be articulated. Pushing emotion while speaking only interferes with the clarity of the story you are telling. It *never* works.

The performance aspect possibly most alien to today's actor, and yet most completely Shakespearean, is the overt intelligence of the Storyteller/Actor/Speaker. Modern drama is dominated by victims, inarticulately groaning their unconscious limitations to an uncomprehending cosmos and an uncaring audience. Shakespeare's creations, on the other hand, even when unable or unwilling to change their circumstances, are remarkable for their utter and complete awareness.

Early Game Scenes

Both scenes from *The Two Gentlemen of Verona* are exemplary of conscious artifice and gamesmanship. In the first, Valentine is trying to maintain a reasonable semblance of courtly speech and behavior toward his beloved Silvia, while Speed, his servant, undermines every attempt, generally answering verse with prose. It is important that both enjoy the sparring intelligently, rather than playing the scene like a couple of semiconscious half-wits. When Silvia comes forward, the permutations increase exponentially, with Speed playing his part of the scene mostly to the audience, a common device in a three-character comic scene. It is customary to have Silvia enter when she is noticed by Valentine, but the First Folio indicates her to be present at the top of the scene. I prefer this latter construction, as it allows Silvia to be a listener for the first part of the scene and then to choose her entrance time with the express purpose of playing Valentine's game.

When later Julia, in disguise as a boy, approaches Silvia to exchange a ring for a portrait on behalf of Proteus, much of the fun of the scene is, of course, in the sexual double entendres derived from Julia's disguise, her obvious infatuation with Proteus, and the words she speaks for the supposedly absent lady, Julia. But the scene also has a deep pathos which can be enhanced by assuming, as the dialogue itself suggests, that Silvia, no dummy by any standards, is aware of Julia's disguise, playing along to determine to her own satisfaction the degree of Julia's love for Proteus. Their exit together at the end of the scene reinforces this further.

In *Henry VI, Part 1,* the first meeting of Margaret and Suffolk, a couple whose on-and-off romance was to dominate the Wars of the Roses, is really about two people playing a game. The victorious Suffolk is obsessed with taking the captive French princess Margaret with him. His asides to his confidant, the audience, are, of course, overheard by Margaret, who then mockingly duplicates his scene. A choice must be made about the heaviness of Margaret's accent, and I suggest that some of it be put on for her captors. Evenly matched in wit, the two may then proceed with the business of the story. Cueing, even some overlapping of lines, is essential to the sense of this scene.

Serious Games

Much more serious in tone is the Humphrey and Elinor scene from *Henry VI, Part 2*. Even here there is, I believe, a sense of play, as Elinor toys with dreams of power which Humphrey, without acknowledging, must at some level share. After all, he protests but never stops her from speaking. There is an intimacy and a sense of shared history here that is best served by stillness and very clear focus.

The famous confrontation between Richard and Anne in *Richard III* can be interpreted as a cursing match or a seduction, and is often considered unplayable by critics too concerned with its logic and by actors too concerned with psychological "truth." Not only is the scene playable, but it carries with it a compelling emotional logic that cannot be denied. Once again it is the game that counts, in this case a very dangerous game in which either party could at any moment become the other's victim. Anne taunts her husband's killer as if she were challenging him to kill her too, and Richard actually places his sword in her hand, telling Anne to dispatch. These, too, are evenly matched opponents, so well matched, in fact, that if the scene is properly cued and played at a solid clip, there is a kind of inevitability about the outcome. Note the repetitions of sounds, words, and phrases bouncing back and forth between the two, especially those words that begin each cued line. The dramatic climax, after Anne drops Richard's sword, is soon followed by ten paired lines ("I would I knew thy heart" through "Vouchsafe to wear this Ring") that scan at six syllables or three "feet" each. This figure, totaling twelve syllables to the pair, is known as an Alexandrine verse and is more common in French poetry and drama. It presents a slower, more stately quality than is generally possible in iambic pentameter. It is as if the two were already walking down the aisle, sharing the meter in perfect accord. In the midst of all this formality, do not forget the public that reinforces it, i.e., the presence of the coffin bearers, King Henry's corpse, and the audience, all witnesses to this perverse union.

A more socially acceptable love scene, though not by the standards of their own society, is Romeo and Juliet's balcony scene. The scene makes no sense unless the audience is a present friend for both lovers, a judge for whom they may perform their feats of poetic derring-do. The winner of this composition and elocution contest may actually vary from performance to performance. Issues to explore include the questions of relative height (how high should the balcony be?), stage position relative to the audience (who is closer to them and when?), and relative darkness (how much of each other do the lovers really get to see?). Because Juliet is stuck in place, it is Romeo who does the moving, and I suggest using the colons in his lines to change position and experiment with different locations about the stage.

Yet another game is the one the Nurse plays with Juliet later on, teasing her by pretending to be alternately out of breath, deaf, and exhausted. If both are aware of the game, and both know it will end, the scene can be kept as light as it needs to be without resorting to bad character acting.

Power Games

As I stated earlier, the more active the language, the less the actor needs to do physically. A corollary is that if great power is involved, the actor need do even less. In *A Midsummer Night's Dream,* the fairies Titania and Oberon are seen to have power over humans and nature—over the seasons themselves, if we are to credit Titania's claims in this scene. After the initial flurry of activity as the couple enter from presumably opposite sides of the stage, the scene becomes still with tension, even menace. The five colons before Titania's exit can be used as moves, either hers or his. Note that two of them happen before a qualifying phrase beginning with "which," thereby punctuating the scene in an interesting, offbeat manner. Note also the utter determination implied by the repeat of the phrase "and for her sake." Puck's presence throughout their argument should not be ignored.

Much more active physically is the Helena and Demetrius scene. It is dominated by active verbs rather than images and may be played in movement punctuated by still moments when Helena has Demetrius pinned down. Any active phrases like his "let me go" need to be taken literally as indications of prior action. A far longer and more complicated scene, which I have not included here, that illustrates the principles of Shakespeare's "blocking" is Act III, Scene 2, in which he manipulates all four lovers (Helena, Demetrius, Hermia, Lysander) with ease, and I recommend it as an exercise for four actors.

Like Oberon and Titania in their world, Antonio and Bassanio define the power structure of *The Merchant of Venice*. Theirs is a simple narrative scene, but rich in implied history and the kind of detail that makes the world of the play immediate and vivid.

When Kate and Petruchio spar in *The Taming of the Shrew*, it is with words and actions both. Repetitions and reversals of meaning are the rule here, suggesting a physical pattern of attack and retreat. It is important that the actions, however, punctuate rather than obscure the verbal play, for the scene can actually work with very little movement but cannot function at all if the words are not understood. The scene also defines cueing at its most essential and powerful. Note the opponents' shifting advantage in terms of lines that cannot be cued. At the top of the scene, Petruchio takes Kate off guard with "Why, what's a movable?" She is caught for a moment without a quick response and has to pause for a brief moment before coming up with "A joyn'd stool." Later, Kate gets the upper hand, and it is Petruchio who hesitates with "A Herald Kate?" and "A combless Cock." Finally, near the end of the scene, Petruchio has regained his control, and a cowed and exhausted Kate can respond to his "It is *extempore*, from my mother wit" only feebly with "A witty mother, witless else her son."

Consenting Couples

I have included Hotspur's farewell to his wife, Lady Percy, from *Henry IV, Part 1*, because of the tremendous variety of language she employs. She begins with a catalogue of technical military terms that need to be fully and clearly articulated so that they may build in intensity only to be undercut by the relatively simple and wholly powerful "Soldiers slain" at its end. Unable to keep Hotspur's attention with this ploy, she resorts to teasing and familiarity, employing a veritable zoo—"Ape," "Weasel," and "Paraquito"—until

Hotspur must repond. Her threat, "Ile break thy little finger *Harry*," argues close physical contact as well. The effect is that we genuinely believe in these two people who obviously care a great deal about each other and yet must part.

Beatrice and Benedick in *Much Ado About Nothing* are equally tied up with each other, but their scene is driven by emotion and has little of the verbal finesse Shakespeare lavishes on so many of his courting couples. It is meant, prose as it is, to be played "fast and furious," and the relative simplicity of the language suggests to me a fair bit of movement: false exits, approaches, and physical contact. The bigger the action, the fuller the scene. Hence Beatrice must be as serious about leaving as she is about forcing Benedick to stop her. It is rare to find a scene this long that is mostly one-liners. Except for Beatrice's "A very even way . . . ," the lines are meant to cue until Beatrice begins to run out of steam in her "Princes and Counties . . ." speech. Note the colons here and in Benedick's last speech, showing a melodramatic hesitancy. Note also the repeated "w" section, with several "will"s, a "With," a "Why," and a "What." Consider the shape of the mouth required to make the sound; it is likely that the two are close to a kiss at this point.

Broad characters and crude comedy are the rule for *The Merry Wives of Windsor*. It is a mistake, however, to make even these extreme folk less aware or intelligent than we would have ourselves be. Mistress Quickly chooses her particularly oblique way of com-municating, as I see it, to be able to more fully observe Falstaff, while Falstaff's impatience is as much an act for his watching cronies as anything else. This is supported by the complete reversal of attitude that Falstaff experiences upon Quickly's exit and Ford's entrance. Now he becomes manipulative and very much in control of the seemingly out-of-control Ford. Ford too, though, especially considering his disguised appearance, seems to me to enjoy his jealousy too much for it to be a totally absorbing obsession. The frequent colons in both scenes most often function as opportunities for comic takes.

The goat-herding Audrey in *As You Like It* is also too often played as a complete dumbbell, but if we invest her with a true wish to capture Touchstone, the court jester, for her own, her tactics become completely clear. Touchstone, too, is captured because he wants to be, and so we see a couple that may be silly in the way they communicate and behave, but who are also very much in love, entirely charming, and indulging in what could be a conscious parody of "romantic" talk. Jaques' commentary, coming as it does at Audrey's pauses, is a useful link to the audience, and I have found it most interesting if his remarks feed Audrey and Touchstone rather than functioning as unheard asides.

The presence of the servant Maria for the first half or so of the first meeting between Viola and Olivia in *Twelfth Night* is also very important, setting up a courtly formality which might not otherwise be there. The scene is full of sexual ambiguity and role reversals, as Viola woos Olivia as proxy for Orsino, the man she actually loves. Rather than assuming blindness or latent lesbianism on Olivia's part, consider instead the possibility of her being fascinated by the very nuance and complexity that Viola brings to her. Later, when Viola meets Feste the Clown, there are even clearer indications that her disguise has been less than completely effective, and Feste gives her a lesson in performance and timing that may prove useful to her next encounter with Olivia.

Indirection

There is no way of pretending that Helena in *All's Well That Ends Well* is anything less than intellectually brilliant, and it may be this quality that has kept her from the popularity she deserves. She is in love and vulnerable, and she can express that vulnerability with precision and thoroughness. Her scene with Parolles is often considered something of a mystery, as this is a relationship that is not explored further anywhere else in the play. Yet the scene does express something of her loneliness and, in the way she bests Parolles verbally, her wit and acumen. Parolles too is more than just a braggart soldier, and he tempers his blustery wit with what needs to be perceived as genuine compassion. Their parting, as early in the play as it appears, can and should bring tears.

Just a few minutes later Helena must brave the redoubtable Countess. She confesses her love for the Countess's son Bertram in terms of great depth and complexity, using images from virtually every discipline of human knowledge, referring to the training given her by her deceased father. The Countess is very much her match though, goading her to express herself and her intentions with full clarity, repeating the word "mother" until she drives Helena to distraction. The scene is structured as several lengthy speeches punctuated by short, quick, explosive bursts of dialogue that bend the scansion of the verse. In the section beginning with the Countess's "To tell me truly" Helena tries unsuccessfully to interrupt the Countess's cross-examination. The scansion here indicates overlapping lines and a momentum that does not break until the colon after "Whereof the world takes note." I like setting the scene in a garden, where the Countess may surround herself by blossoms reminiscent of her own youth.

Another example of directness by indirection is Cassius's conspiratorial approach to Brutus in *Julius Caesar*. He takes his time, building slowly to the argument. But there is a pointedness to the scene from the very start that suggests that both men know right away what is at stake. I cite the number of times each calls the other by name, especially at the beginning of a line. This gives the relationship a formality while allowing for a great deal of personal nuance in each repetition of a name. The public nature of the space is another important element, as it introduces both the danger of interruption and the influence of crowd sounds on their discussion. There is not a great deal of movement called for here, but what there is alternately brings Brutus and Cassius together and then separates them as needed.

The courtship of Troilus and Cressida, especially as it is monitored and chaperoned by Pandarus, has a style to it that is difficult to capture in today's theatre. I have seen it successfully attempted only once, in workshop, by means of ante-bellum southern accoutrements, from accent to costume. Although this approach might wear thin over the course of the complete play, I do recommend this or some other strong choice for the scene to bring the actors to an awareness of style as conscious and intentional.

I have chosen these particular scenes from *Hamlet* because they demonstrate most effectively the complexity of Shakespeare's storytelling and the essential role of the witness. Instead of overinterpreting the relationship between Hamlet and Ophelia, I recommend that actors work mostly on two things: a direct reading of the lines, fast and as punctuated; and an awareness of being overheard. Although not yet a common practice in production, it is nevertheless becoming acceptable to see Hamlet playing at least part of this scene for the listening ears of Claudius and Polonius, hidden offstage. I believe that if we allow Hamlet to communicate his awareness of being overheard to Ophelia, the scene begins to make even more sense as a kind of game that they both perform for the listeners, and the relationship between the two starts to take on some real history and depth. This scene, as culled mostly from the First Folio, probably departs the most from generally accepted punctuation and spelling. The result is a more erratic, less smooth, possibly more exciting performance from both actors.

After playing with Ophelia, directing the Players, and watching the king's reactions to the play within a play, Hamlet is still at play, this time testing Rosencrantz, Guildenstern, and Polonius to see if they have been coached in how to deal with him. The scene is exuberant, full of verbal wit and physical action. Still high on his games and his discoveries, Hamlet comes to confront his mother, still playing, even mocking her turn of phrase. But he provokes an unexpected reaction from her and the hidden Polonius. When Polonius is stabbed, the nature of the scene changes and the fun leaves. Now Hamlet has to get through to Gertrude and make his demands; the Ghost that he sees and she does not is both a distraction and a spur. In many places where Gertrude tries to respond, either her lines or Hamlet's do not scan at an even five feet. I have found that these instances play best as interruptions in what for Hamlet is mostly a monologue, so that he stops talking perhaps only long enough to take a deep breath and then continues.

Listening

The pivotal scene in *Othello,* in which Iago feeds the Moor's jealousy, is full of nuance, echoes, and conscious repetitions. I have actually seen it performed very effectively by two women, possibly because in their version there was none of the macho competitiveness that can get in the way of the language and the listening of each to the other. This is one of those scenes where the language simply must be allowed to do its own work. Othello is not stupid, but he believes Iago's story because he wants to believe it; it suits his expectation. Special attention must be paid to the repetitions here, each man often repeating and questioning the other's words. The abundance of question marks, changed to some other punctuation in most modern editions, suggests serious doubt.

Considerably more complex is the Desdemona and Emilia scene. It has a song, a costume change, and two women with entirely different agendas and perspectives. I think all this makes it Shakespeare's most elaborate scene. Probably most important here is that Desdemona not act, as one student put it, "Desdemona-ish." In other words, it is essential that Desdemona not play the end of the story. The more she projects the tragedy to come, the less the audience is likely to empathize or care in any way. Rather, a lightness, a freewheeling stream of consciousness must prevail—she does sing a song after all, never mind the subject. This is not to say that she, as well as Emilia, is not aware of danger, but rather that the scene must serve to cheer her up, to prepare her for love, not death. Here too listening is very important. Watch the scansion, as it is at best erratic. The inconsistencies provide essential clues to the key issues for both women.

I have combined two scenes from *King Lear* to form a single continuous action leading to the Gloucester "suicide." In some respects the opposite of the *Othello* scene we have just discussed, this has the blinded Gloucester readying himself for death, only to be tricked out of the opportunity by mad Tom o' Bedlam, his own virtuous son Edgar in disguise. As the one in control, Edgar is in touch with the audience at all times; compared with Gloucester's, his senses seem superhuman. The scene is all illusion, from the uphill climb, to the overly detailed description of the Dover cliffs, to Gloucester's fall (on a bare, flat stage), to his rebirth as a soul saved from some demon. Like Othello, Gloucester needs to believe, and Edgar gives him the opportunity. The scene is almost impossible to spoil, but it is the small, detailed choreography of hands, purses, steps, and careful listening (again) that makes it particularly compelling.

In *Macbeth* too, it is listening that provides the central activity for the scene—listening for noises, screams, owls, what have you—for it is obviously too dark to see properly. There is a hushed quality that makes sense only if both Macbeth and the Mrs. are constantly aware of the sounds around them. Lady Macbeth's first speech sets the textual tone for the scene. There is only one line in it that scans in an even, measured fashion, and most are either short or long lines. There is consequently a feeling of run-on speech juxtaposed with frequent catches in breath. Short lines are especially frequent in the scene, and I have had some success overlapping lines from Lady Macbeth's "Consider it not so deeply" through the first "Sleep no more . . ." She, of course, takes action by grabbing the daggers and going off to incriminate the guards, leaving himself to further speculate on the deed. The knocks at the end of the scene should fill in the gaps in the verse scansion, and so run 9, 4, 3, then become continuous, as Macbeth does not stop talking except for the colon of brief consideration after "Wake *Duncan* with thy knocking."

Late Narratives

Shakespeare's last plays are characterized by particularly deliberate storytelling conventions, demanded by the massive sweep of much of the action. For both Antony and Cleopatra, there is a singular awareness of their special place in history. This gives them both a scale of behavior that is highly theatrical. They consciously perform for each other and the audience, represented onstage by Charmian and Cleopatra's other attendants, choosing and dropping attitudes at a moment's notice. The scene included here perfectly balances this public dimension with the intimacy we never really see but to which they frequently allude.

The recognition scene from *Pericles* has been derived from a Third Folio text, as the play does not appear in the First Folio. Even so, this version reinforces the narrative elements by setting the scene mostly in prose, suggesting a rapid-fire pace that denies the sort of self-indulgent emotionality that is so often the hallmark of this kind of potentially sentimental material. As with other scenes I have spoken of, it is important as well that neither Pericles nor Marina play below what would be a normal level of intelligence or awareness. Pericles has refused to speak because of the tragedy he has undergone, but he does listen. Marina appeals to him in every manner she can think of, and her range of performance is extensive. It is best if each recognizes the other fairly early on in the scene, as would logically make sense, but each remains afraid that this is too good to be true.

Leontes' obsessive jealousy in *The Winter's Tale* provides another instance of a single attitude overplayed, and many actors have puzzled over how to make this quality believable. There is no question that Leontes' expression of his jealousy is unreasonable, but if we grant for a moment the potential validity of his perceptions, he is neither stupid nor unaware. Rather, and in particular in this scene with Camillo, he sets complicated, even brilliant tests or snares for those persons he suspects of disloyalty. He is by no means blind, but rather sensitive to every nuance that will support his interpretation of reality. Camillo too is not a mere servant, but a politically canny observer with, ultimately, his own survival in mind. The rhythm of the scene, as with most of Shakespeare's later plays, is erratic, with many departures from regular meter, so many in fact that the scene plays in a jagged, even overtly violent manner.

The Tempest is a kind of ballet that probably featured a fair bit of music and choreography. The scene I have included here is true to that feeling; it is a ballet of power, with Prospero calling the shots, keeping a tight rein on Caliban and waking Miranda from a sleep he probably induced earlier. Prospero must be played with utmost economy, every slightest movement an influence on those around him. The actor playing Caliban must also avoid excessive movement or emotion, relying instead on his history, his connection to the heart of the island, and on his palpably sensing the restrictions Prospero places on him. It is the story the scene tells that is most important. From that story will arise a profound pathos and a deep audience sympathy for both Caliban and Prospero; but if the actors overplay, everything remains muddy, general, and for the most part incomprehensible.

The Two Gentlemen
of Verona

ACT II, SCENE 1—
SPEED, VALENTINE, SILVIA

SPEED

Sir, your Glove.

VALENTINE

Not mine: my Gloves are on.

SPEED

Why then this may be yours: for this is but one.

VALENTINE

Ha? Let me see: I, give it me, it's mine:
Sweet Ornament, that decks a thing divine,
Ah *Silvia, Silvia*.

SPEED

Madam *Silvia*: Madam *Silvia*.

VALENTINE

How now, Sirra?

SPEED

She is not within hearing Sir.

VALENTINE

Why sir, who bade you call her?

SPEED

Your worship sir, or else I mistook.

VALENTINE

Well: you'll still be too forward.

SPEED

And yet I was last chidden for being too slow.

VALENTINE

Go to, sir, tell me: do you know Madam *Silvia*?

SPEED

She that your worship loves?

VALENTINE

Why, how know you that I am in love?

SPEED

Marry by these special marks: first, you have learn'd (like Sir *Proteus*) to wreath your Arms like a Male-content: to relish a Love-song, like a *Robin*-red-breast: to walk alone like one that had the pestilence: to sigh, like a School-boy that had lost his *A,B,C:* to weep like a young wench that had buried her Grandam: to fast, like one that takes diet: to watch, like one that fears robbing: to speak puling, like a beggar at Hallow-Mass: You were wont, when you laughed, to crow like a cock; when you walk'd, to walk like one of the Lions: when you fasted, it was presently after dinner: when you look'd sadly, it was for want of money: And now you are Metamorphis'd with a Mistress, that when I look on you, I can hardly think you are my Master.

VALENTINE

Are all these things perceiv'd in me?

SPEED

They are all perceiv'd without ye.

VALENTINE

Without me? they cannot.

Without you? nay, that's certain: for without you were so simple, none else would: but you are so without these follies, that these follies are within you, and shine through you like the water in an Urinal: that not an eye that sees you, but is a Physician to comment on your Malady.

VALENTINE

But tell me: do'st thou know my Lady *Silvia*?

SPEED

She that you gaze on so, as she sits at supper?

VALENTINE

Hast thou observ'd that? even she I mean.

SPEED

Why sir, I know her not.

VALENTINE

Do'st thou know her by my gazing on her, and yet know'st her not?

SPEED

Is she not hard-favour'd, sir?

VALENTINE

Not so fair (boy) as well favour'd.

SPEED

Sir, I know that well enough.

VALENTINE

What dost thou know?

SPEED

That she is not so fair, as (of you) well-favour'd.

VALENTINE

I mean that her beauty is exquisite,
But her favour infinite.

SPEED

That's because the one is painted, and the other out of all count.

VALENTINE

How painted? and how out of count?

SPEED

Marry sir, so painted to make her fair, that no man counts of her beauty.

VALENTINE

How esteem'st thou me? I account of her beauty.

SPEED

You never saw her since she was deform'd.

VALENTINE

How long hath she been deform'd?

SPEED

Ever since you lov'd her.

VALENTINE

I have lov'd her ever since I saw her,
And still I see her beautiful.

SPEED

If you love her, you cannot see her.

VALENTINE

Why?

SPEED

Because Love is blind: O that you had mine eyes, or your own eyes

had the lights they were wont to have, when you chid at Sir *Proteus,*
for going ungarter'd.

VALENTINE
What should I see then?

SPEED
Your own present folly, and her passing deformity: for he being
in love, could not see to garter his hose; and you, being in love,
cannot see to put on your hose.

VALENTINE
Belike (boy) then you are in love, for last morning
You could not see to wipe my shoes.

SPEED
True sir: I was in love with my bed, I thank you, you swing'd me
for my love, which makes me the bolder to chide you, for yours.

VALENTINE
In conclusion, I stand affected to her.

SPEED
I would you were set, so you affection would cease.

VALENTINE
Last night she enjoin'd me,
To write some lines to one she loves.

SPEED
And have you?

VALENTINE
I have.

SPEED
Are they not lamely writ?

VALENTINE

No (Boy) but as well as I can do them:
Peace, here she comes.

SPEED

Oh excellent motion; oh exceeding Puppet:
Now will he interpret to her.

VALENTINE

Madam & Mistress, a thousand good-morrows.

SPEED

Oh, give ye-good-ev'n: here's a million of manners.

SILVIA

Sir *Valentine,* and servant, to you two thousand.

SPEED

He should give her interest: & she gives it him.

VALENTINE

As you injoin'd me; I have writ your Letter
Unto the secret, nameless friend of yours:
Which I was much unwilling to proceed in,
But for my duty to your Ladyship.

SILVIA

I thank you (gentle Servant) 'tis very Clerkly done.

VALENTINE

Now trust me (Madam) it came hardly-off:
for being ignorant to whom it goes,
I write at random, very doubtfully.

SILVIA

Perchance you think too much of so much pains?

VALENTINE

No (Madam) so it stead you I will write
(Please you command) a thousand times as much:
And yet—

SILVIA

A pretty period: well: I guess the sequel;
And yet I will not name it: and yet I care not.
And yet, take this again: and yet I thank you:
Meaning henceforth to trouble you no more.

SPEED

And yet you will: and yet, another yet.

VALENTINE

What means your Ladyship?
Do you not like it?

SILVIA

Yes, yes: the lines are very quaintly writ,
But (since unwillingly) take them again.
Nay, take them.

VALENTINE

Madam, they are for you.

SILVIA

I, I: you writ them Sir at my request,
But I will none of them: they are for you:
I would have had them writ more movingly:

VALENTINE

Please you, I'll write your Ladyship another.

SILVIA

And when It's writ: for my sake read it over,
And if it please you, so: if not: why so:

VALENTINE
If it please me, (Madam?) what then?

SILVIA
Why if it please you, take it for your labour;
And so good-morrow Servant.

(*Exit* SILVIA)

SPEED
Oh jest unseen: inscrutible: invisible,
As a nose on a man's face, or a Weathercock on a steeple:
My Master sues to her: and she hath taught her Suitor,
He being her Pupil, to become her Tutor.
Oh excellent device, was there ever heard a better?
That my master being scribe,
To himself should write the Letter?

VALENTINE
How now Sir?
What are you reasoning with yourself?

SPEED
Nay: I was rhyming: 'tis you that have the reason.

VALENTINE
To do what?

SPEED
To be a Spokes-man from Madam *Silvia*.

VALENTINE
To whom?

SPEED
To your self: why, she woos you by a figure.

VALENTINE
What figure?

SPEED

By a Letter, I should say,

VALENTINE

Why she hath not writ to me.

SPEED

What need she,
When she hath made you write to your self?
Why, do you not perceive the jest?

VALENTINE

No, believe me.

SPEED

No believing you indeed sir:
But did you perceive her earnest?

VALENTINE

She gave me none, except an angry word.

SPEED

Why she hath given you a Letter.

VALENTINE

That's the Letter I writ to her friend.

SPEED

And that letter hath she deliver'd, & there an end.

VALENTINE

I would it were no worse.

SPEED

I'll warrant you, 'tis as well:
For often have you writ to her: and she in modesty,
Or else for want of idle time, could not again reply,
Or fearing else some messenger, that might her mind discover

Her self hath taught her Love himself, to write unto her lover.
All this I speak in print, for in print I found it.
Why muse you sir, 'tis dinner time.

VALENTINE

I have din'd.

SPEED

I, but hearken sir: though the Cameleon Love can feed on the air,
I am one that am nourish'd by my victuals; and would fain have
meat: oh be not like your Mistress, be moved, be moved.

The Two Gentlemen
of Verona

ACT IV, SCENE 4—
JULIA, SILVIA

JULIA

Gentlewoman, good day: I pray you be my mean
To bring me where to speak with Madam *Silvia*.

SILVIA

What would you with her, if that I be she?

JULIA

If you be she, I do entreat your patience
To hear me speak the message I am sent on.

SILVIA

From whom?

JULIA

From my Master, Sir *Proteus*, Madam.

SILVIA

Oh: he sends you for a Picture?

JULIA

I, Madam.

SILVIA

Ursula, bring my Picture there,
Go, give your Master this: tell him from me,
One *Julia,* that his changing thoughts forget
Would better fit his Chamber, than this Shadow.

JULIA

Madam, please you peruse this Letter;
Pardon me (Madam) I have unadvis'd
Deliver'd you a paper that I should not;
This is the Letter to your Ladyship.

SILVIA

I pray thee let me look on that again.

JULIA

It may not be: good Madam pardon me.

SILVIA

There, hold:
I will not look upon your Master's lines:
I know they are stuff'd with protestations,
And full of new-found oaths, which he will break
As easily as I do tear his paper.

JULIA

Madam, he sends your Ladyship this Ring.

SILVIA

The more shame for him, that he sends it me;
For I have heard him say a thousand times,
His *Julia* gave it him, at his departure:

Though his false finger have profan'd the Ring,
Mine shall not do his *Julia* so much wrong.

JULIA

She thanks you.

SILVIA

What say'st thou?

JULIA

I thank you Madam, that you tender her:
Poor Gentlewoman, my Master wrongs her much.

SILVIA

Do'st thou know her?

JULIA

Almost as well as I do know my self.
To think upon her woes, I do protest
That I have wept a hundred several times.

SILVIA

Belike she thinks that *Proteus* hath forsook her?

JULIA

I think she doth: and that's her cause of sorrow.

SILVIA

Is she not passing fair?

JULIA

She hath been fairer (Madam) than she is,
When she did think my Master lov'd her well;
She, in my judgment, was as fair as you.
But since she did neglect her looking-glass,
And threw her Sun-expelling Masque away,
The air hath starv'd the roses in her cheeks,

And pinch'd the lily-tincture of her face,
That now she is become as black as I.

SILVIA

How tall was she?

JULIA

About my stature: for at *Pentecost,*
When all our Pageants of delight were play'd,
Our youth got me to play the woman's part,
And I was trimm'd in Madam *Julia's* gown,
Which served me as fit, by all men's judgments,
As if the garment had been made for me:
Therefore I know she is about my height,
And at that time I made her weep a good,
For I did play a lamentable part.
(Madam) 'twas *Ariadne,* passioning
For *Theseus'* perjury, and unjust flight;
Which I so lively acted with my tears:
That my poor Mistress moved therewithal,
Wept bitterly: and would I might be dead,
If I in thought felt not her very sorrow.

SILVIA

She is beholding to thee (gentle youth)
Alas (poor Lady) desolate, and left;
I weep my self to think upon thy words:
Here youth: there is my purse; I give thee this
For thy sweet Mistress' sake, because thou lov'st her. Farewell.

JULIA

And she shall thank you for't, if e'er you know her.
A virtuous gentlewoman, mild, and beautiful.
I hope my Master's suit will be but cold,
Since she respects my Mistress' love so much.
Alas, how love can trifle with it self:
Here is her Picture: let me see, I think
If I had such a Tyre, this face of mine

103

Were full as lovely, as is this of hers;
And yet the Painter flatter'd her a little,
Unless I flatter with my self too much.
Her hair is *Auburn,* mine is perfect *Yellow*;
If that be all the difference in his love,
Ile get me such a colour'd Perrywig:
Her eyes are grey as glass, and so are mine:
I, but her fore-head's low, and mine's as high:
What should it be that he respects in her,
But I can make respective in my self,
If this fond Love, were not a blinded god?
Come shadow, come, and take this shadow up,
For 'tis thy rival: O thou senseless form,
Thou shalt be worship'd kiss'd, lov'd, and ador'd;
And were there sense in his Idolatry,
My substance should be statue in thy stead.
Ile use thee kindly, for thy Mistress' sake
That us'd me so: or else by *Jove,* I vow,
I should have scratch'd out your unseeing eyes,
To make my Master out of love with thee.

The First Part of King Henry the Sixth

ACT V, SCENE 3— SUFFOLK, MARGARET

Alarum. Enter SUFFOLK *with* MARGARET *in his hand.*

SUFFOLK
Be what thou wilt, thou art my prisoner.
(*Gazes on her*)
Oh fairest Beauty, do not fear, nor fly:
For I will touch thee but with reverend hands,

I kiss these fingers for eternal peace,
And lay them gently on thy tender side.
Who art thou, say? that I may honor thee.

MARGARET

Margaret my name, and daughter to a King,
The King of Naples, who so ere thou art.

SUFFOLK

An Earl I am, and Suffolk am I call'd
Be not offended Natures miracle,
Thou art alloted to be tane by me:
So doth the Swan her downy Signets save,
Keeping them prisoner undernearth his wings:
Yet if this servile usage once offend,
Go, and be free again, as Suffolk's friend.
(*She is going*)
Oh stay: I have no power to let her pass,
My hand would free her, but my heart says no.
As plays the Sun upon the glassy streams,
Twinkling another counterfetted beam,
So seems this gorgeous beauty to mine eyes.
Fain would I woo her, yet I dare not speak:
Ile call for Pen and Ink, and write my mind:
Fie *De la Pole,* disable not thyself:
Hast not a Tongue? Is she not here?
Wilt thou be daunted at a Woman's sight?
I: Beauty's Princely Majesty is such,
Confounds the tongue, and makes the senses rough.

MARGARET

Say Earl of Suffolk, if thy name be so,
What ransom must I pay before I pass?
For I perceive I am thy prisoner.

SUFFOLK

How canst thou tell she will deny thy suite,
Before thou make a trial of her love?

MARGARET

Why speak'st thou not? What ransom must I pay?

SUFFOLK

She's beautiful; and therefore to be Wooed:
She is a Woman; therefore to be Won.

MARGARET

Wilt thou accept of ransom, yea or no?

SUFFOLK

Fond man, remember that thou hast a wife,
Then how can *Margaret* be thy Paramour?

MARGARET

I were best to leave him, for he will not hear.

SUFFOLK

There all is marr'd: there lies a cooling card.

MARGARET

He talks at random: sure the man is mad.

SUFFOLK

And yet a dispensation may be had.

MARGARET

And yet I would that you would answer me.

SUFFOLK

Ile win this Lady *Margaret*. For whom?
Why for my King: Tush, that's a wooden thing.

MARGARET

He talks of wood: It is some Carpenter.

SUFFOLK

Yet so my fancy may be satisfied,
And peace established between these Realms.
But there remains a scruple in that too:
For though her Father be the King of *Naples,*
Duke of *Anjou* and *Mayne,* yet is he poor,
And our Nobility will scorn the match.

MARGARET

Hear ye Captain? Are you not at leisure?

SUFFOLK

It shall be so, disdain they ne'r so much:
Henry is youthful, and will quickly yield.
Madam, I have a secret to reveal.

MARGARET

What though I be inthral'd, he seems a knight
And will not any way dishonor me.

SUFFOLK

Lady, vouchsafe to listen what I say.

MARGARET

Perhaps I shall be rescu'd by the French,
And then I need not crave his courtesy.

SUFFOLK

Sweet Madam, give me hearing in a cause.

MARGARET

Tush, women have been captivate ere now.

SUFFOLK

Lady, wherefore talk you so?

MARGARET

I cry you mercy, 'tis but *Quid* for *Quo*.

SUFFOLK

Say gentle Princess, would you not suppose
Your bondage happy, to be made a Queen?

MARGARET

To be a Queen in bondage, is more vile,
Than is a slave, in base servility:
For Princes should be free.

SUFFOLK

And so shall you,
If happy England's Royal King be free.

MARGARET

Why what concerns his freedom unto me?

SUFFOLK

Ile undertake to make thee *Henry's* Queen,
to put a Golden Scepter in thy hand,
And set a precious Crown upon thy head,
If thou wilt condescend to be my—

MARGARET

What?

SUFFOLK

His love.

MARGARET

I am unworthy to be *Henry's* wife.

SUFFOLK

No gentle Madam, I unworthy am
To woo so fair a Dame to be his wife,

And have no portion in the choice my self.
How say you Madam, are ye so content?

And if my Father please, I am content.

SUFFOLK
Then call our Captains and our Colours forth,
And Madam, at your Father's Castle walls,
We'll crave a parley, to confer with him.

The Second Part of
King Henry the Sixth

ACT I, SCENE 2—
ELINOR, HUMPHREY
(DUCHESS AND DUKE OF GLOSTER), MESSENGER

ELINOR
Why droops my Lord like over-ripen'd Corn,
Hanging the head at Ceres plenteous load?
Why doth the Great Duke *Humphrey* knit his brows,
As frowning at the Favours of the world?
Why are thine eyes fixt to the sullen earth,
Gazing on that which seems to dim thy sight?
What seest thou there? King *Henry's* Diadem,
Inchac'd with all the Honours of the world?
If so, Gaze on, and grovel on thy face,
Until thy head be circled with the same.
Put forth thy hand, reach at the glorious Gold.
What, is't too short? Ile lengthen it with mine,
And having both together heav'd it up,
We'll both together lift our heads to heaven,

And never more abase our sight so low,
As to vouchsafe one glance unto the ground.

HUMPHREY

O *Nell,* sweet *Nell,* if thou dost love thy Lord,
Banish the Canker of ambitious thoughts:
And may that thought, when I imagine ill
Against my King and Nephew, virtuous *Henry,*
Be my last breathing in this mortal world.
My troublous dreams this night, doth make me sad.

ELINOR

What dream'd my Lord, tell me, and Ile requite it
With sweet rehearsal of my morning's dream.

HUMPHREY

Me thought this staff mine Office-badge in Court.
Was broke in twain: by whom, I have forgot,
But as I think, it was by the Cardinal,
And on the pieces of the broken Wand
Were plac'd the heads of *Edmond* Duke of Somerset,
And *William de la Pole* first Duke of Suffolk.
This was my dream, what it doth bode God knows.

ELINOR

Tut, this was nothing but an argument,
That he that breaks a stick of Gloster's grove,
Shall lose his head for his presumption.
But list to me my *Humphrey,* my sweet Duke:
Me thought I sat in Seat of Majesty,
In the Cathedral Church of Westminster,
And that the Chair where Kings & Queens were crown'd
Where *Henry* and Dame *Margaret* kneel'd to me,
And on my head did set the Diadem.

HUMPHREY

Nay, *Elinor,* then must I chide outright:
Presumptuous Dame, ill-nurtur'd *Elinor,*
Art thou not second Woman in the Realm?
And the Protector's wife belov'd of him?
Has thou not worldly pleasure at command,
Above the reach or compass of thy thought?
And wilt thou still be hammering Treachery,
To tumble down thy husband, and thy self,
From top of Honor, to Disgrace's feet?
Away from me, and let me hear no more.

ELINOR

What, what, my Lord? Are you so cholerick
With *Elinor,* for telling but her dreams?
Next time Ile keep my dreams unto my self,
And not be check'd.

HUMPHREY

Nay be not angry, I am pleas'd again.

(*Enter* MESSENGER)

MESSENGER

My Lord Protector, 'tis his Highness pleasure,
You do prepare to ride unto *Saint Albans,*
Where as the King and Queen do mean to Hawk.

HUMPHREY

I go. Come *Nell* thou wilt ride with us?

(*Exit* HUMPHREY)

ELINOR

Yes my good Lord, Ile follow presently.
Follow I must, I cannot go before,
While Gloster bears this base and humble mind.

Were I a man, a Duke, and next of blood,
I would remove these tedious stumbling blocks,
And smooth my way upon their headless necks.
And being a woman, I will not be slack
To play my part in Fortune's Pageant.

The Life and Death of Richard the Third

ACT I, SCENE 2—
LADY ANNE,
RICHARD DUKE OF GLOUCESTER,
GENTLEMAN

ANNE

Come, now toward Chertsey with your holy Load,
Taken from Paul's, to be interred there.
And still as you are weary of this weight,
Rest you, whiles I lament King Henry's Corse.

(*Enter* RICHARD DUKE OF GLOUCESTER)

RICHARD

Stay you that bear the Corse, and set it down.

ANNE

What black Magician conjures up this Fiend,
To stop devoted charitable deeds?

RICHARD

Villains set down the Corse, or by St. Paul,
Ile make a Corse of him that disobeys.

GENTLEMAN

My Lord Stand back, and let the Coffin pass.

RICHARD

Unmanner'd Dog,
Stand'st thou when I command:
Advance thy Halbert higher than my breast,
Or by St. Paul Ile strike thee to my Foot,
And spurn upon thee Beggar for thy boldness.

ANNE

What do you tremble? are you all afraid?
Alas, I blame you not, for you are Mortal,
And Mortal eyes cannot endure the Devil.
Avaunt thou dreadful minister of Hell;
Thou had'st but power over his Mortal body,
His Soul thou canst not have: Therfore be gone.

RICHARD

Sweet Saint, for Charity, be not so curst.

ANNE

Foul Devil,
For God's sake hence, and trouble us not,
For thou hast made the happy earth thy Hell:
Fill'd it with cursing cries, and deep exclaims:
If thou delight to view thy heinous deeds,
Behold this pattern of thy Butcheries.
Oh Gentlemen, see, see dead *Henry's* wounds,
Open their congeal'd mouths, and bleed afresh.
Blush, blush, thou lump of foul Deformity:
For 'tis thy presence that exhales this blood
From cold and empty Veins where no blood dwells.
Thy Deeds unhuman and unnatural,
Provokes this Deluge most unnatural.
O God! which this Blood mad'st, revenge his death:
O Earth! which this Blood drink'st, revenge his death.

Either Heav'n with Lightning strike the murd'rer dead:
Or Earth gape open wide, and eat him quick,
As thou dost swallow up this good King's blood,
Which this Hell-govern'd arm hath butchered.

RICHARD

Lady, you know no Rules of Charity.
Which renders good for bad, Blessings for Curses.

ANNE

Villain, thou know'st no law of God nor Man,
No Beast so fierce, but knows some touch of pity.

RICHARD

But I know none, and therefore am no Beast.

ANNE

O wonderful, when devils tell the truth!

RICHARD

More wonderful, when Angels are so angry:
Vouchsafe (divine perfection of a Woman)
Of these supposed Crimes, to give me leave
By circumstance, but to acquit my self.

ANNE

Vouchsafe (defus'd infection of a man)
Of these known evils, but to give me leave
By circumstance, to curse thy cursed Self.

RICHARD

Fairer than tongue can name thee, let me have
Some patient leisure to excuse my self.

ANNE

Fouler than heart can think thee,
Thou can'st make no excuse current,
But to hang thy self.

RICHARD

By such despair, I should accuse my self.

ANNE

And by despairing shalt thou stand excus'd,
For doing worthy Vengeance on thy self,
That did'st unworthy slaughter upon others.

RICHARD

Say I slew them not.

ANNE

Then say they were not slain:
But dead they are, and devilish slave by thee.

RICHARD

I did not kill your Husband.

ANNE

Why then he is alive.

RICHARD

Nay, he is dead, and slain by Edward's hands.

ANNE

In thy foul throat thou Ly'st,
Queen *Margaret* saw
Thy murd'rous Falchion smoking in his blood:
The which, thou once did'st bend against her breast,
But that thy Brothers beat aside the point.

RICHARD

I was provoked by her sland'rous tongue,
That laid their guilt, upon my guiltless Shoulders.

ANNE

Thou wast provoked by thy bloody mind,
That never dream'st on ought but Butcheries:
Did'st thou not kill this King?

RICHARD

I grant ye.

ANNE

Do'st grant me Hedge-hog,
Then God grant me too
Thou may'st be damned for that wicked deed,
O he was gentle, mild, and virtuous.

RICHARD

The better for the King of heaven that hath him.

ANNE

He is in heaven, where thou shalt never come.

RICHARD

Let him thank me, that holp to send him thither:
For he was fitter for that place than earth.

ANNE

And thou unfit for any place but hell.

RICHARD

Yes one place else, if you will hear me name it.

ANNE

Some dungeon.

RICHARD

Your Bed-chamber.

ANNE

Ill rest betide the chamber where thou liest.

RICHARD

So will it Madam, till I lie with you.

ANNE

I hope so.

RICHARD

I know so. But gentle Lady *Anne*,
To leave this keen encounter of our wits,
And fall something into a slower method.
Is not the causer of the timeless deaths
Of these *Plantagenets, Henry* and *Edward*,
As blameful as the Executioner.

ANNE

Thou wast the cause, and most accurst effect.

RICHARD

Your beauty was the cause of that effect:
Your beauty, that did haunt me in my sleep,
To undertake the death of all the world,
So I might live one hour in your sweet bosom.

ANNE

If I thought that, I tell thee Homicide,
These Nails should rent that beauty from my Cheeks.

RICHARD

These eyes could not endure that beauty's wrack,
You should not blemish it, if I stood by;
As all the world is cheered by the Sun,
So I by that: It is my day, my life.

ANNE

Black night o'er-shade thy day, and death thy life.

RICHARD

Curse not thy self fair Creature,
Thou art both.

ANNE

I would I were, to be reveng'd on thee.

RICHARD

It is a quarrel most unnatural,
To be reveng'd on him that loveth thee.

ANNE

It is a quarrel just and reasonable,
To be reveng'd on him that kill'd my Husband.

RICHARD

He that bereft thee Lady of thy Husband,
Did it to help thee to a better Husband.

ANNE

His better doth not breathe upon the earth.

RICHARD

He lives, that loves thee better than he could.

ANNE

Name him.

RICHARD

Plantagenet.

ANNE

Why that was he.

RICHARD

The selfsame name, but one of better Nature.

ANNE

Where is he?

RICHARD

Here:
(*She spits at him*)
Why dost thou spit at me?

ANNE

Would it were mortal poison, for thy sake.

RICHARD

Never came poison from so sweet a place.

ANNE

Never hung poison on a fouler Toad.
Out of my sight, thou dost infect mine eyes.

RICHARD

Thine eyes (sweet Lady) have infected mine.

ANNE

Would they were Basilisks, to strike thee dead.

RICHARD

I would they were, that I might die at once:
For now they kill me with a living death.
Those eyes of thine, from mine have drawn salt Tears;
Sham'd their Aspects with store of childish drops:
These eyes, which never shed remorseful tear,
No, when my Father Yorke, and *Edward* wept,
To hear the piteous moan that Rutland made
When black-fac'd *Clifford* shook his sword at him.
Nor when thy warlike Father like a Child,
Told the sad story of my Father's death,
And twenty times, made pause to sob and weep:
That all the standers by had wet their cheeks
Like Trees bedash'd with rain. In that sad time,

119

My manly eyes did scorn an humble tear:
And what these sorrows could not thence exhale,
Thy Beauty hath, and made them blind with weeping.
I never sued to Friend, nor Enemy:
My Tongue could never learn sweet smoothing word.
But now thy Beauty is propos'd my Fee,
My proud heart sues, and prompts my tongue to speak.
(*She looks scornfully at him*)
Teach not thy lip such Scorn; for it was made
For kissing Lady, not for such contempt.
If thy revengeful heart cannot forgive,
Lo here I lend thee this sharp-pointed Sword,
Which if thou please to hide in this true breast,
And let the Soul forth that adoreth thee,
I lay it naked to the deadly stroke,
And humbly beg the death upon my knee.
(*He lays his breast open. She offers at it with his sword*)
Nay do not pause: For I did kill King *Henry*,
But 'twas thy Beauty that provoked me.
Nay now dispatch: 'Twas I that stabb'd young *Edward*,
But 'twas thy Heavenly face that set me on.
(*She falls the sword*)
Take up the Sword again, or take up me.

ANNE

Arise Dissembler, though I wish thy death,
I will not be thy Executioner.

RICHARD

Then bid me kill my self, and I will do it.

ANNE

I have already.

RICHARD

That was in thy rage:
Speak it again, and even with the word,
This hand, which for thy love, did kill thy Love,

Shall for thy love, kill a far truer Love,
To both their deaths shalt thou be accessary.

ANNE

I would I knew thy heart.

RICHARD

'Tis figur'd in my tongue.

ANNE

I fear me, both are false.

RICHARD

Then never Man was true.

ANNE

Well, well, put up your Sword.

RICHARD

Say then my Peace is made.

ANNE

That shalt thou know hereafter.

RICHARD

But shall I live in hope.

ANNE

All men I hope live so.

RICHARD

Vouchsafe to wear this Ring.

ANNE

To take is not to give.

RICHARD

Look how my Ring incompasseth thy finger,
Even so thy Breast incloseth my poor heart:
Wear both of them, for both of them are thine.
And if thy poor devoted Servant may
But beg one favour at thy gracious hand,
Thou dost confirm his happiness for ever.

ANNE

What is it?

RICHARD

That it may please you leave these sad designs,
To him that hath most cause to be a Mourner,
And presently repair to Crosby House:
Where (after I have solemnly interr'd
At Chertsy Monast'ry this Noble King,
And wet his Grave with my Repentant Tears)
I will with all expedient duty see you,
For diverse unknown Reasons, I beseech you,
Grant me this Boon.

ANNE

With all my heart, and much it joys me too,
To see you are become so penitent.

RICHARD

Bid me farewell.

ANNE

'Tis more than you deserve:
But since you teach me how to flatter you,
Imagine I have said farewell already.

The Tragedy of
Romeo and Juliet

ACT II, SCENE 2—
ROMEO, JULIET

ROMEO

He jests at Scars that never felt a wound,
But soft, what light through yonder window breaks?
It is the East, and *Juliet* is the Sun,
Arise fair Sun and kill the envious Moon,
Who is already sick and pale with grief,
That thou her Maid art far more fair than she:
Be not her Maid since she is envious,
Her Vestal livery is but sick and green,
And none but fools do wear it, cast it off:
It is my Lady, O it is my Love, O that she knew she were,
She speaks, yet she says nothing, what of that?
Here eye discourses, I will answer it:
I am too bold 'tis not to me she speaks:
Two of the fairest stars in all the Heaven,
Having some business do entreat her eyes,
To twinkle in their Spheres till they return.
What if her eyes were there, they in her head,
The brightness of her cheek would shame those stars,
As day-light doth a Lamp, her eye in heaven,
Would through the airy Region stream so bright,
That Birds would sing, and think it were not night:
See how she leans her cheek upon her hand.
O that I were a Glove upon that hand,
That I might touch that cheek.

JULIET

Ay me.

ROMEO

She speaks.
Oh speak again bright Angel, for thou art
As glorious to this night being o'er my head,
As is a winged messenger of heaven:
Unto the white upturned wond'ring eyes
Of mortals that fall back to gaze on him,
When he bestrides the lazy puffing Clouds,
And falls upon the bosom of the air.

JULIET

O *Romeo, Romeo*, wherefore art thou *Romeo*?
Deny thy Father and refuse thy name:
Or if thou wilt not, be but sworn my Love,
And Ile no longer be a *Capulet*.

ROMEO

Shall I hear more, or shall I speak at this?

JULIET

'Tis but thy name that is my Enemy:
Thou art thy self, though not a *Montague,*
What's *Montague*? it is nor hand nor foot,
Nor arm, nor face, O be some other name
Belonging to a man.
What's in a name? that which we call a Rose,
by any other word would smell as sweet,
So *Romeo* would, were he not *Romeo* call'd,
Retain that dear perfection which he owes,
Without that title *Romeo*, doff thy name,
And for thy name which is no part of thee,
Take all my self.

ROMEO

I take thee at thy word:
Call me but Love, and Ile be new baptiz'd,
Hence forth I never will be *Romeo*.

JULIET

What man art thou, that thus bescreen'd in night
So stumblest on my counsel?

ROMEO

By a name,
I know not how to tell thee who I am:
My name dear Saint, is hateful to my self,
Because it is an Enemy to thee,
Had I it written, I would tear the word.

JULIET

My ears have not yet drunk a hundred words
Of thy tongue's uttering, yet I know the sound.
Art thou not *Romeo,* and a *Montague?*

ROMEO

Neither fair Maid, if either thee dislike.

JULIET

How cam'st thou hither.
Tell me, and wherefore?
The Orchard walls are high, and hard to climb,
And the place death, considering who thou art,
If any of my kinsmen find thee here.

ROMEO

With Love's light wings
Did I o'er-perch these Walls,
For stony limits cannot hold Love out,
And what Love can do, that dares Love attempt:
Therefore thy kinsmen are no stop to me.

JULIET

If they see thee, they will murder thee.

ROMEO

Alack there lies more peril in thine eye,
Than twenty of their Swords, look thou but sweet,
And I am proof against their enmity.

JULIET

I would not for the world they saw thee here.

ROMEO

I have night's cloak to hide me from their eyes
And but thou love me, let them find me here,
My life were better ended by their hate,
Than death prorogued wanting of thy Love.

JULIET

By whose direction found'st thou out this place?

ROMEO

By Love that first did prompt me to enquire,
He lent me counsel, and I lent him eyes,
I am no Pilot, yet wert thou as far
As that vast shore wash'd with the farthest Sea,
I should adventure for such Merchandise.

JULIET

Thou knowest the mask of night is on my face,
Else would a Maiden blush bepaint my cheek,
For that which thou hast heard me speak to night,
Fain would I dwell on form, fain, fain, deny
What I have spoke, but farewell Compliment,
Dost thou Love? I know thou wilt say I,
And I will take thy word, yet if thou swear'st,
Thou may'st prove false: at Lovers' perjuries
They says *Jove* laugh'd, oh gentle *Romeo,*
If thou dost Love, pronounce it faithfully:
Or if thou think'st I am too quickly won,
Ile frown and be perverse, and say thee nay,
So thou wilt woo: But else not for the world.

In truth fair *Montague* I am too fond:
And therefore thou mayest think my behavior light,
But trust me Gentleman, Ile prove more true,
Than those that have coying to be strange,
I should have been more strange, I must confess,
But that thou over heard'st ere I was 'ware
My true Love's passion, therefore pardon me,
And not impute this yielding to light Love,
Which the dark night hath so discovered.

ROMEO

Lady, by yonder Moon I vow,
That tips with silver all these Fruit tree tops.

JULIET

O swear not by the Moon, th'inconstant Moon,
That monthly changes in her circled Orb,
Least that thy Love prove likewise variable.

ROMEO

What shall I swear by?

JULIET

Do not swear at all:
Or if thou wilt swear by thy gracious self,
Which is the God of my Idolatry,
And Ile believe thee.

ROMEO

If my heart's dear love—

JULIET

Well do not swear, although I joy in thee:
I have no joy of this contract tonight,
It is too rash, too unadvis'd, too sudden,
Too like the lightning which doth cease to be
Ere one can say, it lightens, Sweet good night:
This bud of Love by Summer's ripening breath,

May prove a beauteous Flower when next we meet:
Goodnight, goodnight, as sweet repose and rest,
Come to thy heart, as that within my breast.

ROMEO

O wilt thou leave me so unsatisfied?

JULIET

What satisfaction can'st thou have to night?

ROMEO

Th'exchange of thy Love's faithful vow for mine.

JULIET

I gave thee mine before thou did'st request it:
And yet I would it were to give again.

ROMEO

Would'st thou withdraw it,
For what purpose Love?

JULIET

But to be frank and give it thee again,
And yet I wish but for the thing I have,
My bounty is as boundless as the Sea,
My Love as deep, the more I give to thee
The more I have, for both are Infinite:
I hear some noise within dear Love adieu:
(*Calls within*)
Anon good Nurse, sweet *Montague* be true:
Stay but a little, I will come again.

ROMEO

O blessed blessed night, I am afear'd
Being in night, all this is but a dream,
Too flattering sweet to be substantial.

JULIET

Three words dear *Romeo*
And goodnight indeed,
If that thy bent of Love be Honourable,
Thy purpose marriage, send me word tomorrow,
By one that Ile procure to come to thee,
Where and what time thou wilt perform the rite,
And all my fortunes at thy foot Ile lay,
And follow thee my Lord throughout the world.
(*Within:* Madam)
I come, anon: but if thou meanest not well,
I do beseech thee
(*Within:* Madam)
(By and by I come)
To cease thy strife, and leave me to my grief,
Tomorrow will I send.

ROMEO

So thrive my soul.

JULIET

A thousand times goodnight.

(*Exit*)

ROMEO

A thousand times the worse to want thy light,
Love goes toward Love as school-boys from their books
But Love from Love, towards school with heavy looks.

(*Enter* JULIET *again*)

JULIET

Hist Romeo hist: O for a Falc'ner's voice,
To lure this Tassel gentle back again,
Bondage is hoarse, and may not speak aloud,
Else would I tear the Cave where Echo lies,

And make her airy tongue more hoarse, then
With repetition of my *Romeo*.

ROMEO

It is my soul that calls upon my name.
How silver sweet, sound Lovers' tongues by night,
Like softest Music to attending ears.

JULIET

Romeo.

ROMEO

My dear.

JULIET

What a clock tomorrow
Shall I send to thee?

ROMEO

By the hour of nine.

JULIET

I will not fail, 'tis twenty years till then,
I have forgot why I did call thee back.

ROMEO

Let me stand here till thou remember it.

JULIET

I shall forget, to have thee still stand there,
Rememb'ring how I Love thy company.

ROMEO

And Ile still stay, to have thee still forget,
Forgetting any other home but this.

JULIET

'Tis almost morning, I would have thee gone,
And yet no further than a wanton's Bird,
That lets it hop a little from his hand,
Like a poor prisoner in his twisted Gyves,
And with a silken thread plucks it back again,
So loving Jealous of his liberty.

ROMEO

I would I were thy Bird.

JULIET

Sweet so would I,
Yet I should kill thee with much cherishing:
Good night, good night.
Parting is such sweet sorrow,
That I shall say goodnight, till it be morrow.
Sleep dwell upon thine eyes, peace in thy breast.

ROMEO

Would I were sleep and peace so sweet to rest.

The Tragedy of
Romeo and Juliet

ACT II, SCENE 5—
JULIET, NURSE

JULIET

The clock struck nine when I did send the Nurse,
In half an hour she promis'd to return,
Perchance she cannot meet him: that's not so:
Oh she is lame, Love's Herald should be thoughts,
Which ten times faster glides than the Sun's beams,

Driving back shadows over lowering hills.
Therefore do nimble Pinion'd Doves draw Love,
And therefore hath the wind-swift *Cupid* wings:
Now is the Sun upon the highmost hill
Of this day's journey, and from nine till twelve,
I three long hours, yet she is not come.
Had she affections and warm youthful blood,
She would be as swift in motion as a ball,
My words would bandy her to my sweet Love,
And his to me, but old folks,
Many fain as they were dead,
Unwieldy, slow, heavy, and pale as lead.
(*Enter* NURSE)
O God she comes, O honey Nurse what news?
Hast thou met with him? send thy man away.

NURSE

Peter stay at the gate.

JULIET

Now good sweet Nurse:
O Lord, why lookest thou sad?
Though news be sad, yet tell them merrily.
If good thou sham'st the music of sweet news,
By playing it to me, with so sour a face.

NURSE

I am a weary, give me leave awhile,
Fie how my bones ache, what a jaunt have I had?

JULIET

I would thou had'st my bones, and I thy news:
Nay come I pray thee speak, good good Nurse speak.

NURSE

Jesu what haste? can you not stay a while?
Do you not see that I am out of breath?

JULIET

How art thou out of breath, when thou hast breath
To say to me, that thou art out of breath?
The excuse that thou dost make in this delay,
Is longer than the tale thou dost excuse.
Is thy news good or bad? answer to that,
Say either, and Ile stay the circumstance:
Let me be satisfied, is't good or bad?

NURSE

Well, you have made a simple choice, you know not how to choose
a man: *Romeo,* no not he though his face be better than any man's,
yet his legs excels all men's, and for a hand, and a foot, and a body,
though they be not to be talkt on, yet they are past compare: he
is not the flower of courtesy, but Ile warrant him as gentle a Lamb:
go thy ways wench, serve God. What have you din'd at home?

JULIET

No no: but all this did I know before
What says he of our marriage? what of that?

NURSE

Lord how my head aches, what a head have I?
It beats as it would fall in twenty pieces.
My back at t'other side: O my back, my back:
Beshrew your heart for sending me about
To catch my death with jaunting up and down.

JULIET

I'faith: I am sorry that thou are not well.
Sweet sweet, sweet Nurse, tell me what says my Love?

NURSE

Your Love says like an honest Gentleman,
And a courteous, and a kind, and a handsome,
And I warrant a virtuous: where is your Mother?

JULIET

Where is my Mother?
Why she is within, where should she be?
How oddly thou repli'st:
Your Love says like a Gentleman:
Where is your Mother?

NURSE

O God's Lady dear,
Are you so hot? marry come up I trow,
Is this the Poultis for my aching bones?
Henceforward do your messages your self.

JULIET

Here's such a coil, come what says *Romeo*?

NURSE

Have you got leave to go to shrift today?

JULIET

I have.

NURSE

Then hie you hence to Friar *Lawrence'* Cell,
There stays a Husband to make you a wife:
Now comes the wanton blood up in your cheeks,
They'll be in Scarlet straight at any news:
Hie you to Church, I must an other way,
To fetch a Ladder by the which your Love
Must climb a bird's nest Soon at night,
Go Ile to dinner, hie you to the Cell.

JULIET

Hie to high Fortune, honest Nurse, farewell.

A Midsummer Night's Dream

ACT II, SCENE 1—
OBERON, TITANIA, PUCK

(Enter the King of Fairies at one door with his train, and the Queen at another with hers)

OBERON

Ill met by Moon-light,
Proud *Titania*.

TITANIA

What, jealous *Oberon*? Fairy skip hence.
I have forsworn his bed and company.

OBERON

Tarry rash Wanton; am not I thy Lord?

TITANIA

Then I must be thy Lady: but I know
When thou wast stol'n away from Fairy Land,
And in the shape of *Corin,* sat all day.
Playing on pipes of Corn, and versing love
To amorous *Phillida*. Why art thou here
Come from the farthest steep of *India*?
But that forsooth the bouncing *Amazon*
Your buskin'd Mistress, and your Warrior love,
To *Theseus* must be Wedded; and you come,
To give their bed joy and prosperity.

OBERON

How canst thou thus for shame *Titania*,
Glance at my credit, with *Hippolyta*?
Knowing I know thy love to *Theseus*?

Didst thou not lead him through the glimmering night
From *Peregenia,* whom he ravished?
And make him with fair Eagles break his faith
With *Ariadne,* and *Atiopa*?

TITANIA

These are the forgeries of jealousy,
And never since the middle Summer's spring
Met we on hill, in dale, forest, or mead,
By paved fountain, or by rushy brook,
Or in the beached margent of the sea,
To dance our ringlets to the whistling Wind,
But with thy brawls thou hast disturb'd our sport.
Therefore the Winds, piping to us in vain,
As in revenge, have suck'd up from the sea
Contagious fogs: Which falling in the Land,
Hath every petty River made so proud,
That they have over-borne their Continents.
The Ox hath therefore stretch'd his yoke in vain,
The Ploughman lost his sweat, and the green Corn
Hath rotted, ere his youth attain'd a beard:
The fold stands empty in the drowned field,
And Crows are fatted with the murrion flock,
The nine men's Morris is fill'd up with mud,
And the quaint Mazes in the wanton green,
For lack of tread are undistinguishable.
The human mortals want their winter here,
No night is now with hymn or carol blest;
Therefore the Moon (the governess of floods)
Pale in her anger, washes all the air;
That Rheumatic diseases do abound.
And through this distemperature, we see
The seasons alter; hoared headed frosts
Fall in the fresh lap of the crimson Rose,
And on old Hyem's chin and Icy crown,
An odorous Chaplet of sweet Summer buds
Is as in mock'ry set. The Spring, the Summer,
The childing Autumn, angry Winter change

Their wonted Liveries, and the mazed world,
By their increase, now knows not which is which;
And this same progeny of evils,
Comes from our debate, from our dissension,
We are their parents and original.

OBERON

Do you amend it then, it lies in you,
Why should *Titania* cross her *Oberon*?
O do but beg a little changeling boy,
To be my Henchman.

TITANIA

Set your heart at rest,
The Fairy land buys not the child of me,
His mother was a Vot'ress of my Order,
And in the spiced *Indian* air, by night
Full often hath she gossip'd by my side,
And sat with me on *Neptune's* yellow sands,
Marking th'embarked traders on the flood,
When we have laugh'd to see the sails conceive,
And grow big bellied with the wanton wind:
Which she with pretty and with swimming gait,
Following (her womb then rich with my young squire)
Would imitate, and sail upon the Land,
To fetch me trifles, and return again,
As from a voyage, rich with merchandise.
But she being mortal, of that boy did die,
And for her sake I do rear up her boy,
And for her sake I will not part with him.

OBERON

How long within this wood intend you stay?

TITANIA

Perchance till after *Theseus'* wedding day.
If you will patiently dance in our Round,

And see our Moon-light revels, go with us;
If not, shun me and I will spare your haunts.

OBERON

Give me that boy, and I will go with thee.

TITANIA

Not for thy Fairy Kingdom. Fairies away:
We shall chide down right, if I longer stay.
(*Exeunt*)

OBERON

Well, go thy way: thou shalt not from this grove,
Till I torment thee for this injury.
My gentle *Puck* come hither; thou remembrest
Since once I sat upon a promontory,
And heard a Mermaid on a Dolphin's back,
Uttering such dulcet and harmonious breath,
That the rude sea grew civil at her song,
And certain stars shot madly from their Spheres,
To hear the Sea-maid's music.

PUCK

I remember.

OBERON

That very time I saw (but thou could'st not)
Flying between the cold Moon and the earth,
Cupid all arm'd; a certain aim he took
At a fair Vestal, throned by the West,
And loos'd his love-shaft smartly from his bow,
As it should pierce a hundred thousand hearts,
But I might see young *Cupid's* Fiery shaft
Quench'd in the chaste beams of the wat'ry Moon;
And the imperial Vot'ress passed on,
In maiden meditation, fancy free.
Yet mark'd I where the bolt of *Cupid* fell.
It fell upon a little western flower;
Before, milk-white; now purple with love's wound,

138

And maidens call it, Love in idleness.
Fetch me that flower; the herb I show'd thee once,
The juice of it, on sleeping eye-lids laid,
Will make or man or woman madly dote
Upon the next live creature that it sees.
Fetch me this herb, and be thou here again,
Ere the *Leviathan* can swim a league.

PUCK

Ile put a girdle about the earth, in forty minutes.

OBERON

Having once this juice,
Ile watch *Titania,* when she is asleep,
And drop the liquor of it in her eyes:
The next thing when she waking looks upon,
(Be it on Lion, Bear, or Wolf, or Bull,
On meddling Monkey, or on busy Ape)
She shall pursue it with the soul of love.
And ere I take this charm off from her sight,
(As I can take it with another herb)
Ile make her render up her Page to me.

A Midsummer Night's Dream

ACT II, SCENE 1—
DEMETRIUS, HELENA

(*Enter* DEMETRIUS, HELENA following him)

DEMETRIUS

I love thee not, therefore pursue me not,
Where is *Lysander,* and fair *Hermia*?
The one Ile slay, the other slayeth me.

Thou told'st me they were stol'n into this wood;
And here am I, and wood within this wood,
Because I cannot meet my *Hermia*.
Hence, get thee gone, and follow me no more.

HELENA

You draw me, you hard-hearted Adamant,
But yet you draw not Iron, for my heart
Is true as steel. Leave you your power to draw,
And I shall have power to follow you.

DEMETRIUS

Do I entice you? do I speak you fair?
Or rather do I not in plainest truth,
Tell you I do not, nor I cannot love you?

HELENA

And even for that do I love thee the more;
I am your spaniel, and *Demetrius,*
The more you beat me, I will fawn on you.
Use me but as your spaniel; spurn me, strike me,
Neglect me, lose me; only give me leave
(Unworthy as I am) to follow you.
What worser place can I beg in your love,
(And yet a place of high respect with me)
Than to be used as you do your dog.

DEMETRIUS

Tempt not too much the hatred of my spirit,
For I am sick when I do look on thee.

HELENA

And I am sick when I look not on you:

DEMETRIUS

You do impeach your modesty too much,
To leave the City, and commit your self
Into the hands of one that loves you not,

To trust the opportunity of night,
And the ill counsel of a desert place,
With the rich worth of your virginity.

HELENA

Your virtue is my privilege: for that
It is not night when I do see your face.
Therefore I think I am not in the night,
Nor doth this wood lack worlds of company,
For you in my respect are all the world.
Then how can it be said I am alone,
When all the world is here to look on me?

DEMETRIUS

Ile run from thee, and hide me in the brakes,
And leave thee to the mercy of wild beasts.

HELENA

The wildest hath not such a heart as you;
Run when you will, the story shall be chang'd:
Apollo flies, and *Daphne* holds the chase;
The Dove pursues the Griffin, the mild Hind
Makes speed to catch the Tiger. Bootless speed,
When cowardice pursues, and valour flies.

DEMETRIUS

I will not stay thy questions, let me go;
Or if thou follow me, do not believe,
But I shall do thee mischief in the wood.

HELENA

I, in the Temple, in the Town, and Field
You do me mischief. Fie *Demetrius,*
Your wrongs do set a scandal on my sex:
We cannot fight for love, as men may do;
We should be woo'd, and were not made to woo.
I follow thee, and make a heaven of hell,
To die upon the hand I love so well.

The Merchant of Venice

ACT I, SCENE 1—
ANTONIO, BASSANIO

ANTONIO

Well: tell me now, what Lady is the same
To whom you swore a secret Pilgrimage
That you today promis'd to tell me of?

BASSANIO

Tis not unknown to you *Antonio*
How much I have disabled mine estate,
By something showing a more swelling port
Than my faint means would grant continuance:
Nor do I now make moan to be abridg'd
From such a noble rate, but my chief care
Is to come fairly off from the great debts
Wherein my time something too prodigal
Hath left me gag'd: to you Antonio
I owe the most in money, and in love,
And from your love I have a warranty
To unburden all my plots and purposes,
How to get clear of all the debts I owe.

ANTONIO

I pray you good *Bassanio* let me know it,
And if it stand as you your self still do,
Within the eye of honour, be assur'd
My purse, my person, my extremest means
Lie all unlock'd to your occasions.

BASSANIO

In my school days, when I had lost one shaft
I shot his fellow of the selfsame flight
The selfsame way, with more advised watch
To find the other forth, and by adventuring both,
I oft found both. I urge this child-hood proof,
Because what follows is pure innocence.
I owe you much, and like a willful youth,
That which I owe is lost: but if you please
To shoot another arrow that self way
Which you did shoot the first, I do not doubt,
As I will watch the aim: or to find both,
Or bring your latter hazard back again,
And thankfully rest debtor for the first.

ANTONIO

You know me well, and herein spend but time
To wind about my love with circumstance,
And out of doubt you do more wrong
In making question of my uttermost
Than if you had made waste of all I have:
Then do but say to me what I should do
That in your knowledge may by me be done,
And I am press'd unto it: therefore speak.

BASSANIO

In *Belmont* is a Lady richly left,
And she is fair, and fairer than that word,
Of wond'rous virtues, sometimes from her eyes
I did receive fair speechless messages:
Her name is *Portia,* nothing undervalu'd
To *Cato's* daughter, *Brutus' Portia,*
Nor is the wide world ignorant of her worth,
For the four winds blow in from every coast
Renowned suitors, and her sunny locks
Hang on her temples like a golden fleece,
And many *Jasons* come in quest of her.

O my *Antonio,* had I but the means
To hold a rival place with one of them,
I have a mind presages me such thrift,
That I should questionless be fortunate.

ANTONIO

Thou know'st that all my fortunes are at sea,
Neither have I money, nor commodity
To raise a present sum, therefore go forth
Try what my credit can in *Venice* do,
That shall be rack'd even to the uttermost,
To furnish thee to *Belmont* to fair *Portia.*
Go presently inquire, and so will I
Where money is, and I no question make
To have it of my trust, or for my sake.

The Taming of the Shrew

ACT II, SCENE 1—
PETRUCHIO, KATHERINE

PETRUCHIO

Good morrow *Kate,* for that's your name I hear.

KATHERINE

Well have you heard, but something hard of hearing:
They call me *Katherine,* that do talk of me.

PETRUCHIO

You lie in faith, for you are call'd plain *Kate,*
And bonny *Kate,* and sometimes *Kate* the curst:
But *Kate,* the prettiest *Kate* in Christendom,
Kate of *Kate*-hall, my super-dainty *Kate,*
For dainties are all *Kates,* and therefore *Kate*

Take this of me, *Kate* of my consolation,
Hearing thy mildness prais'd in every Town,
Thy virtues spoke of, and thy beauty sounded,
Yet not so deeply as to thee belongs,
My self am mov'd to woo thee for my wife.

KATHERINE

Mov'd, in good time, let him that mov'd you hither
Remove you hence: I knew you at the first
You were a moveable.

PETRUCHIO

Why, what's a moveable?

KATHERINE

A join'd stool.

PETRUCHIO

Thou hast hit it: come sit on me.

KATHERINE

Asses were made to bear, and so are you.

PETRUCHIO

Women were made to bear, and so are you.

KATHERINE

No such Jade as you, if me you mean.

PETRUCHIO

Alas good *Kate,* I will not burden thee,
For knowing thee to be but young and light.

KATHERINE

Too light for such a swain as you to catch,
And yet as heavy as my weight should be.

PETRUCHIO

Should be, should: buzz.

KATHERINE

Well ta'en, and like a buzzard.

PETRUCHIO

Oh slow-wing'd Turtle, shall a buzzard take thee?

KATHERINE

I for a Turtle, as he takes a buzzard.

PETRUCHIO

Come, come you Wasp, i'faith you are too angry.

KATHERINE

If I be waspish, best beware my sting.

PETRUCHIO

My remedy is then to pluck it out.

KATHERINE

I, if the fool could find it where it lies.

PETRUCHIO

Who knows not where a Wasp does wear his sting? In his tail.

KATHERINE

In his tongue?

PETRUCHIO

Whose tongue?

KATHERINE

Yours if you talk of tails, and so farewell.

PETRUCHIO

What with my tongue in your tail.
Nay, come again, good Kate, I am a Gentleman.

KATHERINE

That Ile try.

(She strikes him)

PETRUCHIO

I swear Ile cuff you if you strike again.

KATHERINE

So may you lose your arms,
If you strike me, you are no Gentleman,
And if no Gentleman, why then no arms.

PETRUCHIO

A Herald *Kate*? Oh put me in thy books.

KATHERINE

What is your Crest, a Coxcomb?

PETRUCHIO

A combless Cock, so *Kate* will be my Hen.

KATHERINE

No Cock of mine, you crow too like a craven.

PETRUCHIO

Nay come *Kate,* come: you must not look so sour.

KATHERINE

It is my fashion when I see a Crab.

PETRUCHIO

Why here's no crab, and therefore look not sour.

KATHERINE

There is, there is.

PETRUCHIO

Then show it me.

KATHERINE

Had I a glass, I would.

PETRUCHIO

What, you mean my face?

KATHERINE

Well aim'd of such a young one.

PETRUCHIO

Now by St. George I am too young for you.

KATHERINE

Yet you are wither'd.

PETRUCHIO

'Tis with cares.

KATHERINE

I care not.

PETRUCHIO

Nay hear you *Kate*. In soothe you 'scape not so.

KATHERINE

I chafe you if I tarry. Let me go.

PETRUCHIO

No, not a whit, I find you passing gentle:
'Twas told me you were rough, and coy, and sullen,
And now I find report a very liar:
For thou art pleasant, gamesome, passing courteous,
But slow in speech: yet sweet as spring-time flowers.
Thou canst not frown, thou canst not look askance,
Nor bite the lip, as angry wenches will,
Nor hast thou pleasure to be cross in talk:
But thou with mildness entertain'st thy wooers,
With gentle conference, soft, and affable.
Why does the world report that *Kate* doth limp?

Oh sland'rous world: *Kate* like the hazel twig
Is straight, and slender, and as brown in hue
As hazel nuts, and sweeter than the kernels:
Oh let me see thee walk: thou dost not halt.

KATHERINE

Go fool, and whom thou keep'st command.

PETRUCHIO

Did ever *Dian* so become a Grove
As *Kate* this chamber with her princely gait:
O be thou *Dian,* and let her be *Kate,*
And then let *Kate* be chaste, and *Dian* sportful.

KATHERINE

Where did you study all this goodly speech?

PETRUCHIO

It is *extempore,* from my mother wit.

KATHERINE

A witty mother, witless else her son.

PETRUCHIO

Am I not wise?

KATHERINE

Yes, keep you warm.

PETRUCHIO

Marry so I mean sweet *Katherine* in thy bed:
And therefore setting all this chat aside,
Thus in plain terms: your father hath consented
That you shall be my wife; your dowry 'greed on,
And will you, nill you, I will marry you.
Now *Kate,* I am a husband for your turn,
For by this light, whereby I see thy beauty,
Thy beauty that doth make me like thee well,
Thou must be married to no man but me,

(*Enter* BAPTISTA, GREMIO, TRANIO)
For I am he am born to tame you *Kate,*
And bring you from a wild *Kate* to a *Kate*
Conformable as other household *Kates*:
Here comes your father, never make denial,
I must, and will have *Katherine* to my wife.

The First Part of Henry the Fourth

ACT II, SCENE 3— HOTSPUR, LADY PERCY, SERVANT

HOTSPUR
How now Kate, I must leave you within these two hours.

LADY PERCY
O my good Lord, why are you thus alone?
For what offence have I this fortnight been
A banish'd woman from my *Harry's* bed?
Tell me (sweet Lord) what is't that takes from thee
Thy stomach, pleasure, and thy golden sleep?
Why dost thou bend thine eye upon the earth?
And start so often when thou sitt'st alone?
Why hast thou lost the fresh blood in thy cheeks?
And given my Treasures and my rights of thee
To thick-ey'd musing, and curst melancholy?
In my faint-slumbers, I by thee have watcht,
And heard thee murmur tales of Iron Wars:
Speak terms of manage to thy bounding Steed,
Cry courage to the field. And thou hast talk'd
Of Sallies, and Retires; Trenches, Tents,
Of Palizadoes, Frontiers, Parapets,
Of Basilisks, of Canon, Culverin,

Of Prisoners ransom, and of Soldiers slain,
And all the current of a heady fight.
Thy spirit within thee hath been so at War,
And thus hath so bestirr'd thee in thy sleep,
That beads of sweat hath stood upon thy Brow,
Like bubbles in a late-disturbed Stream;
And in thy face strange motions have appear'd,
Such as we see when men restrain their breath
On some great sudden haft. O what portents are these?
Some heavy business hath my Lord in hand,
And I must know it: else he loves me not.

HOTSPUR

What ho; is *Gilliams* with the Packet gone?

SERVANT

He is my Lord, an hour agone.

HOTSPUR

Hath *Butler* brought those horses from the Sheriff?

SERVANT

One horse, my Lord, he brought even now.

HOTSPUR

What Horse? A Roan, a crop ear, it is not.

SERVANT

It is my Lord.

HOTSPUR

That Roan shall be my Throne. Well, I will back him straight.
Esperance, bid *Butler* lead him forth into the Park.

LADY PERCY

But hear you, my Lord.

HOTSPUR

What say'st thou my Lady?

LADY PERCY

What is it carries you away?

HOTSPUR

Why, my horse (my Love) my horse.

LADY PERCY

Out you mad-headed Ape, a Weasel hath not such a deal of Spleen, as you are tost with. In sooth Ile know your business *Harry,* that I will. I fear my Brother *Mortimer* doth stir about his Title, and hath sent for you to line his enterprise. But if you go—

HOTSPUR

So far a foot, I shall be weary, Love.

LADY PERCY

Come, come, you Paraquito, answer me directly unto this question, that I shall ask. Indeed Ile break thy little finger *Harry,* if thou wilt not tell me true.

HOTSPUR

Away, away you trifler: Love, I love thee not,
I care not for thee *Kate*: this is no world
To play with Mammets, and to tilt with lips.
We must have bloody Noses, and crack'd Crownes,
And pass them current too. Gods me, my horse.
What sayst thou Kate? what wold'st thou have with me?

LADY PERCY

Do ye not love me? Do ye not indeed?
Well, do not then. For since you love me not,
I will not love my self. Do you not love me?
Nay, tell me if thou speak'st in jest, or no.

HOTSPUR

Come, wilt thou see me ride?
And when I am a horseback, I will swear
I love thee infinitely. But hark you *Kate,*
I must not have you henceforth, question me,

Whether I go: nor reason whereabout.
Whether I must, I must: and to conclude,
This Evening must I leave thee, gentle *Kate*.
I know you wife, but yet no further wife
Than *Harry Percy's* wife. Constant you are.
But yet a woman: and for secrecy,
No Lady closer. For I will believe
Thou wilt not utter what thou do'st not know,
And so far wilt I trust thee, gentle Kate.

LADY PERCY

How so far?

HOTSPUR

Not an inch further. But hark you *Kate,*
Whither I go, thither shall you go too:
To day will I set forth, to morrow you.
Will this content you *Kate?*

LADY PERCY

It must of force.

(*Exeunt*)

Much Ado About Nothing

ACT IV, SCENE 1—
BENEDICK, BEATRICE

BENEDICK

Lady *Beatrice,* have you wept all this while?

BEATRICE

Yea, and I will weep a while longer.

BENEDICK

I will not desire that.

BEATRICE

You have no reason, I do it freely.

BENEDICK

Surely I do believe your fair cousin is wrong'd.

BEATRICE

Ah, how much might the man deserve of me that would right her!

BENEDICK

Is there any way to show such friendship?

BEATRICE

A very even way, but no such friend.

BENEDICK

May a man do it?

BEATRICE

It is a man's office, but not yours.

BENEDICK

I do love nothing in the world so well as you, is not that strange?

BEATRICE

As strange as the thing I know not, it were as possible for me to say, I loved nothing so well as you, but believe me not, and yet I lie not, I confess nothing, nor I deny nothing, I am sorry for my cousin.

BENEDICK

By my sword *Beatrice* thou lov'st me.

BEATRICE

Do not swear by it and eat it.

BENEDICK

I will swear by it that you love me, and I will make him eat it that says I love not you.

BEATRICE

Will you not eat your word?

BENEDICK

With no sauce that can be devised to it, I protest I love thee.

BEATRICE

Why then God forgive me.

BENEDICK

What offence sweet Beatrice?

BEATRICE

You have stayed me in a happy hour, I was about to protest I loved you.

BENEDICK

And do it with all thy heart.

BEATRICE

I love you with so much of my heart, that none is left to protest.

BENEDICK

Come, bid me do any thing for thee.

BEATRICE

Kill *Claudio.*

BENEDICK

Ha, not for the wide world.

BEATRICE

You kill me to deny, farewell.

BENEDICK

Tarry sweet *Beatrice*.

BEATRICE

I am gone, though I am here, there is no love in you, nay I pray you let me go.

BENEDICK

Beatrice.

BEATRICE

In faith I will go.

BENEDICK

We'll be friends first.

BEATRICE

You dare easier be friends with me, than fight with mine enemy.

BENEDICK

Is *Claudio* thine enemy?

BEATRICE

Is a not approved in the height a villain, that hath slandered, scorned, dishonoured my kinswoman? O that I were a man! what, bear her in hand until they come to take hands, and then with public accusation uncovered slander, unmitigated rancour? O God that I were a man! I would eat his heart in the market-place.

BENEDICK

Hear me *Beatrice*.

BEATRICE

Talk with a man out at a window, a proper saying.

BENEDICK

Nay but *Beatrice*.

BEATRICE

Sweet *Hero,* she is wronged, she is slandered, she is undone.

BENEDICK

Beat——?

BEATRICE

Princes and Counties! surely a Princely testimony, a goodly Count, Comfect, a sweet Gallant surely, O that I were a man for his sake! or that I had any friend would be a man for my sake! But manhood is melted into curtsies, valour into complement, and men are only turned into tongue, and trim ones too: he is now as valiant as *Hercules,* that only tells a lie, and swears it: I cannot be a man with wishing, therefore I will die a woman with grieving.

BENEDICK

Tarry good *Beatrice*, by this hand I love thee.

BEATRICE

Use it for my love some other way than swearing by it.

BENEDICK

Think you in your soul the Count *Claudio* hath wrong'd *Hero*?

BEATRICE

Yea, as sure as I have a thought, or a soul.

BENEDICK

Enough, I am engaged, I will challenge him, I will kiss your hand, and so leave you: by this hand *Claudio* shall render me a dear account: as you hear of me, so think of me: go comfort your cousin, I must say she is dead, and so farewell.

The Merry Wives
of Windsor

ACT II, SCENE 2—
MISTRESS QUICKLY, FALSTAFF

QUICKLY

Give your worship good morrow.

FALSTAFF

Good-morrow, good-wife.

QUICKLY

Not so, and't please your worship.

FALSTAFF

Good maid then.

QUICKLY

Ile be sworn,
As my mother was the first hour I was born.

FALSTAFF

I do believe the swearer; what with me?

QUICKLY

Shall I vouchsafe your worship a word, or two?

FALSTAFF

Two thousand (fair woman) and Ile vouchsafe the hearing.

QUICKLY

There is one Mistress *Ford,* (Sir) I pray come a little nearer this
ways: I my self dwell with M. Doctor *Caius*:

FALSTAFF

Well, on; Mistress *Ford,* you say.

QUICKLY

Your worship says very true: I pray your worship come a little
nearer this ways.

FALSTAFF

I warrant thee, no-body hears: mine own people, mine own people.

QUICKLY

Are they so? heaven bless them, and make them his Servants.

FALSTAFF

Well; Mistress *Ford,* what of her?

QUICKLY

Why, Sir; she's a good-creature; Lord, Lord, your Worship's a wanton: well: heaven forgive you, and all of us, I pray—

FALSTAFF

Mistress *Ford*: Come, Mistress *Ford.*

QUICKLY

Marry this is the short, and the long of it: you have brought her
into such a Canaries, as 'tis wonderful: the best Courtier of them
all (when the Court lay at *Windsor*) could never have brought her
to such a Canary: yet there has been Knights, and Lords, and Gentlemen, with their Coaches; I warrant you Coach after Coach, letter
after letter, gift after gift, smelling so sweetly; all Musk, and so
rushling, I warrant you, in silk and gold, and in such alligant terms,
and in such wine and sugar of the best, and the fairest, that would
have won any woman's heart: and I warrant you, they could never
get an eye-wink of her: I had my self twenty Angels given me this
morning, but I defy all Angels (in any such sort, as they say) but
in the way of honesty: and I warrant you, they could never get her
so much as sip on a cup with the proudest of them all, and yet

there has been Earls: nay, (which is more) Pensioners, but I warrant you all is one with her.

FALSTAFF

But what says she to me? be brief my good she-*Mercury*.

QUICKLY

Marry, she hath receiv'd your Letter: for the which she thanks you a thousand times; and she gives you notice, that her husband will be absence from his house, between ten and eleven.

FALSTAFF

Ten, and eleven.

QUICKLY

I, forsooth: and then you may come and see the picture (she says) that you wot of: Master *Ford* her husband will be from home: alas, the sweet woman leads an ill life with him: he's a very jealousy-man; she leads a very frampold life with him, (good heart.)

FALSTAFF

Ten, and eleven.
Woman, commend me to her, I will not fail her.

QUICKLY

Why, you say well: But I have another messenger to your worship: Mistress *Page* hath her hearty commendations to you too: and let me tell you in your ear, she's as fartuous a civil modest wife, and one (I tell you) that will not miss you morning not evening prayer, as any is in *Windsor,* who e'er be the other: and she bade me tell your worship, that her husband is seldom from home, but she hopes there will come a time. I never knew a woman so dote upon a man; surely I think you have charms, la: yes in truth.

FALSTAFF

Not I, I assure thee; letting the attraction of my good parts aside, I have no other charms.

QUICKLY

Blessing on your heart for't.

FALSTAFF

But I pray thee tell me this: has *Ford's* wife, and *Page's* wife acquainted each other, how they love me?

QUICKLY

That were a jest indeed: they have not so little grace I hope, that were a trick indeed: but Mistress *Page* would desire you to send her your little Page of all loves: her husband has a marvelous infection to the little Page: and truly Master *Page* is an honest man: never a wife in *Windsor* leads a better life than she does: do what she will, say what she will, take all, pay all, go to bed when she list, rise when she list, all is as she will: and truly she deserves it; for if there be a kind woman in *Windsor,* she is one: you must send her your Page, no remedy.

FALSTAFF

Why, I will.

QUICKLY

Nay, but do so then, and look you, he may come and go between you both: and in any case have a nay-word, that you may know one another's mind, and the Boy never need to understand any thing; for 'tis not good that children should know any wickedness: old folks you know, have discretion, as they say, and know the world.

FALSTAFF

Fare-thee-well, commend me to them both: there's my purse, I am yet thy debtor: Boy, go along with this woman, this news distracts me.

The Merry Wives
of Windsor

ACT II, SCENE 2—
FORD, FALSTAFF

FORD

Bless you sir.

FALSTAFF

And you sir: would you speak with me?

FORD

I make bold, to press, with so little preparation upon you.

FALSTAFF

You're welcome, what's your will?

FORD

Sir, I am a Gentleman that have spent much, my name is *Broome.*

FALSTAFF

Good Master *Broome,* I desire more acquaintance of you.

FORD

Good Sir *John,* I sue for yours: not to charge you, for I must let you understand, I think my self in better plight for a Lender, than you are: the which hath something embolden'd me to this unseason'd intrusion: for they say, if money go before, all ways do lie open.

FALSTAFF

Money is a good Soldier (Sir) and will on.

FORD

Troth, and I have a bag of money here troubles me: if you will
help to bear it (Sir *John*) take all, or half, for easing me of the
carriage.

FALSTAFF

Sir, I know not how I may deserve to be your Porter.

FORD

I will tell you sir, if you will give me the hearing.

FALSTAFF

Speak (good Master *Broome*) I shall be glad to be your Servant.

FORD

Sir, I hear you are a Scholar: (I will be brief with you) and you
have been a man long known to me, though I had never so good
means as desire, to make my self acquainted with you. I shall discover a thing to you, wherein I must very much lay open mine own
imperfection: but (good Sir *John*) as you have one eye upon my
follies, as you hear them unfolded, turn another into the Register
of your own, that I may pass with a reproof the easier, sith you
your self know how easy it is to be such an offender.

FALSTAFF

Very well Sir, proceed.

FORD

There is a Gentlewoman in this Town, her husband's name is *Ford*.

FALSTAFF

Well Sir.

FORD

I have long lov'd her, and I protest to you, bestowed much on her:
followed her with a doting observance: engrossed opportunities to
meet her: fee'd every slight occasion that could but niggardly give
me sight of her: not only bought many presents to give her, but

have given largely to many, to know what she would have given: briefly, I have pursu'd her, as Love hath pursued me, which hath been on the wing of all occasions: but whatsoever I have merited, either in my mind, or in my means, mead I am sure I have received none, unless Experience be a jewel, that I have purchased at an infinite rate, and that hath taught me to say this,

> Love like a shadow flies, when substance Love pursues,
> Pursuing that that flies, and flying what pursues.

FALSTAFF

Have you receiv'd no promise of satisfaction at her hands?

FORD

Never.

FALSTAFF

Have you importun'd her to such a purpose?

FORD

Never.

FALSTAFF

Of what quality was your love then?

FORD

Like a fair house, built on another man's ground, so that I have lost my edifice, by mistaking the place where I erected it.

FALSTAFF

To what purpose have you unfolded this to me?

FORD

When I have told you that, I have told you all: Some say, that though she appear honest to me, yet in other places she enlargeth her mirth so far, that there is shrewd construction made of her. Now (Sir *John*) here is the heart of my purpose: you are a gentleman of excellent breeding, admirable discourse, of great admittance, authentic in your place and person, generally allow'd for your many war-like, court-like, and learned preparations.

FALSTAFF

O Sir.

FORD

Believe it, for you know it: there is money, spend it, spend it, spend more; spend all I have, only give me so much of your time in exchange of it, as to lay an amiable siege to the honesty of this *Ford's* wife: use your Art of wooing; win her to consent to you: if any man may, you may as soon as any.

FALSTAFF

Would it apply well to the vehemency of your affection that I should win what you would enjoy? Methinks you prescribe to your self very preposterously.

FORD

O, understand my drift: she dwells so securely on the excellency of her honor, that the folly of my soul dares not present it self: she is too bright to be look'd against. Now, could I come to her with any detection in my hand; my desires had instance and argument to commend themselves, I could drive her then from the ward of her purity, her reputation, her marriage-vow, and a thousand other her defences, which now are too-too strongly embattled against me: what say you to't, Sir *John*?

FALSTAFF

Master *Broome,* I will first make bold with your money: next, give me your hand: and last, as I am a gentleman, you shall, if you will, enjoy *Ford's* wife.

FORD

O good Sir.

FALSTAFF

I say you shall.

FORD

Want no money (Sir John) you shall want none.

FALSTAFF

Want no *Mistress Ford* (Master *Broome*) you shall want none: I shall
be with her (I may tell you) by her own appointment, even as you
came in to me, her assistant or go-between, parted from me: I say
I shall be with her between ten and eleven: for at that time the
jealous-rascally-knave her husband will be forth: come you to me
at night, you shall know how I speed.

FORD

I am blessed in your acquaintance: do you know *Ford* Sir?

FALSTAFF

Hang him (poor Cuckoldly knave) I know him not: yet I wrong
him to call him poor: They say the jealous wittolly-knave hath
masses of money, for the which his wife seems to me well-favoured:
I will use her as the key of the Cuckoldly-rogue's Coffer, and there's
my harvest-home.

FORD

I would you knew *Ford,* sir, that you might avoid him, if you
saw him.

FALSTAFF

Hang him, mechanical-salt-butter rogue; I will stare him out of his
wits: I will awe him with my cudgel: it shall hang like a Meteor o'er
the Cuckold's horns: Master *Broome,* thou shalt know, I will pre-
dominate over the peasant, and thou shalt lie with his wife. Come
to me soon at night: *Ford's* a knave, and I will aggravate his style:
thou (Master *Broome*) shalt know him for knave, and Cuckold. Come
to me soon at night.

(*Exit*)

FORD

What a damn'd Epicurean-Rascal is this? my heart is ready to crack
with impatience: who says this is improvident jealousy? my wife

hath sent to him, the hour is fixt, the match is made: would any man have thought this? See the hell of having a false woman . . .

As You Like It

ACT III, SCENE 3—
CLOWN,
AUDREY, JAQUES

CLOWN

Come apace good *Audrey,* I will fetch up your Goats, *Audrey:* and how *Audrey* am I the man yet? Doth my simple feature content you?

AUDREY

Your features, Lord warrant us: what features?

CLOWN

I am here with thee, and thy Goats, as the most capricious Poet honest *Ovid* was among the Goths.

JAQUES

O knowledge ill inhabited, worse than Jove in a thatch'd house.

CLOWN

When a man's verses cannot be understood, nor a man's good wit seconded with the forward child, understanding: it strikes a man more dead than a great reckoning in a little room: truly, I would the Gods had made thee poetical.

AUDREY

I do not know what Poetical is: is it honest in deed and word: is it a true thing?

CLOWN

No truly: for the truest poetry is the most faining, and Lovers are given to Poetry: and what they swear in Poetry, may be said as Lovers, they do fain.

AUDREY

Do you wish then that the Gods had made me Poetical?

CLOWN

I do truly: for thou swear'st to me thou art honest: Now if thou wert a Poet, I might have some hope that thou didst fain.

AUDREY

Would you not have me honest?

CLOWN

No truly, unless thou wert hard favor'd: for honesty coupled to beauty, is to have Honey a sauce to Sugar.

JAQUES

A material fool.

AUDREY

Well, I am not fair, and therefore I pray the Gods make me honest.

CLOWN

Truly, and to cast away honesty upon a foul slut were to put good meat into an unclean dish.

AUDREY

I am not a slut, though I thank the Gods I am foul.

CLOWN

Well, praised be the Gods, for thy foulness; sluttishness may come hereafter. But be it, as it may be, I will marry thee: and to that end, I have been with Sir *Oliver Mar-text,* the Vicar of the next village, who hath promis'd to meet me in this place of the Forest, and to couple us.

JAQUES
I would fain see this meeting.

AUDREY
Well, the Gods give us joy.

CLOWN
Amen. A man may if he were of a fearful heart, stagger in this attempt: for here we have no Temple but the wood, no assembly but horn-beasts. But what though? Courage. As horns are odious, they are necessary. It is said, many a man knows no end of his goods; right: Many a man has good Horns, and knows no end of them. Well, that is the dowry of his wife, 'tis none of his own getting; horns, even so poor men alone: No, no, the noblest Deer hath them as huge as the Rascal: Is the single man therefore blessed? No, as a wall'd Town is more worthier than a village, so is the forehead of a married man, more honorable than the bare brow of a bachelor: and by how much defence is better than no skill, by so much is a horn more precious than to want.

Twelfth Night

ACT I, SCENE 5—
VIOLA, OLIVIA, MARIA

VIOLA
The honorable Lady of the house, which is she?

OLIVIA
Speak to me, I shall answer for her: your will.

VIOLA
Most radiant, exquisite, and unmatchable beauty. I pray you tell me if this be the Lady of the house, for I never saw her. I would be loathe to cast away my speech: for besides that it is excellently

well penn'd, I have taken great pains to con it. Good Beauties, let me sustain no scorn; I am very comptible, even to the least sinister usage.

OLIVIA

Are you a Comedian?

VIOLA

No my profound heart: and yet (by the very fangs of malice, I swear) I am not that I play. Are you the Lady of the house?

OLIVIA

If I do not usurp my self, I am.

VIOLA

Most certain, if you are she, you do usurp your self: for what is yours to bestow, is not yours to reserve. But this is from my Commission: I will on with my speech in your praise, and then show you the heart of my message.

OLIVIA

Come to what is important in't: I forgive you the praise.

VIOLA

Alas, I took great pains to study it, and 'tis Poetical.

OLIVIA

It is the more like to be feigned, I pray you keep it in. I heard you were saucy at my gates, and allowed your approach rather to wonder at you, than to hear you. If you be mad, be gone: if you have reason, be brief: 'tis not that time of Moon with me, to make one in so skipping a dialogue.

MARIA

Will you hoist sail sir, here lies your way.

VIOLA

No good swabber, I am to hull here a little longer. Some mollification for your Giant, sweet Lady; tell me your mind, I am a messenger.

OLIVIA

Sure you have some hideous matter to deliver when the courtesy of it is so fearful. Speak your office.

VIOLA

It alone concerns your ear: I bring no overture of war, no taxation of homage; I hold the Olive in my hand: my words are as full of peace, as matter.

OLIVIA

Yet you began rudely. What are you? What would you?

VIOLA

The rudeness that hath appear'd in me, have I learn'd from my entertainment. What I am, and what I would, are as secret as maiden-head: to your ears, Divinity; to any others, profanation.

OLIVIA

Give us the place alone,
We will hear this divinity. Now sir, what is your text.

VIOLA

Most sweet Lady.

OLIVIA

A comfortable doctrine, and much may be said of it. Where lies your text?

VIOLA

In *Orsino's* bosom.

OLIVIA

In his bosom? In what chapter of his bosom?

VIOLA

To answer by the method, in the first of his heart.

OLIVIA

O, I have read it: it is heresy. Have you no more to say?

VIOLA

Good Madam, let me see your face.

OLIVIA

Have you any Commission from your Lord, to negotiate with my face: you are now out of your Text: but we will draw the Curtain, and show you the picture. Look you sir, such a one I was this present: Is't not well done?

VIOLA

Excellently done, if God did all.

OLIVIA

'Tis in grain sir, 'twill endure wind and weather.

VIOLA

'Tis beauty truly blent, whose red and white,
Nature's own sweet, and cunning hand laid on:
Lady, you are the cruell'st she alive,
If you will lead these graces to the grave,
And leave the world no copy.

OLIVIA

O sir, I will not be so hard-hearted: I will give out diverse schedules of my beauty. It shall be Inventoried and every particle and utensil labell'd to my will: As, Item two lips indifferent red, Item two grey eyes, with lids to them: Item, one neck, one chin, and so forth. Were you sent hither to praise me?

VIOLA

I see you what you are, you are too proud:
But if you were the devil, you are fair:
My Lord, and master loves you: O such love

Could be but recompens'd, though you were crown'd
The non-pareil of beauty.

OLIVIA

How does he love me?

VIOLA

With adorations, fertile tears,
With groans that thunder love, with sighs of fire.

OLIVIA

Your Lord does know my mind, I cannot love him.
Yet I suppose him virtuous, know him noble,
Of great estate, of fresh and stainless youth;
In voices well divulg'd, free, learn'd, and valiant,
And in dimension, and the shape of nature,
A gracious person; But yet I cannot love him:
He might have took his answer long ago.

VIOLA

If I did love you in my master's flame,
With such a suff'ring, such a deadly life:
In your denial, I would find no sense,
I would not understand it.

OLIVIA

Why, what would you?

VIOLA

Make me a willow Cabin at your gate,
And call upon my soul within the house,
Write loyal Cantons of contemned love,
And sing them loud even in the dead of night:
Hallow your name to the reverberate hills,
And make the babbling Gossip of the air,
Cry out *Olivia*: O you should not rest
Between the elements of air, and earth,
But you should pity me.

OLIVIA

You might do much:
What is your Parentage?

VIOLA

Above my fortunes, yet my state is well:
I am a Gentleman.

OLIVIA

Get you to your Lord:
I cannot love him: let him send no more,
Unless (perchance) you come to me again,
To tell me how he takes it: Fare you well:
I thank you for your pains: spend this for me.

VIOLA

I am no fee'd post, Lady; keep your purse,
My Master, not my self, lacks recompense.
Love make his heart of flint, that you shall love,
And let your fervor like my master's be,
Plac'd in contempt: Farewell fair cruelty.

(*Exit*)

OLIVIA

What is your Parentage?
Above my fortunes, yet my state is well;
I am a Gentleman. Ile be sworn thou art,
Thy tongue, thy face, thy limbs, actions, and spirit,
Do give thee five-fold blazon: not too fast: soft, soft,
Unless the Master were the man. How now?
Even so quickly may one catch the plague?
Methinks I feel this youth's perfections
With an invisible, and subtle stealth
To creep in at mine eyes.

Twelfth Night

ACT III, SCENE 1—
VIOLA, CLOWN

VIOLA

Save thee Friend and thy Music: dost thou live by thy Tabor?

CLOWN

No sir, I live by the Church.

VIOLA

Art thou a Churchman?

CLOWN

No such matter, sir, I do live by the Church: For, I do live at my house, and my house doth stand by the Church.

VIOLA

So thou may'st say the King's lies by a beggar, if a beggar dwell near him: or the Church stands by thy Tabor, if thy Tabor stand by the Church.

CLOWN

You have said sir: To see this age: A sentence is but a cheveril glove to a good wit, how quickly the wrong side may be turn'd outward.

VIOLA

Nay, that's certain: they that dally nicely with words, may quickly make them wanton.

CLOWN

I would therefore my sister had had no name Sir.

VIOLA

Why man?

CLOWN

Why sir, her name's a word, and to dally with that word, might make my sister wanton: But indeed, words are very Rascals, since bonds disgrac'd them.

VIOLA

Thy reason man?

CLOWN

Troth sir, I can yield you none without words, and words are grown so false, I am loath to prove reason with them.

VIOLA

I warrant thou art a merry fellow, and car'st for nothing.

CLOWN

Not so sir, I do care for something: but in my conscience sir, I do not care for you: if that be to care for nothing sir, I would it would make you invisible.

VIOLA

Art not thou the Lady *Olivia's* fool?

CLOWN

No indeed sir, the Lady *Olivia* has no folly, she will keep no fool sir, until she be married, and fools are as like husbands, as Pilchards are to Herrings, the Husbands the bigger, I am indeed not her fool, but her corrupter of words.

VIOLA

I saw thee late at the Count *Orsino's*.

CLOWN

Foolery sir, does walk about the Orb like the Sun, it shines every where. I would be sorry sir, but the Fool should be as oft with your Master, as with my Mistress: I think I saw your wisdom there.

VIOLA

Nay, and thou pass upon me, Ile no more with thee. Hold there's expenses for thee.

CLOWN

Now Jove in his next commodity of hair, send thee a beard.

VIOLA

By my troth Ile tell thee, I am almost sick for one, though I would not have it grow on my chin. Is thy Lady within?

CLOWN

Would not a pair of these have bred sir?

VIOLA

Yes being kept together, and put to use.

CLOWN

I would play Lord *Pandarus* of *Phrygia* sir, to bring a *Cressida* to this *Troilus*.

VIOLA

I understand you sir, 'tis well begg'd.

CLOWN

The matter I hope is not great; begging, but a beggar: *Cressida* was a beggar. My Lady is within sir. I will conster to them whence you come, who you are and what you would are out of my welkin, I might have said Element, but the word is over-worn.

(*Exit*)

VIOLA

This fellow is wise enough to play the fool,
And to do that well, craves a kind of wit:
He must observe their mood on whom he jests,
The quality of persons, and the time:
And like the Haggard, check at every Feather

That comes before his eye. This is a practice,
As full of labour as a Wise-man's Art:
For folly that he wisely shows, is fit;
But wisemen's folly fall'n, quite taint their wit.

All's Well That Ends Well

ACT I, SCENE 1—
HELENA, PAROLLES, PAGE

HELENA

My imagination
Carries no favour in't but *Bertram*.
I am undone, there is no living, none,
If *Bertram* be away. 'Twere all one,
That I should love a bright particular star,
And think to wed it, he is so above me
In his bright radiance and colateral light,
Must I be comforted, not in his sphere;
Th'ambition in my love thus plagues it self:
The hind that would be mated by the Lion
Must die for love. 'Twas pretty, though a plague
To see him every hour to sit and draw
His arched brows, his hawking eye, his curls
Of every line and trick of his sweet favour.
But now he's gone, and my idolatrous fancy
Must sanctify his Relics. Who comes here?
(*Enter* PAROLLES)
One that goes with him: I love him for his sake,
And yet I know him a notorious Liar,
Think him a great way fool, folly a coward,
Yet these fixt evils sit so fit in him,
That they take place, when Vertue's steely bones

Looks bleak i'th' cold wind: withall, full oft we see
Cold wisdom waiting on superfluous folly.

PAROLLES

Save you fair Queen.

HELENA

And you Monarch.

PAROLLES

No.

HELENA

And no.

PAROLLES

Are you meditating on virginity?

HELENA

I: you have some stain of soldier in you: Let me ask you a question.
Man is enemy to virginity, how may we barracado it against him?

PAROLLES

Keep him out.

HELENA

But he assails, and our virginity though valiant, in the defence yet
is weak: unfold to us some warlike resistance.

PAROLLES

There is none: Man setting down before you, will undermine you,
and blow you up.

HELENA

Bless our poor Virginity from underminers and blowers up. Is there
no Military policy how Virgins might blow up men?

PAROLLES

Virginity being blown down, Man will quicklier be blown up: marry
in blowing him down again, with the breach your selves made, you

lose your City. It is not politick, in the Common-wealth of Nature, to preserve virginity. Loss of Virginity, is rational increase, and there was never Virgin got, till virginity was first lost. That you were made of, is mettal to make Virgins. Virginity, by beeing once lost, may be ten times found: by being ever kept, it is ever lost: 'tis too cold a companion: Away with't.

HELENA

I will stand for't a little, though therefore I die a Virgin.

PAROLLES

There's little can be said in't, 'tis against the rule of Nature. To speak on the part of virginity, is to accuse your Mothers; which is most infallible disobedience. He that hangs himself is a Virgin: Virginity murders itself, and should be buried in highways out of all sanctified limit, as a desperate Offendress against Nature. Virginity breeds mites, much like a Cheese, consumes it self to the very paring, and so dies with feeding his own stomach. Besides, Virginity is peevish, proud, idle, made of self-love, which is the most inhibited sin in the Cannon. Keep it not, you cannot choose but loose by't. Out with't: within ten year it will make it self two, which is a goodly increase, and the principal it self not much the worse. Away with't.

HELENA

How might one do sir, to lose it to her own liking?

PAROLLES

Let me see. Marry ill, to like him that ne'r it likes. 'Tis a commodity will lose the gloss with lying: The longer kept, the less worth: Off with't while 'tis vendible. Answer the time of request, Virginity like an old Courtier, wears her cap out of fashion, richly suited, but unsuitable, just like the brooch & the toothpick, which were not now: your Date is better in your Pie and your Porridge, then in your cheek: and your virginity, is like one of our French wither'd pears, it lookes ill, it eats drily, marry 'tis a wither'd pear: it was formerly better, marry yet 'tis a wither'd pear: Will you any thing with it?

HELENA

Not my virginity yet:
There shall your Master have a thousand loves,
A Mother, and a Mistress, and a friend,
A Phoenix, Captain, and an enemy,
A guide, a Goddess, and a Sovereign,
A Counsellor, a Traitoress, and a Dear:
His humble ambition, proud humility:
His jarring, concord: and his discord, dulcet:
His faith, his sweet disaster: with a world
Of pretty fond adoptious christendoms
That blinking Cupid gossips. Now shall he:
I know not what he shall, God send him well,
The Court's a learning place, and he is one.

PAROLLES

What one i'faith?

HELENA

That I wish well, 'tis pity.

PAROLLES

What's pity?

HELENA

That wishing well had not a body in't,
Which might be felt, that we the poorer born,
Whose baser stars do shut us up in wishes,
Might with effects of them follow our friends,
And show what we alone must think, which never
Returns us thanks.

(*Enter* PAGE)

PAGE

Monsieur *Parolles*,
My Lord calls for you.

PAROLLES

Little Helen farewell, if I can remember thee, I will think of thee
at Court.

HELENA

Monsieur *Parolles,* you were born under a charitable star.

PAROLLES

Under *Mars* I.

HELENA

I especially think, under *Mars.*

PAROLLES

Why under *Mars?*

HELENA

The wars hath so kept you under, that you must needs be born
under *Mars.*

PAROLLES

When he was predominant.

HELENA

When he was retrograde I think rather.

PAROLLES

Why think you so?

HELENA

You go so much backward when you fight.

PAROLLES

That's for advantage

HELENA

So is running away,
When fear proposes the safety:
But the composition that your valour and fear makes in you, is a
virtue of a good wing, and I like the wear well.

PAROLLES

I am so full of business, I cannot answer thee acutely: I will return
perfect Courtier, in the which my instruction shall serve to natu-
ralize thee, so thou wilt be capable of a Courtier's counsel, and
understand what advice shall thrust upon thee, else thou diest in
thine unthankfulness, and thine ignorance makes thee away, farewell: When thou hast leisure, say thy prayers: when thou hast none,
remember thy Friends: Get thee a good husband, and use him as
he uses thee: So farewell.

HELENA

Our remedies oft in our selves do lie,
Which we ascribe to heaven: the fated sky
Gives us free scope, only doth backward pull
Our slow designs, when we our selves are dull.
What power is it, which mounts my love so high,
That makes me see, and cannot feed mine eye?
The mightiest space in fortune, Nature brings
To join like, likes; and kiss like native things.
Impossible be strange attempts to those
That weigh their pains in sense, and do suppose
What hath been, cannot be. Who ever strove
To show her merit, that did miss her love?
(The King's disease) my project may deceive me,
But my intents are fixt, and will not leave me.

All's Well That Ends Well

ACT I, SCENE 3—
COUNTESS, HELENA

COUNTESS

Even so it was with me when I was young:
If ever we are nature's, these are ours, this thorn
Doth to our Rose of youth rightly belong
Our blood to us, this to our blood is borne,
It is the show, and seal of nature's truth,
Where love's strong passion is imprest in youth,
By our remembrances of days forgone,
Such were our faults, or then we thought them none,
Her eye is sick on't, I observe her now.

HELENA

What is your pleasure Madam?

COUNTESS

You know *Helen* I am a mother to you.

HELENA

Mine honorable Mistress.

COUNTESS

Nay a mother, why not a mother? when I said a mother
Methought you saw a serpent, what's in mother,
That you start at it? I say I am your mother,
And put you in the Catalogue of those
That were enwombed mine, 'tis often seen
Adoption strives with nature, and choice breeds
A native slip to us from foreign seeds:
You nere opprest me with a mother's groan,

Yet I express to you a mother's care,
(God's mercy maiden) does it curd thy blood
To say I am thy mother? what's the matter,
That this distemper'd messenger of wet?
The many color'd Iris rounds thine eye?
—Why, that you are my daughter?

HELENA

That I am not.

COUNTESS

I say I am your Mother.

HELENA

Pardon Madam.
The Count Rosillion cannot be my brother:
I am from humble, he from honor'd name:
No note upon my Parents, his all noble,
My Master, my dear Lord he is, and I
His servant live, and will his vassal die:
He must not be my brother.

COUNTESS

Nor I your Mother.

HELENA

You are my mother Madam, would you were
So that my Lord your son were not my brother,
Indeed my mother, or were you both our mothers,
I care no more for, than I do for heaven,
So I were not his sister, cant no other,
But I your daughter, he must be my brother.

COUNTESS

Yes *Helen,* you might be my daughter in law,
God shield you mean it not, daughter and mother
So strive upon your pulse; what pale again?
My fear hath catcht your fondness! now I see

The mystery of your loveliness, and find
Your salt tear's head, now to all sense 'tis gross:
You love my son, invention is asham'd
Against the proclamation of thy passion
To say thou dost not: therefore tell me true,
But tell me then 'tis so, for look, thy cheeks
Confess it 'ton tooth to th'other, and thine eyes
See it so grossly shown in thy behaviours,
That in their kind they speak it, only sin
And hellish obstinacy tie thy tongue
That truth should be suspected, speak, is't so?
If it be so, you have wound a goodly clewe:
If it be not, forswear't how ere I charge thee,
As heaven shall work in me for thine avail
To tell me truly.

HELENA

Good Madam pardon me.

COUNTESS

Do you love my Son?

HELENA

Your pardon noble Mistress.

COUNTESS

Love you my Son?

HELENA

Do not you love him Madam?

COUNTESS

Go not about; my love hath in't a bond
Whereof the world takes note: Come, come, disclose:
The state of your affection, for your passions
Have to the full appeach'd.

186

HELENA

Then I confesse
Here on my knee, before high heaven and you,
That before you, and next unto high heaven, I love your Son:
My friends were poor but honest, so's my love:
Be not offended, for it hurts not him
That he is lov'd of me; I follow him not
By any token of presumptuous suite,
Nor would I have him, till I do deserve him,
Yet never know how that desert should be:
I know I love in vain, strive against hope:
Yet in this captious, and intenible Sieve.
I still pour in the waters of my love
And lack not to lose still; thus *Indian* like
Religious in mine error, I adore
The Sun that looks upon his worshipper,
But knows of him no more. My dearest Madam,
Let not your hate encounter with my love,
For loving where you do; but if your self,
Whose aged honor cites a virtuous youth,
Did ever, in so true a flame of liking,
Wish chastely, and love dearly, that your *Dian*
Was both her self and love, O then give pity
To her whose state is such, that cannot choose
But lend and give where she is sure to loose;
That seeks not to find that, her search implies,
But riddle like, lives sweetly where she dies.

COUNTESS

Had you not lately an intent, speak truly,
To go to *Paris*?

HELENA

Madam I had.

COUNTESS

Wherefore? tell true.

HELENA

I will tell truth, by grace it self I swear:
You know my Father left me some prescriptions
Of rare and prov'd effects, such as his reading
And manifest experience, had collected
For general sovereignty: and that he will'd me
In heedfull'st reservation to bestow them,
As notes, whose faculties inclusive were,
More than they were in note: Amongst the rest
There is a remedy, approv'd, set down,
To cure the desperate languishings whereof
The King is render'd lost.

COUNTESS

This was your motive for *Paris,* was it, speak?

HELENA

My Lord, your son, made me to think of this;
Else *Paris,* and the medicine, and the King,
Had from the conversation of my thoughts,
Haply been absent then.

COUNTESS

But think you *Helen,*
If you should tender your supposed aide,
He would receive it? He and his Physicians
Are of a mind, he, that they cannot help him:
They, that they cannot help, how shall they credit
A poor unlearned Virgin, when the Schools
Embowel'd of their doctrine, have left off
The danger to it self.

HELENA

There's something in't
More than my Father's skill, which was the great'st
Of his profession, that his good receipt,
Shall for my legacy be sanctified
By th'luckiest stars in heaven, and would your honor
But give me leave to try success, I'd venture

The well lost life of mine, on his Grace's cure,
By such a day, an hour.

COUNTESS

Do'st thou believe't?

HELENA

I Madam knowingly.

COUNTESS

Why *Helen* thou shalt have my leave and love,
Means and attendants, and my loving greetings
To those of mine in Court, Ile stay at home
And pray God's blessing into thy attempt:
Begone tomorrow, and be sure of this,
What I can help thee to, thou shalt not miss.

The Tragedy of
Julius Caesar

ACT I, SCENE 2—
CASSIUS, BRUTUS

CASSIUS

Will you go see the order of the course?

BRUTUS

Not I.

CASSIUS

I pray you do.

BRUTUS

I am not Gamesome: I do lack some part
Of that quick Spirit that is in *Antony*:

Let me not hinder *Cassius* your desires;
Ile leave you.

CASSIUS

Brutus, I do observe you now of late:
I have not from your eyes, that gentleness
And show of Love, as I was wont to have:
You bear too stubborn, and too strange a hand
Over your Friend, that loves you.

BRUTUS

Cassius,
Be not deceiv'd: If I have veil'd my look,
I turn the trouble of my Countenance
Merely upon my self. Vexed I am
Of late, with passions of some difference,
Conceptions only proper to my self,
Which give some soil (perhaps) to my Behaviours:
But let not therefore my good Friends be griev'd
(Among which number *Cassius* be you one)
Nor construe any further my neglect,
Then that poor *Brutus* with himself at war,
Forgets the shows of Love to other men.

CASSIUS

Then *Brutus,* I have much mistook your passion,
By means whereof, this Breast of mine hath buried
Thoughts of great value, worthy Cogitations.
Tell me good *Brutus,* Can you see your face?

BRUTUS

No *Cassius*:
For the eye sees not it self but by reflection,
By some other things.

CASSIUS

'Tis just,
And it is very much lamented *Brutus,*

That you have no such Mirrors, as will turn
Your hidden worthiness into your eye,
That you might see your shadow:
I have heard,
Where many of the best respect in Rome,
(Except immortal *Caesar*) speaking of *Brutus*,
And groaning underneath this Ages yoke,
Have wish'd, that Noble *Brutus* had his eyes.

BRUTUS

Into what dangers, would you
Lead me *Cassius*?
That you would have me seek into my self,
For that which is not in me?

CASSIUS

Therefore good *Brutus,* be prepar'd to hear:
And since you know, you cannot see your self
So well as by Reflections; I your Glass,
Will modestly discover to your self
That of your self, which you yet know not of.
And be not jealous on me, gentle *Brutus*:
Were I a common Laughter, or did use
To stale with ordinary Oaths my love
To every new Protester: if you know,
That I do fawn on men, and hug them hard,
And after scandal them: Or if you know,
That I profess my self in Banqueting
To all the Rout, then hold me dangerous.

(*Flourish, and Shout*)

BRUTUS

What means this Shouting?
I do fear, the People choose *Caesar*
For their King.

CASSIUS

I, do you fear it?
Then must I think you would not have it so.

BRUTUS

I would not *Cassius,* yet I love him well:
But wherefore do you hold me here so long?
What is it, that you would impart to me?
If it be ought toward the general good,
See Honor in one eye, and Death i'th' other,
And I will look on both indifferently:
For let the Gods so speed me, as I love
The name of Honor, more than I fear death.

CASSIUS

I know that virtue to be in you *Brutus,*
As well as I do know your outward favour.
Well, Honor is the subject of my Story:
I cannot tell, what You and other men
Think of this life: But for my single self,
I had as lief not be, as live to be
In awe of such a thing, as I my self.
I was born free as *Caesar,* so were you,
We both have fed as well, and we can both
Endure the Winters cold, as well as he.
For once, upon a Raw and Gusty day,
The troubled Tiber, chafing with her Shores,
Caesar said to me, Dar'st thou *Cassius* now
Leap in with me into this angry Flood,
And swim to yonder Point? Upon the word,
Accoutred as I was, I plunged in,
And bade him follow: so indeed he did.
The Torrent roar'd, and we did buffet it
With lusty Sinews, throwing it aside,
And stemming it with hearts of Controversy.
But ere we could arrive the Point propos'd,
Caesar cried, Helpe me *Cassius,* or I sink.
I (as *Aeneas,* our great Ancestor,

Did from the Flames of Troy, upon his shoulder
The old *Anchyses* bear) so, from the waves of Tiber
Did I the tired *Caesar*: And this Man,
Is now become a God, and *Cassius* is
A wretched Creature, and must bend his body,
If *Caesar* carelessly but nod on him.
He had a Fever when he was in Spain,
And when the Fit was on him, I did mark
How he did shake: 'Tis true, this God did shake,
His Coward lips did from their colour fly,
And that same Eye, whose bend doth awe the World,
Did lose his Lustre: I did hear him groan:
I, and that Tongue of his, that bade the Romans
Mark him, and write his Speeches in their Books,
Alas, it cried, Give me some drink *Titinius*,
As a sick Girl: Ye Gods, it doth amaze me,
A man of such feeble a temper should
So get the start of the Majestic world,
And bear the Palm alone.

(*Shout. Flourish*)

BRUTUS

Another general shout?
I do believe, that these applauses are
For some new Honors, that are heap'd on *Caesar*.

CASSIUS

Why man, he doth bestride the narrow world
Like a Colossus, and we petty men
Walk under his huge legs, and peep about
To find our selves dishonourable Graves.
Men at sometime, are Masters of their Fates.
The fault (dear *Brutus*) is not in our Stars,
But in our Selves, that we are underlings.
Brutus and *Caesar*: What should be in that *Caesar*?
Why should that name be sounded more than yours:

Write them together: Yours, is as fair a Name:
Sound them, it doth become the mouth as well:
Weigh them, it is as heavy: Conjure with 'em,
Brutus will start a Spirit as soon as *Caesar*.
Now in the names of all the Gods at once,
Upon what meat doth this our *Caesar* feed,
That he is grown so great? Age, thou art sham'd.
Rome, thou hast lost the breed of Noble Bloods.
When went there by an Age, since the great Flood,
But it was fam'd with more than with one man?
When could they say (till now) that talk'd of Rome,
That her wide Walks incompast but one man?
Now is it Rome indeed, and Room enough
When there is in it but one only man.
O! you and I, have heard our Fathers say,
There was a *Brutus* once, that would have brook'd
Th'eternal Devil to keep his State in Rome,
As easily as a King.

BRUTUS

That you do love me, I am nothing jealous:
What you would work me to, I have some aim:
How I have thought of this, and of these times
I shall recount hereafter. For this present,
I would not so (with love I might intreat you)
Be any further mov'd: What you have said,
I will consider: what you have to say
I will with patience hear, and find a time
Both meet to hear, and answer such high things.
Till then, my Noble Friend, chew upon this:
Brutus had rather be a Villager,
Than to repute himself a Son of Rome
Under these hard Conditions, as this time
Is like to lay upon us.

CASSIUS

I am glad that my weak words
Have struck but this much show of fire from *Brutus*.

194

Troilus and Cressida

ACT III, SCENE 2—
PANDARUS, TROILUS, CRESSIDA

PANDARUS

Have you seen my Cousin?

TROILUS

No *Pandarus*: I stalk about her door
Like a strange soul upon the Stygian banks
Staying for waftage. O be thou my *Charon*,
And give me swift transportance to those fields,
Where I may wallow in the Lily beds
Propos'd for the deserver. O gentle *Pandarus*,
From *Cupid's* shoulder pluck his painted wings,
And fly with me to *Cressid*.

PANDARUS

Walk here i'th'Orchard, Ile bring her straight.

(*Exit* PANDARUS)

TROILUS

I am giddy; expectation whirls me round,
Th'imaginary relish is so sweet,
That it enchants my sense: what will it be
When that the wat'ry palates taste indeed
Love's thrice reputed Nectar? Death I fear me
Sounding destruction, or some joy too fine,
Too subtle, potent, and too sharp in sweetness,
For the capacity of my ruder powers;
I fear it much, and I do fear besides,

That I shall lose distinction in my joys,
As doth a battle, when they charge on heaps
The enemy flying.

(*Enter* PANDARUS)

PANDARUS
She's making her ready, she'll come straight: you must be witty
now, she does so blush, and fetches her wind so short, as if she
were 'fraid with a sprite: Ile fetch her; it is the prettiest villain, she
fetches her breath so short as a new ta'en Sparrow.

(*Exit* PANDARUS)

TROILUS
Even such a passion doth embrace my bosom:
My heart beats thicker than a fev'rous pulse,
And all my powers do their bestowing lose,
Like vassalage at unawares encount'ring
The eye of Majesty.

(*Enter* PANDARUS *and* CRESSIDA)

PANDARUS
Come, come, what need you blush?
Shame's a baby; here she is now, swear the oaths now to her, that
you have sworn to me. What are you gone again, you must be
watched ere you be made tame, must you? come your ways, come
your ways, and you draw backward we'll put you i'the fills: why do
you not speak to her? Come draw this curtain, and let's see your
picture. Alas the day, how loath you are to offend day light? and
'twere dark you'ld close sooner: So, so, rub on, and kiss the mistress;
how now, a kiss in fee-farm? build there Carpenter, the air is sweet.
Nay, you shall fight your hearts out ere I part you. The Falcon, as
the Tercel, for all the Ducks i'th' River: go to, go to.

TROILUS
You have bereft me of all words Lady.

PANDARUS

Words pay no debts; give her deeds: but she'll bereave you of the deeds too, if she call your activity in question: what billing again? here's "in witness whereof the Parties interchangeably—" Come in, come in, Ile go get a fire?

CRESSIDA

Will you walk in my Lord?

TROILUS

O *Cressida,* how often have I wish'd me thus?

CRESSIDA

Wish'd my Lord? the gods grant? O my Lord.

TROILUS

What should they grant? what makes this pretty abruption: what too curious dreg espies my sweet Lady in the fountain of our love?

CRESSIDA

More dregs than water, if my tears have eyes.

TROILUS

Fears make devils of Cherubins, they never see truly.

CRESSIDA

Blind fear, that seeing reason leads, finds safer footing than blind reason, stumbling without fear: to fear the worst, oft cures the worse.

TROILUS

Oh let my Lady apprehend no fear,
In all *Cupid's* Pageant there is presented no monster.

CRESSIDA

Not nothing monstrous neither?

TROILUS

Nothing but our undertakings, when we vow to weep as seas, live in fire, eat rocks, tame Tigers; thinking it harder for our Mistress to devise imposition enough, than for us to undergo any difficulty imposed. This the monstrosity in love Lady, that the will is infinite, and the execution confin'd; that the desire is boundless, and the act a slave to limit.

CRESSIDA

They say all Lovers swear more performance than they are able, and yet reserve an ability that they never perform: vowing more than the perfection of ten; and discharging less than the tenth part of one. They that have the voice of Lions, and the act of Hares: are they not Monsters?

TROILUS

Are there such? such are not we: Praise us as we are tasted, allow us as we prove: our head shall go bare till merit crown it: no perfection in reversion shall have a praise in present: we will not name desert before his birth, and being born his addition shall be humble: few words to fair faith. *Troilus* shall be such to *Cressid,* as what envy can say worst, shall be a mock for his truth; and what truth can speak truest, not truer than *Troilus.*

CRESSIDA

Will you walk in my Lord?

(*Enter* PANDARUS)

PANDARUS

What blushing still? have you not done talking yet?

CRESSIDA

Well Uncle, what folly I commit, I dedicate to you.

PANDARUS

I thank you for that: if my Lord get a Boy of you, you'll give him me: be true to my Lord, if he flinch, chide me for it.

TROILUS

You know now your hostages: your Uncle's word and my firm faith.

PANDARUS

Nay, Ile give my word for her too: our kindred though they be
long ere they are woo'd, they are constant being won: they are
Burrs I can tell you, they'll stick where they are thrown.

CRESSIDA

Boldness comes to me now, and brings me heart: Prince *Troilus*,
I have lov'd you night and day, for many weary months.

TROILUS

Why was my *Cressid* then so hard to win?

CRESSIDA

Hard to seem won: but I was won my Lord
With the first glance; that ever—pardon me,
If I confess much you will play the tyrant:
I love you now, but not till now so much
But I might master it; in faith I lie:
My thoughts were like unbridled children grown
Too head-strong for their mother: see we fools,
Why have I blabb'd: who shall be true to us
When we are so unsecret to our selves?
But though I lov'd you well, I woo'd you not,
And yet good faith I wish'd my self a man;
Or that we women had men's privilege
Of speaking first. Sweet, bid me hold my tongue,
For in this rapture I shall surely speak
The thing I shall repent: see, see, your silence
Coming in Dumbness, from my weakness draws
My soul of counsel from me. Stop my mouth.

TROILUS

And shall, albeit sweet Music issues thence.

PANDARUS

Pretty i'faith.

CRESSIDA

My Lord, I do beseech you pardon me,
'Twas not my purpose thus to beg a kiss:
I am asham'd; O Heavens, what have I done!
For this time will I take my leave my Lord.

TROILUS

Your leave sweet *Cressid*?

PANDARUS

Leave: and you take leave till to morrow morning.

CRESSIDA

Pray you content you.

TROILUS

What offends you Lady?

CRESSIDA

Sir, mine own company.

TROILUS

You cannot shun your self.

CRESSIDA

Let me go and try:
I have a kind of self resides with you:
But an unkind self, that it self will leave,
To be another's fool. Where is my wit?
I would be gone: I speak I know not what.

TROILUS

Well know they what they speak, that speak so wisely.

CRESSIDA

Perchance my Lord, I show more craft than love,
And fell so roundly to a large confession,
To Angle for your thoughts: but you are wise,
Or else you love not: for to be wise and love,
Exceeds man's might, that dwells with gods above.

TROILUS

O that I thought it could be in a woman:
As if it can, I will presume in you,
To feed for aye her lamp and flames of love,
To keep her constancy in plight and youth,
Out-living beauties outward, with a mind
That doth renew swifter than blood decays:
Or that persuasion could but thus convince me,
That my integrity and truth to you,
Might be affronted with the match and weight
Of such a winnow'd purity in love:
How were I then up-lifted! but alas,
I am as true, as truth's simplicity,
And simpler than the infancy of truth.

CRESSIDA

In that Ile war with you.

TROILUS

O virtuous fight,
When right with right wars who shall be most right:
True swains in love, shall in the world to come
Approve their truths by *Troilus,* when their times,
Full of protest, of oath and big compare;
Wants similes, truth tir'd with iteration,
As true as steel, as plantage to the Moon:
As Sun to day: as Turtle to her mate:
As Iron to Adamant: as Earth to th'Center:
Yet after all comparisons of truth,
(As truth's authentic author to be cited)
As true as *Troilus,* shall crown up the Verse,
And sanctify the numbers.

CRESSIDA

Prophet may you be:
If I be false, or swerve a hair from truth,
When time is old and hath forgot it self:
When water drops have worn the Stones of *Troy*;

And blind oblivion swallow'd Cities up;
And mighty States characterless are grated
To dusty nothing; yet let memory,
From false to false, among false Maids in love,
Upbraid my falsehood, when they've said as false
As Air, as Water, as Wind, as sandy earth;
As Fox to Lamb; as Wolf to Heifer's Calf;
Pard to the Hind, or Stepdame to her Son;
Yea, let them say, to stick the heart of falsehood,
As false as *Cressid*.

PANDARUS

Go to, a bargain made: seal it, seal it, Ile be the witness; here I
hold your hand: here my Cousin's, if ever you prove false one to
another, since I have taken such pains to bring you together, let
all pitiful goers between be call'd to the world's end after my name:
call them all Panders; let all constant men be *Troilus*, all false women
Cressids, and all brokers between, Panders: say, Amen.

TROILUS

Amen.

CRESSIDA

Amen.

PANDARUS

Amen.
Whereupon I will show you a Chamber, which bed, because it shall
not speak of your pretty encounters, press it to death: away.
And Cupid grant all tongue-tied Maidens here,
Bed, Chamber, and Pander, to provide this gear.

The Tragedy
of Hamlet

ACT III, SCENE 1—
HAMLET, OPHELIA

HAMLET

Thus Conscience does make Cowards of us all,
And thus the Native hew of Resolution
Is sicklied o'er, with the pale cast of Thought,
And enterprizes of great pith and moment,
With this regard their Currents turn away,
And lose the name of Action. Soft you now,
The fair *Ophelia*? Nymph, in thy Orisons
Be all my sins remembered.

OPHELIA

Good my Lord,
How does your Honor for this many a day?

HAMLET

I humbly thank you: well, well, well.

OPHELIA

My Lord, I have Remembrances of yours,
That I have longed long to re-deliver.
I pray you now, receive them.

HAMLET

No, no, I never gave you ought.

OPHELIA

My honor'd Lord, I know right well you did,
And with them words of so sweet breath compos'd,

As made the things more rich, than perfume left:
Take these again, for to the Noble mind
Rich gifts wax poor, when givers prove unkind.
There my Lord.

HAMLET
Ha, ha: Are you honest?

OPHELIA
My Lord.

HAMLET
Are you fair?

OPHELIA
What means your Lordship?

HAMLET
That if you be honest and fair, your Honesty should admit no discourse to your Beauty.

OPHELIA
Could Beauty my Lord, have better Commerce than your Honesty?

HAMLET
I truly: for the power of Beauty, will sooner transform Honesty from what it is, to a Bawd, then the force of Honesty can translate Beauty into his likeness. This was sometime a Paradox, but now the time gives it proof. I did love you once.

OPHELIA
Indeed my Lord, you made me believe so.

HAMLET
You should not have believed me. For virtue cannot so inoculate our old stock, but we shall rellish of it. I loved you not.

OPHELIA

I was the more deceived.

HAMLET

Get thee to a Nunnery. Why would'st thou be a breeder of Sinners? I am my self indifferent honest, but yet I could accuse me of such things, that it were better my Mother had not borne me. I am very Proud, revengeful, Ambitious, with more offences at my beck, than I have thoughts to put them in imagination, to give them shape, or time to act them in. What should such Fellows as I do, crawling between Heaven and Earth. We are arrant Knaves all, believe none of us. Goe thy ways to a Nunnery. Where's your Father?

OPHELIA

At home, my Lord.

HAMLET

Let the doors be shut upon him, that he may play the Fool no way, but in's own house. Farewell.

OPHELIA

O help him, you sweet Heavens.

HAMLET

If thou doest Marry, Ile give thee this Plague for thy Dowry. Be thou as chaste as Snow, thou shalt not escape Calumny. Get thee to a Nunnery. Go, Farewell. Or if thou wilt needs Marry, marry a fool: for Wise men know well enough, what monsters you make of them. To a Nunnery go, and quickly too. Farewell.

OPHELIA

O heavenly Powers, restore him.

HAMLET

I have heard of your pratlings too well enough. God has given you one pace, and you make your self another: you gidge, you amble, and you lisp, and nickname God's creatures, and make your Wantonness, your Ignorance. Go too, Ile no more on't, it hath made me mad. I say, we will have no more Marriages. Those that are married already, all but one shall live, the rest shall keep as they are. To a Nunnery, go.

(*Exit* HAMLET)

OPHELIA

O what a Noble mind is here o'er-thrown?
The Courtiers, Soldiers, Schollers: Eye, tongue, sword,
The'expectancie and Rose of the fair State,
The glass of Fashion, and the mould of Form,
The'observ'd of all Observers, quite, quite down.
Have I of Ladies most deject and wretched,
That suck'd the Honey of his Musick Vows:
Now see that Noble, and most Sovereign Reason,
Like sweet Bells jangled out of tune, and harsh,
That unmatch'd Form and Feature of blown youth,
Blasted with extasy. Oh woe is me,
T'have seen what I have seen: see what I see.

The Tragedy of Hamlet

ACT III, SCENE 2—
HAMLET, HORATIO,
ROSENKRANTZ, GUILDENSTERN,
POLONIUS

HAMLET

Why let the strucken Deer go weep,
The Hart ungalled play:
For some must watch, while some must sleep;
So runs the world away.
Would not this Sir, and a Forest of Feathers, if the rest of my Fortunes turn Turk with me; with two Provincial Roses on my rac'd Shoes, get me a Fellowship in a cry of Players sir.

HORATIO

Halfe a share.

HAMLET

A whole one I,
For thou dost know: Oh *Damon* deer,
This Realm dismantled was of Jove himself,
And now reigns here.
A very very Pajock.

HORATIO

You might have Rim'd.

HAMLET

Oh good *Horatio,* Ile take the Ghost's word for a thousand pound.
Did'st perceive?

HORATIO

Very well my Lord.

HAMLET

Upon the talk of the poisoning?

HORATIO

I did very well note him.

(*Enter* ROSENKRANTZ *and* GUILDENSTERN)

HAMLET

Oh, ha: Come some Music. Come the Recorders:
For if the King like not the Comedy,
Why then belike he likes it not perdy.
Come some Music.

GUILDENSTERN

Good my Lord, vouchsafe me a word with you.

HAMLET

Sir, a whole History.

GUILDENSTERN

The King, sir.

HAMLET

I sir, what of him?

GUILDENSTERN

Is in his retirement, marvellous distemper'd.

HAMLET

With drink Sir?

GUILDENSTERN

No my Lord, rather with choler.

HAMLET

Your wisdom should show it self more richer, to signify this to his Doctor: for me to put him to his Purgation, would perhaps plunge him into far more Choler.

GUILDENSTERN

Good my Lord put your discourse into some frame, and start not so wildly from my affair.

HAMLET

I am tame Sir, pronounce.

GUILDENSTERN

The Queen your Mother, in most great affliction of spirit, hath sent me to you.

HAMLET

You are welcome.

GUILDENSTERN

Nay, good my Lord, this courtesy is not of the right breed. If it shall please you to make me a wholesome answer, I will do your

Mother's commandment: if not, your pardon, and my return shall be the end of my Business.

HAMLET

Sir, I cannot.

GUILDENSTERN

What, my Lord?

HAMLET

Make you a wholesome answer: my wit's diseas'd. But sir, such answers as I can make, you shall command: or rather you say, my Mother: therefore no more but to the matter. My Mother you say.

ROSENKRANTZ

Then thus she says: your behavior hath stroke her into amazement, and admiration.

HAMLET

Oh wonderful Son, that can so astonish a Mother. But is there no sequel at the heels of this Mother's admiration?

ROSENKRANTZ

She desires to speak with you in her Closet, ere you go to bed.

HAMLET

We shall obey, were she ten times our Mother. Have you any further Trade with us?

ROSENKRANTZ

My Lord, you once did love me.

HAMLET

So do I still, by these pickers and stealers.

ROSENKRANTZ

Good my Lord, what is your cause of distemper? You do freely bar the door of your own Liberty, if you deny your griefs to your Friend.

HAMLET

Sir I lack Advancement.

ROSENKRANTZ

How can that be, when you have the voice of the King himself, for your Succession in Denmark?

HAMLET

I, but while the grass grows, the Proverb is something musty.
(*Enter one with a Recorder*)
O the Recorder. Let me see, to withdraw with you, why do you go about to recover the wind of me, as if you would drive me into a toil?

GUILDENSTERN

O my Lord, if my Duty be too bold, my love is too unmannerly.

HAMLET

I do not well understand that. Will you play upon this Pipe?

GUILDENSTERN

My Lord, I cannot.

HAMLET

I pray you.

GUILDENSTERN

Believe me, I cannot.

HAMLET

I do beseech you.

GUILDENSTERN

I know no touch of it, my Lord.

HAMLET

'Tis as easy as lying: govern these Ventiges with you finger and thumb, give it breath with your mouth, and it will discourse most excellent Music. Look you, these are the stops.

GUILDENSTERN

But these cannot I command to any utterance of harmony, I have not the skill.

HAMLET

Why look you now, how unworthy a thing you make of me: you would play upon me; you would seem to know my stops: you would pluck out the heart of my Mystery; you would sound me from my lowest Note, to the top of my Compass: and there is much Music, excellent Voice, in this little Organ, yet cannot you make it. Why do you think, that I am easier to be played on, than a Pipe? Call me what Instrument you will, though you can fret me, you cannot play upon me. God bless you Sir.

(*Enter* POLONIUS)

POLONIUS

My Lord; the Queen would speak with you, and presently.

HAMLET

Do you see that Cloud? that's almost in shape like a Camel.

POLONIUS

By'th'Mass, and it's like a Camel indeed.

HAMLET

Me thinks it is like a Weasel.

POLONIUS

It is back'd like a Weasel.

HAMLET

Or like a Whale?

POLONIUS

Very like a Whale.

HAMLET

Then I will come to my Mother, by and by:
They fool me to the top of my bent.
I will come by and by.

POLONIUS

I will say so.

(*Exit*)

HAMLET

By and by, is easily said. Leave me Friends:
'Tis now the very witching time of night,
When Churchyards yawn, and Hell it self breathes out
Contagion to this world. Now could I drink hot blood,
And do such bitter business as the day
Would quake to look on. Soft now, to my Mother:
Oh Heart, lose not thy Nature; let not ever
The Soul of *Nero,* enter this firm bosom:
Let me be cruel, not unnatural.
I will speak Daggers to her, but use none:
My Tongue and Soul in this be Hypocrits.
How in my words somever she be shent,
To give them Seals, never my Soul consent.

The Tragedy of Hamlet

ACT III, SCENE 4—
POLONIUS, HAMLET, QUEEN, GHOST

POLONIUS

Look you lay home to him,
Tell him his pranks have been too broad to bear with,
And that your Grace hath screen'd, and stood between

Much heat, and him. Ile silence me e'en here:
Pray you be round with him.

HAMLET
(*Within*)
Mother, mother, mother.

QUEEN
Ile warrant you, fear me not.
Withdraw, I hear him comming.

(*Enter* HAMLET)

HAMLET
Now Mother, what's the matter?

QUEEN
Hamlet, thou hast thy Father much offended.

HAMLET
Mother, you have my Father much offended.

QUEEN
Come, come, you answer with an idle tongue.

HAMLET
Go, go, you question with an idle tongue.

QUEEN
Why how now *Hamlet*?

HAMLET
What's the matter now?

QUEEN
Have you forgot me?

HAMLET

No by the Rood, not so:
You are the Queen, your Husband's Brother's wife,
But would you were not so. You are my Mother.

QUEEN

Nay, then Ile set those to you that can speak.

HAMLET

Come, come, and sit you down, you shall not budge:
You go not till I set you up a glass,
Where you may see the inmost part of you?

QUEEN

What wilt thou do? thou wilt not murder me?
Help, help, hoa.

POLONIUS

What hoa, help, help, help.

HAMLET

How now, a Rat? dead for a Ducat, dead.

(*Kills* POLONIUS)

POLONIUS

Oh I am slain.

QUEEN

Oh me, what hast thou done?

HAMLET

Nay I know not, is it the King?

QUEEN

Oh what a rash, and bloody deed is this?

HAMLET

A bloody deed, almost as bad good Mother,
As kill a King, and marry with his Brother.

QUEEN

As kill a King?

HAMLET

I Lady, 'twas my word.
Thou wretched, rash, intruding fool farewell,
I took thee for thy Betters, take thy Fortune,
Thou find'st to be too busy, is some danger.
Leave wringing of your hands, peace, sit you down,
And let me wring your heart, for so I shall
If it be made of penetrable stuff;
If damned Custom have not braz'd it so,
That it is proof and bulwark against Sense.

QUEEN

What have I done, that thou dar'st wag thy tongue,
In noise so rude against me?

HAMLET

Such an Act
That blurs the grace and blush of Modesty,
Calls Virtue Hypocrite, takes off the Rose
From the fair forehead of an innocent love,
And makes a blister there. Makes marriage vows
As false as Dicer's Oathes. Oh such a deed,
As from the body of Contraction plucks
The very soul, and sweet Religion makes
A rapsody of words. Heaven's face doth glow,
Yea this solidity and compound mass,
With tristful visage as against the doom,
Is thought-sick at the act.

QUEEN

Aye me; what act, that roars so loud, & thunders in the index.

HAMLET

Look here upon this Picture, and on this,
The counterfeit presentment of two Brothers:
See what a grace was seated on his Brow,
Hyperion's curls, the front of Jove himself,
An eye like Mars, to threaten or command
A Station, like the Herald Mercury
New lighted on a heaven-kissing hill:
A Combination, and a form indeed,
Where every God did seem to set his Seal,
To give the world assurance of a man.
This was your Husband. Look you now what follows.
Here is your Husband, like a Mildew'd ear
Blasting his wholesom breath. Have you eyes?
Could you on this fair Mountain leave to feed,
And batten on this Moor? Ha? Have you eyes?
You cannot call it Love: For at your age,
The hey-day in the blood is tame, it's humble,
And waits upon the Judgment: and what Judgment
Would step from this, to this? what devil was't,
That thus hath cozen'd you at hoodman-blind?
O Shame! where is thy Blush? Rebellious Hell,
If thou canst mutine in a Matron's bones,
To flaming youth, let Virtue be as wax,
And melt in her own fire. Proclaim no shame,
When the compulsive Ardor gives the charge,
Since Frost itself, as actively doth burn,
As Reason panders Will.

QUEEN

O *Hamlet,* speak no more.
Thou turn'st mine eyes into my very soul,
And there I see such black and grained spots,
As will not leave their Tinct.

HAMLET

Nay, but to live
In the rank sweat of an enseamed bed,

Stew'd in Corruption; honeying and making love
Over the nasty Sty.

QUEEN

Oh speak to me, no more,
These words like Daggers enter in mine ears.
No more sweet *Hamlet*.

HAMLET

A Murderer, and a Villain:
A Slave, that is not twentieth part the tythe
Of your precedent Lord. A vice of Kings,
A Cutpurse of the Empire and the Rule.
That from a shelf, the precious Diadem stole,
And put it in his Pocket.

QUEEN

No more.

(*Enter* GHOST)

HAMLET

A King of shreds and patches.
Save me; and hover o'er me with your wings
You heavenly Guards. What would you gracious figure?

QUEEN

Alas he's mad.

HAMLET

Do you not come your tardy Son to chide,
That laps't in Time and Passion, lets go by
Th'important acting of your dread command? Oh say.

GHOST

Do not forget: this Visitation
Is but to whet thy almost blunted purpose.

But look, Amazement on thy Mother sits;
O step between her, and her fighting Soul,
Conceit in weakest bodies, strongest works.
Speak to her *Hamlet*.

HAMLET

How is it with you Lady?

QUEEN

Alas, how is't with you?
That you do bend your eye on vacancy,
And with their corporal air do hold discourse.
Forth at your eyes, your spirits wildly peep,
And as the sleeping Soldiers in th' Alarm,
Your bedded hair, like life in excrements,
Start up, and stand an end. Oh gentle Son,
Upon the heat and flame of thy distemper
Sprinkle cool patience. Whereon do you look?

HAMLET

On him, on him: look you how pale he glares,
His form and cause conjoin'd, preaching to stones,
Would make them capable. Do not look upon me,
Least with this piteous action you convert
My stern effects: then what I have to do,
Will want true colour; tears perchance for blood.

QUEEN

To who do you speak this?

HAMLET

Do you see nothing there?

QUEEN

Nothing at all, yet all that is I see.

HAMLET

Nor did you nothing hear?

QUEEN

No, nothing but our selves.

HAMLET

Why look you there: look how it steals away:
My Father in his habit, as he liv'd,
Look where he goes even now out at the Portal.

(*Exit*)

QUEEN

This is the very coinage of your Brain,
This bodiless Creation extasy is very cunning in.

HAMLET

Extasy?
My Pulse as yours doth temperately keep time,
And makes as healthfull Music. It is not madness
That I have uttered; bring me to the Test
And I the matter will re-word: which madness
Would gambol from. Mother, for love of Grace,
Lay not a flattering Unction to your soul,
That not your trespass, but my madness speaks:
It will but skin and film the Ulcerous place,
Whil'st rank Corruption mining all within,
Infects unseen. Confess your self to Heaven,
Repent what's past, avoid what is to come,
And do not spread the Compost o'er the Weeds,
To make them rank. Forgive me this my Virtue,
For in the fatness of this pursy times,
Virtue it self, of vice must pardon beg,
Yea curb, and woo, for leave to do him good.

QUEEN

Oh *Hamlet,*
Thou hast cleft my heart in twain.

O throw away the worser part of it,
And live the purer with the other half.
Good night, but go not to mine Uncle's bed,
Assume a Virtue, if you have it not, refrain to night,
And that shall lend a kind of easiness
To the next abstinence. Once more goodnight,
And when you are desirous to be blest,
Ile blessing beg of you. For this same Lord,
I do repent: but heaven hath pleas'd it so,
To punish me with this, and this with me,
That I must be their Scourge and Minister.
I will bestow him, and will answer well
The death I gave him: so again, good night.
I must be cruel, only to be kind;
Thus bad begins, and worse remains behind.

QUEEN

What shall I do?

HAMLET

Not this by no means that I bid thee do:
Let the blunt King tempt you again to bed,
Pinch Wanton on you: cheek, call you his Mouse,
And let him for a pair of reechy kisses,
Or paddling in your neck with his damn'd Fingers,
Make you to ravel all this matter out,
That I essentially am not in madness,
But mad in craft. 'Twere good you let him know,
For who that's but a Queen, fair, sober, wife,
Would from a Paddock, from a Bat, a Gib,
Such dear concernings hide. Who would do so,
No in despite of Sense and Secrecy,
Unpeg the Basket on the house's top:
Let the Birds fly, and like the famous Ape
To try Conclusions in the Basket, creep
And break your own neck down.

QUEEN

Be thou assur'd, if words be made of breath,
And breath of life: I have no life to breathe
What thou hast said to me.

HAMLET

I must to England, you know that?

QUEEN

Alack I had forgot: 'Tis so concluded on.

HAMLET

This man shall set me packing:
Ile lug the Guts into the Neighbor room,
Mother goodnight. Indeed this counsellor
Is now most still, most secret, and most grave,
Who was in life, a foolish prating Knave.
Come sir, to draw toward an end with you.
Good night Mother.

The Tragedy of Othello

ACT III, SCENE 3—
IAGO, OTHELLO

IAGO

My Noble Lord.

OTHELLO

What dost thou say, *Iago*?

IAGO

Did *Michael Cassio*
When he woo'd my Lady, know of your love?

OTHELLO

He did, from first to last:
Why dost thou ask?

IAGO

But for a satisfaction of my Thought,
No further harm.

OTHELLO

Why of thy thought, *Iago*?

IAGO

I did not think he had been acquainted with her.

OTHELLO

O yes, and went between us very oft.

IAGO

Indeed?

OTHELLO

Indeed? I indeed. Discern'st thou ought in that?
Is he not honest?

IAGO

Honest, my Lord?

OTHELLO

Honest? I, Honest.

IAGO

My Lord, for ought I know.

OTHELLO

What do'st thou think?

IAGO

Think, my Lord?

OTHELLO

Think, my Lord? Alas, thou echo'st me;
As if there were some Monster in thy thought
Too hideous to be shown. Thou dost mean something:
I heard thee say even now, thou lik'st not that,
When *Cassio* left my wife. What did'st thou not like?
And when I told thee, he was of my Counsel,
Of my whole course of wooing; thou cried'st, Indeed?
And did'st contract, and purse thy brow together,
As if thou then had'st shut up in thy Brain
Some horrible Conceit. If thou do'st love me,
Show me thy thought.

IAGO

My Lord, you know I love you.

OTHELLO

I think thou do'st:
And for I know thou'rt full of Love, and Honesty,
And weigh'st thy words before thou giv'st them breath,
Therefore these stops of thine, fright me the more:
For such things in a false disloyal Knave
Are tricks of Custom: but in a man that's just,
They're close dilations, working from the heart,
That Passion cannot rule.

IAGO

For *Michael Cassio,*
I dare be sworn, I think that he is honest.

OTHELLO

I think so too.

IAGO

Men should be what they seem,
Or those that be not, would they might seem none.

OTHELLO

Certain, men should be what they seem.

IAGO

Why then I think *Cassio's* an honest man.

OTHELLO

Nay, yet there's more in this?
I pray thee speak to me, as to thy thinkings,
As thou dost ruminate, and give thy worst of thoughts
The worst of words.

IAGO

Good my Lord pardon me,
Though I am bound to every Act of duty,
I am not bound to that: All Slaves are free:
Utter my Thoughts? Why say, they are vile, and false?
As where's that Palace, wherein foul things
Sometimes intrude not? Who has that breath so pure,
Wherein uncleanly Apprehensions
Keep Leets, and Law-days, and in Sessions sit
With meditations lawful?

OTHELLO

Thou do'st conspire against thy Friend (*Iago*)
If thou but think'st him wrong'd, and mak'st his ear
A stranger to thy Thoughts.

IAGO

I do beseech you,
Though I perchance am vicious in my guess
(As I confess it is my Nature's plague
To spy into Abuses, and of my jealousy
Shapes faults that are not) that your wisdom
From one, that so imperfectly conceits,
Would take no notice, nor build your self a trouble
Out of his scattering, and unsure observance:
It were not for your quiet, nor your good,

Nor for my Manhood, Honesty, and Wisdom,
To let you know my thoughts.

OTHELLO

What dost thou mean?

IAGO

Good name in Man, and woman (dear my Lord)
Is the immediate Jewel of their Souls;
Who steals my purse, steals trash:
'Tis something, nothing;
'Twas mine, 'tis his, and has been slave to thousands:
But he that filches from me my good Name,
Robs me of that, which not enriches him,
And makes me poor indeed.

OTHELLO

Ile know thy Thoughts.

IAGO

You cannot, if my heart were in your hand,
Nor shall not, whil'st 'tis in my custody.

OTHELLO

Ha?

IAGO

Oh, beware my Lord, of jealousy,
It is the green-ey'd Monster, which doth mock
The meat it feeds on. That Cuckold lives in bliss,
Who certain of his Fate, loves not his wronger:
But oh, what damned minutes tells he o'er,
Who dotes, yet doubts: Suspects, yet soundly loves?

OTHELLO

O misery.

IAGO

Poor, and Content, is rich, and rich enough,
But Riches fineless, is as poor as Winter,

To him that ever fears he shall be poor:
Good Heaven, the Souls of all my Tribe defend
From Jealousy.

OTHELLO

Why? why is this?
Think'st thou, I'ld make a Life of Jealousy;
To follow still the changes of the Moon
With fresh suspicions? No: to be once in doubt,
Is to be resolv'd: Exchange me for a Goat,
When I shall turn the business of my Soul
To such exsufflicate, and blow'd Surmises,
Matching thy inference. 'Tis not to make me Jealous,
To say my wife is fair, feeds well, loves company,
Is free of Speech, Sings, Plays, and Dances:
Where Virtue is, these are more virtuous.
Nor from mine own weak merits, will I draw
The smallest fear, or doubt of her revolt,
For she had eyes, and chose me. No *Iago*,
Ile see before I doubt; when I doubt, prove;
And on the proof, there is no more but this,
Away at once with Love, or Jealousy.

IAGO

I am glad of this: For now I shall have reason
To show the Love and Duty that I bear you
With franker spirit. Therefore (as I am bound)
Receive it from me. I speak not yet of proof:
Look to your wife, observe her well with *Cassio*,
Wear your eyes, thus: not Jealous, nor Secure:
I would not have your free, and Noble Nature,
Out of self-Bounty, be abus'd: Look too't:
I know our Country disposition well:
In Venice, they do let Heaven see the pranks
They dare not show their Husbands.
Their best Conscience,
Is not to leav't undone, but kept unknown.

226

OTHELLO

Dost thou say so?

IAGO

She did deceive her Father, marrying you,
And when she seem'd to shake, and fear your looks,
She lov'd them most.

OTHELLO

And so she did.

IAGO

Why go to then:
She that so young could give out such a Seeming
To seal her Father's eyes up, close as Oak,
He thought 'twas Witchcraft.
But I am much to blame:
I humbly do beseech you of your pardon
For too much loving you.

OTHELLO

I am bound to thee for ever.

IAGO

I see this hath a little dash'd your Spirits:

OTHELLO

Not a jot, not a jot.

IAGO

Trust me, I fear it has:
I hope you will consider what is spoke
Comes from your Love.
But I do see y'are mov'd:
I am to pray you, not to strain my speech
To grosser issues, nor to larger reach,
Than to Suspicion.

OTHELLO

I will not.

IAGO

Should you do so (my Lord)
My speech should fall unto such vile success,
Which my Thoughts aim'd not.
Cassio's my worthy Friend:
My Lord, I see y'are mov'd.

OTHELLO

No, not much mov'd:
I do not think but *Desdemona's* honest.

IAGO

Long live she so;
And long live you to think so.

OTHELLO

And yet how Nature erring from it self—

IAGO

I, there's the point:
As (to be bold with you)
Not to affect many proposed Matches
Of her own Clime, Complexion, and Degree,
Whereto we see in all things, Nature tends:
Foh, one may smell in such, a will most rank,
Foul dispositions, Thoughts unnatural.
But (pardon me) I do not in position
Distinctly speak of her, though I may fear
Her will, recoiling to her better judgment,
May fall to match you with her Country forms,
And happily repent.

OTHELLO

Farewell, farewell:
If more thou dost perceive, let me know more:

Set on thy wife to observe.
Leave me *Iago*.

IAGO

My Lord, I take my leave.

OTHELLO

Why did I marry?
This honest Creature (doubtless)
Sees, and knows more, much more than he unfolds.

IAGO

My Lord, I would I might entreat your Honor
To scan this thing no farther: Leave it to time,
Although 'tis fit that *Cassio* have his Place;
For sure he fills it up with great Ability;
Yet if you please, to hold him off a-while:
You shall by that perceive him, and his means:
Note if your Lady strain his Entertainment
With any strong, or vehement importunity,
Much will be seen in that: In the mean time,
Let me be thought too busy in my fears,
(As worthy cause I have to fear I am)
And hold her free, I do beseech your Honor.

OTHELLO

Fear not my government.

IAGO

I once more take my leave.
(*Exit*)
This Fellow's of exceeding honesty.
And knows all Quantities with a learn'd Spirit
Of human dealings. If I do prove her Haggard,
Though that her jesses were my dear heart-strings,
I'ld whistle her off, and let her down the wind
To prey at Fortune. Haply, for I am black,
And have not those soft parts of Conversation

That Chamberers have: Or for I am declin'd
Into the vale of years (yet that's not much)
She's gone. I am abus'd, and my relief
Must be to loathe her. Oh Curse of Marriage!
That we can call these delicate Creatures ours,
And not their Appetites? I had rather be a toad,
And live upon the vapour of a Dungeon,
Than keep a corner in the thing I love
For others' uses. Yet 'tis the plague to Great-ones,
Prerogativ'd are they less than the Base,
'Tis destiny unshunnable, like death:
Even then, this forked plague is Fated to us,
When we do quicken. Look where she comes.

The Tragedy of Othello

ACT IV, SCENE 3—
EMILIA, DESDEMONA

EMILIA

How goes it now? He looks gentler than he did.

DESDEMONA

He says he will return incontinent,
And hath commanded me to go to bed,
And bid me to dismiss you.

EMILIA

Dismiss me?

DESDEMONA

It was his bidding: therefore good *Emilia,*
Give me my nightly wearing, and adieu.
We must not now displease him.

EMILIA

I, would you had never seen him.

DESDEMONA

So would not I: my love doth so approve him,
That even his stubbornness, his checks, his frowns,
(Prithee un-pin me) have grace and favour.

EMILIA

I have laid those Sheets you bade me on the bed.

DESDEMONA

All's one: good Father, how foolish are our minds?
If I do die before, prithee shroud me
In one of those same Sheets.

EMILIA

Come, come: you talk.

DESDEMONA

My Mother had a Maid call'd *Barbary*,
She was in love: and he she lov'd prov'd mad,
And did forsake her. She had a Song of Willow,
An old thing 'twas: but it express'd her Fortune,
And she died singing it. That Song tonight,
Will not go from my mind: I have much to do,
But to go hang my head all at one side
And sing it like poor *Barbary*; prithee dispatch.

EMILIA

Shall I go fetch your Night-gown?

DESDEMONA

No, un-pin me here,
This *Lodovico* is a proper man.

EMILIA

A very handsome man.

DESDEMONA

He speaks well.

EMILIA

I know a Lady in Venice would have walk'd barefoot to Palestine
for a touch of his nether lip.

DESDEMONA

> *The poor Soul sat singing, by a Sycamore tree.*
> *Sing all a green Willow:*
> *Her hand on her bosom, her head on her knee,*
> *Sing Willow, Willow, Willow.*
> *The fresh Streams ran by her, and murmur'd her moans,*
> *Sing Willow, etc.*
> *Her salt tears fell from her, and softened the stones,*
> *Sing Willow, etc.* (Lay by these)
> *Willow, Willow.* (Prithee hie thee: He'll come anon)
> *Sing all a green Willow must be my Garland.*
> *Let no body blame him, his scorn I approve.*

(Nay that's not next. Hark, who is't that knocks?)

EMILIA

It's the wind.

DESDEMONA

> *I call'd my Love false Love: but what said he then?*
> *Sing Willow, etc.*
> *If I court me more women, you'll couch with more men.*

So get thee gone, good night: mine eyes do itch:
Doth that bode weeping?

EMILIA

'Tis neither here, nor there.

DESDEMONA

I have heard it said so. O these Men, these men!
Do'st thou in conscience think (tell me *Emilia*)

That there be women do abuse their husbands
In such gross kind?

EMILIA

There be some such, no question.

DESDEMONA

Would'st thou do such a deed for all the world?

EMILIA

Why, would not you?

DESDEMONA

No, by this Heavenly light.

EMILIA

Nor I neither, by this Heavenly light:
I might do't as well i'th' dark.

DESDEMONA

Would'st thou do such a deed for all the world?

EMILIA

The world's a huge thing:
It is a great price, for a small vice.

DESDEMONA

In troth, I think thou would'st not.

EMILIA

In troth I think I should, and undo't when I had done. Marry, I would not do such a thing for a joint Ring, nor for measures of Lawn, nor for Gowns, Petticoats, nor Caps, nor any petty exhibition. But for all the whole world: why, who would not make her husband a Cuckold, to make him a Monarch? I should venture Purgatory for't.

DESDEMONA

Beshrew me, if I would do such a wrong
For the whole world.

EMILIA

Why, the wrong is but a wrong i'th' world: and having the world
for your labour, 'tis a wrong in your own world, and you might
quickly make it right.

DESDEMONA

I do not think there is any such woman.

EMILIA

Yes, a dozen: and as many to th' vantage, as would store the world
they play'd for.
But I do think it is their Husbands' faults
If Wives do fall: (Say, that they slack their duties,
And pour our Treasures into foreign laps;
Or else break out in peevish Jealousies,
Throwing restraint upon us: Or say they strike us,
Or scant our former having in despite)
Why we have galls: and though we have some Grace,
Yet have we some Revenge. Let Husbands know,
Their wives have sense like them: They see, and smell,
And have their Palates both for sweet, and sour,
As Husbands have. What is it that they do,
When they change us for others? Is it Sport?
I think it is: and doth Affection breed it?
I think it doth. Is't Frailty that thus errs?
It is so too. And have not we Affections?
Desires for Sport? and Frailty, as men have?
Then let them use us well: else let them know,
The ills we do, their ills instruct us so.

DESDEMONA

Good night, good night:
Heaven me such uses send,
Not to pick bad, from bad: but by bad, mend.

The Tragedy of King Lear

ACT IV, SCENE 1
AND ACT IV, SCENE 5—
GLOUCESTER, EDGAR

GLOUCESTER

Sirrah, naked fellow.

EDGAR

Poor Tom's a-cold. I cannot daub it further.

GLOUCESTER

Come hither fellow.

EDGAR

And yet I must:
Bless thy sweet eyes, they bleed.

GLOUCESTER

Know'st thou the way to Dover?

EDGAR

Both stile, and gate; Horseway, and foot-path: poor Tom hath been scared out of his good wits. Bless thee good man's son, from the foul Fiend.

GLOUCESTER

Here take this purse, ye whom the heav'ns plagues
Have humbled to all strokes: that I am wretched
Makes thee the happier: Heavens deal so still:
Let the superfluous, and Lust-dieted man,
That slaves your ordinance, that will not see
Because he does not feel, feel your powre quickly:

So distribution should undo excess,
And each man have enough. Dost thou know Dover?

EDGAR

I Master.

GLOUCESTER

There is a Cliff, whose high and bending head
Looks fearfully in the confined Deep:
Bring me but to the very brim of it,
And Ile repay the misery thou do'st bear
With something rich about me: from that place,
I shall no leading need.

EDGAR

Give me thy arm;
Poor Tom shall lead thee.

(*Exeunt*)
(*Enter* GLOUCESTER, and EDGAR)

GLOUCESTER

When shall I come to th'top of that same hill?

EDGAR

You do climb up it now. Look how we labor.

GLOUCESTER

Me thinks the ground is even.

EDGAR

Horrible steep.
Hark, do you hear the Sea?

GLOUCESTER

No truly.

EDGAR

Why then your other senses grow imperfect
By your eyes anguish.

GLOUCESTER

So may it be indeed.
Me thinks thy voice is alter'd, and thou speak'st
In better phrase and matter than thou did'st.

EDGAR

Y'are much deceiv'd: In nothing am I chang'd
But in my Garments.

GLOUCESTER

Me thinks y'are better spoken.

EDGAR

Come on Sir,
Here's the place: stand still: how fearful
And dizzy 'tis, to cast one's eyes so low,
The Crows and Choughs, that wing the midway air
Show scarce so gross as Beetles. Half way down
Hangs one that gathers Sampire: dreadful Trade:
Me thinks he seems no bigger than his head.
The Fishermen, that walk'd upon the beach
Appear like Mice: and yond tall Anchoring Bark,
Diminish'd to her Cock: her Cock, a Buoy
Almost too small for sight. The murmuring Surge,
That on th'unnumbred idle Pebble chafes
Cannot be heard so high. Ile look no more,
Least my brain turn, and the deficient sight
Topple down headlong.

GLOUCESTER

Set me where you stand.

EDGAR

Give me your hand:
You are now within a foot of th'extreme Verge:
For all beneath the Moon would I not leap upright.

GLOUCESTER

Let go my hand:
Here Friend's another purse: in it, a jewel
Well worth a poor mans taking. Fairies, and Gods
Prosper it with thee. Go thou further off,
Bid me farewell, and let me hear thee going.

EDGAR

Now fare ye well, good Sir.

GLOUCESTER

With all my heart.

EDGAR

Why I do trifle thus with his despair,
Is done to cure it.

GLOUCESTER

O you mighty Gods!
This world I do renounce, and in your sights
Shake patiently my great affliction off:
If I could bear it longer, and not fall
To quarrel with your great opposeless wills,
My snuff, and loathed part of Nature should
Burn it self out. If *Edgar* live, O bless him:
Now Fellow, fare thee well.

EDGAR

Gone Sir, farewell:
And yet I know not how conceit may rob
The Treasury of life, when life it self
Yields to the Theft. Had he been where he thought,
By this had thought been past. Alive or dead?

Hoa, you Sir: Friend, hear you, Sir, speak:
Thus might he pass indeed: yet he revives.
What are you Sir?

GLOUCESTER

Away, and let me die.

EDGAR

Had'st thou been ought
But Gossamer, Feathers, Air,
(So many fathom down precipitating)
Thoud'st shiver'd like an Egg: but thou do'st breathe:
Hast heavy substance, bleed'st not, speak'st, art sound,
Ten Masts at each, make not the altitude
Which thou hast perpendicularly fell,
Thy life's a Miracle, Speak yet again.

GLOUCESTER

But have I falne, or no?

EDGAR

From the dread Summit of this Chalky Bourne
Look up a height, the shrill-gorg'd Lark so far
Cannot be seen, or heard: do but look up.

GLOUCESTER

Alack, I have no eyes:
Is wretchedness depriv'd that benefit
To end it self by death? 'Twas yet some comfort,
When misery could beguile the Tyrant's rage,
And frustrate his proud will.

EDGAR

Give me your arm.
Up, so: How is't? Feel you your Legs? You stand.

GLOUCESTER

Too well, too well.

EDGAR

This is above all strangeness,
Upon the crown o' th' Cliff. What thing was that
Which parted from you?

GLOUCESTER

A poor unfortunate Beggar.

EDGAR

As I stood here below, me thought his eyes
Were two full Moons: he had a thousand Noses,
Horns welk'd, and waved like the enraged Sea:
It was some Fiend: Therefore thou happy Father,
Think that the clearest Gods, who make them Honors
Of men's Impossibilities, have preserved thee.

GLOUCESTER

I do remember now: henceforth Ile bear
Affliction, till it do cry out it self
Enough, enough, and die. That thing you speak of,
I took it for a man: often 'twould say
The Fiend, the Fiend, he led me to that place.

EDGAR

Bear free and patient thoughts.

The Tragedy of Macbeth

ACT II, SCENE 2—
LADY MACBETH, MACBETH

LADY MACBETH

That which hath made them drunk, hath made me bold:
What hath quench'd them, hath given me fire.
Hark, peace: it was the Owl that shriek'd,

The fatal Bell-man, which gives the stern'st good-night.
He is about it, the Doors are open:
And the surfeited Grooms do mock their charge
With Snores. I have drugg'd their Possets,
That Death and Nature do contend about them,
Whether they live or die.

(*Enter* MACBETH)

MACBETH

Who's there? what hoa?

LADY MACBETH

Alack, I am afraid they have awak'd,
And 'tis not done: The'attempt, and not the deed,
Confounds us: hark: I lay'd their Daggers ready,
He could not miss 'em. Had he not resembled
My Father as he slept, I had done't.
My Husband?

MACBETH

I have done the deed:
Didst thou not hear a noise?

LADY MACBETH

I heard the Owl scream, and the Cricket cry.
Did you not speak?

MACBETH

When?

LADY MACBETH

Now.

MACBETH

As I descended?

LADY MACBETH

I.

MACBETH

Hark, who lies i'th'second Chamber?

LADY MACBETH

Donalbaine.

MACBETH

This is a sorry sight.

LADY MACBETH

A foolish thought, to say a sorry sight.

MACBETH

There's one did laugh in's sleep,
And one cried Murder, that they did wake each other:
I stood, and heard them: But they did say their Prayers,
And addrest them again to sleep.

LADY MACBETH

There are two lodg'd together.

MACBETH

One cried God bless us, and Amen the other,
As they had seen me with these Hangman's hands:
List'ning their fear, I could not say Amen,
When they did say God bless us.

LADY MACBETH

Consider it not so deeply.

MACBETH

But wherefore could not I pronounce Amen?
I had most need of Blessing, and Amen stuck in my throat.

LADY MACBETH

These deeds must not be thought
After these ways: so, it will make us mad.

MACBETH

Me thought I heard a voice cry, Sleep no more:
Macbeth does murder Sleep, the innocent Sleep,
Sleep that knits up the ravel'd Sleeve of Care,
The death of each day's Life, sore Labor's Bath,
Balm of hurt Minds, great Nature's second Course,
Chief nourisher in Life's Feast.

LADY MACBETH

What do you mean?

MACBETH

Still it cried, Sleep no more to all the House:
Glamis hath murther'd Sleep, and therefore *Cawdor*
Shall sleep no more: *Macbeth* shall sleep no more.

LADY MACBETH

Who was it, that thus cried? why worthy *Thane,*
You do unbend your Noble strength, to think
So brain-sickly of things: Go get some Water,
And wash this filthy Witness from your Hand.
Why did you bring these Daggers from the place?
They must lie there: go carry them, and smear
The sleepy Grooms with blood.

MACBETH

Ile go no more:
I am afraid, to think what I have done:
Look on't again, I dare not.

LADY MACBETH

Infirm of purpose:
Give me the Daggers: the sleeping, and the dead,
Are but as Pictures: 'tis the Eye of Child-hood,
That fears a painted Devil. If he do bleed,
Ile gild the Faces of the Grooms withal,
For it must seem their Guilt.

(*Exit*)
(*Knock within*)

MACBETH

Whence is that knocking?
How is't with me, when every noise appals me?
What Hands are here? hah: they pluck out mine Eyes.
Will all great *Neptune's* Ocean wash this blood
Clean from my Hand? no: this my Hand will rather
The multitudinous Seas incarnadine,
Making the Greeny one, Red.

(*Enter* LADY MACBETH)

LADY MACBETH

My Hands are of your colour: but I shame
To wear a Heart so white.
(*Knock*)
I hear a knocking at the South entry:
Retire we to our Chamber:
A little Water clears us of this deed.
How easy is it then? your Constancy
Hath left you unattended.
(*Knock*)
Hark, more knocking.
Get on your Night-Gown, least occasion call us,
And show us to be Watchers: be not lost
So poorly in your thoughts

MACBETH

To know my deed,
(*Knock*)
'Twere best not know my self
Wake *Duncan* with thy knocking:
I would thou could'st.

(*Exeunt*)

The Tragedy of
Antony and Cleopatra

ACT I, SCENE 3—
CLEOPATRA, ANTONY

CLEOPATRA

I am sick, and sullen.

ANTONY

I am sorry to give breathing to my purpose.

CLEOPATRA

Help me away dear *Charmian,* I shall fall,
It cannot be thus long, the sides of Nature
Will not sustain it.

ANTONY

Now my dearest Queen.

CLEOPATRA

Pray you stand farther from me.

ANTONY

What's the matter?

CLEOPATRA

I know by that same eye there's some good news.
What says the married woman you may go?
Would she had never given you leave to come.
Let her not say 'tis I that keep you here,
I have no power upon you: Hers you are.

ANTONY

The Gods best know.

CLEOPATRA

Oh never was there Queen
So mightily betrayed: yet at the first
I saw the Treasons planted.

ANTONY

Cleopatra.

CLEOPATRA

Why should I think you can be mine, & true,
(Though you in swearing shake the Throned Gods)
Who have been false to *Fulvia*?
Riotous madness,
To be entangled with those mouth-made vows,
Which break themselves in swearing.

ANTONY

Most sweet Queen.

CLEOPATRA

Nay pray you seek no color for your going,
But bid farewell, and go:
When you sued staying,
Then was the time for words: No going then,
Eternity was in our Lips, and Eyes,
Bliss in our brows bent: none our parts so poor,
But was a race of Heaven. They are so still,
Or thou the greatest Soldier of the world,
And turn'd the greatest Liar.

ANTONY

How now Lady?

CLEOPATRA

I would I had thy inches, thou should'st know
There were a heart in Egypt.

ANTONY

Hear me Queen:
The strong necessity of Time, commands
Our Services awhile: but my full heart
Remains in use with you. Our Italy,
Shines o'er with civil Swords: *Sextus Pompeius*
Makes his approaches to the Port of Rome,
Equality of two Domestic powers,
Breed scrupulous faction: The hated grown to strength
Are newly grown to Love: The condemn'd *Pompey*,
Rich in his Father's Honor, creeps apace
Into the hearts of such, as have not thrived
Upon the present state, whose Numbers threaten,
And quietness grown sick of rest, would purge
By any desperate change: My more particular,
And that which most with you should safe my going,
Is *Fulvia's* death.

CLEOPATRA

Though age from folly could not give me freedom
It does from childishness. Can *Fulvia* die?

ANTONY

She's dead my Queen.
Look here, and at thy Sovereign leisure read
The Garboils she awak'd: at the last, best,
See when, and where she died.

CLEOPATRA

O most false Love!
Where be the Sacred Vials thou should'st fill
With sorrowful water? Now I see, I see,
In *Fulvia's* death, how mine receiv'd shall be.

ANTONY

Quarrel no more, but be prepar'd to know
The purposes I bear: which are, or cease,
As you should give th'advice. By the fire

That quickens Nilus slime, I go from hence
Thy Soldier, Servant, making Peace or War,
As thou affects.

CLEOPATRA

Cut my Lace, *Charmian* come,
But let it be, I am quickly ill, and well,
So *Antony* loves.

ANTONY

My precious Queen forbear,
And give true evidence to his Love, which stands
An honorable Trial.

CLEOPATRA

So *Fulvia* told me.
I prithee turn aside, and weep for her,
Then bid adieu to me, and say the tears
Belong to Egypt. Good now, play one Scene
Of excellent dissembling, and let it look
Like perfect Honor.

ANTONY

You'll heat my blood no more?

CLEOPATRA

You can do better yet: but this is meetly.

ANTONY

Now by Sword.

CLEOPATRA

And Target. Still he mends.
But this is not the best. Look prithee *Charmian,*
How this Herculean Roman does become
The carriage of his chase.

ANTONY

I'll leave you Lady.

CLEOPATRA

Courteous Lord, one word:
Sir, you and I must part, but that's not it:
Sir, you and I have lov'd, but there's not it:
That you know well, something it is I would:
Oh, my Oblivion is a very *Antony,*
And I am all forgotten.

ANTONY

But that your Royalty
Holds Idleness your subject, I should take you
For Idleness it self.

CLEOPATRA

'Tis sweating Labor,
To bear such Idleness so near the heart
As *Cleopatra* this. But Sir, forgive me,
Since my becomings kill me, when they do not
Eye well to you. Your Honor calls you hence,
Therefore be deaf to my unpitied Folly.
And all the Gods go with you. Upon your Sword
Sit Laurel victory, and smooth success
Be strew'd before your feet.

ANTONY

Let us go.
Come: Our separation so abides and flies,
That thou residing here, goes yet with me;
And I hence fleeting, here remain with thee.
Away.

Pericles, Prince of Tyre

ACT V, SCENE 1—
MARINA, PERICLES

MARINA

Hail, sir, my Lord, lend ear.

PERICLES

Hum, ha.

MARINA

I am a maid, my Lord, that ne'er before invited eyes, but have been gazed on like a Comet: she speaks, my Lord, that may be, hath endured a grief might equal yours, of both were justly weighed, though wayward fortune did malign my state, my derivation was from ancestors who stood equivalent with mighty Kings, but time hath rooted out my parentage, and to the world and awkward casualties, bound me in servitude, I will desist, but there is something glows upon my cheek, and whispers in mine ear, *Go not till he speak*.

PERICLES

My fortunes, parentage, good parentage to equal mine; was it not thus, what say you?

MARINA

I said, my Lord, if you did know my parentage, you would not do me violence.

PERICLES

I do think so, pray you turn your eyes upon me, y'are like something that, what Country-women, here of these shores?

MARINA

No, nor of any shores, yet I was mortally brought forth, and am no other than I appear.

PERICLES

I am great with woe, and shall deliver weeping: my dearest wife was like this maid, and such a one my daughter might have been: my Queen's square brows, her stature to an inch, as wand-like straight, as silver-voic't, her eyes as jewel-like, and cast as richly, in pace another *Juno*, who starves the ears she feeds, and makes them hungry, the more she gives them speech; where do you live?

MARINA

Where I am but a stranger, from the deck you may discern the place.

PERICLES

Where were you bred? and how achiev'd you these endowments which you make more rich to owe?

MARINA

If I should tell my history, it would seem like lies disdain'd in the reporting.

PERICLES

Prithee speak, falseness cannot come from thee, for thou lookest modest as *Justice*, and thou seem'st a *Pallas* for the crowned truth to dwell in, I will believe thee, and make my senses credit thy relation, to points that seem impossible, for thou look'st like one I loved indeed; what were thy friends? Did'st thou not stay when I did push thee back; which was when I perceived thee that thou cam'st from good descent.

MARINA

So indeed I did.

PERICLES

Report thy parentage, I think thou said'st thou had'st been tost from wrong to injury, and that thou thought'st thy griefs might equal mine, if both were opened.

MARINA

Some such thing I said, and said no more, but what my thoughts did warrant me was likely.

PERICLES

Tell thy story, if thine considered prove the thousand part of my endurance, thou art a man, and I have suffered like a girl, yet thou do'st look like patience, gazing on Kings' graves, and smiling extremity out of act, what were thy friends? how lost thou thy name, my most kind virgin? recount I do beseech thee, Come, sit by me.

MARINA

My name is *Marina*.

PERICLES

Oh I am mockt, and thou by some insenced god sent hither to make the world to laugh at me.

MARINA

Patience, good sir, or here Ile cease.

PERICLES

Nay Ile be patient, thou little know'st how thou dost startle me to call thyself *Marina*.

MARINA

The name was given me by one that had some power, my father and a King.

PERICLES

How, a King's daughter, and call'd *Marina*?

MARINA

You said you would believe me, but not to be a troubler of your peace, I will end here.

PERICLES

But are you flesh and blood?
Have you a working pulse, and are no Fairy?

Motion? well speak on, where were you born?
And wherefore call'd *Marina*?

MARINA

Call'd *Marina*, for I was born at sea.

PERICLES

At sea? who was thy mother?

MARINA

My mother was the Daughter of a King, who died the minute I
was born, as my good Nurse *Lychorida* hath oft delivered weeping.

PERICLES

O stop there a little, this is the rarest dream
That e'er dull sleep did mock sad fools withal,
This cannot be my daughter; buried! well, where were you bred?
Ile hear you more to the bottom of your story and never inter-
rupt you.

MARINA

You scorn, believe me 'twere best I did give o'er.

PERICLES

I will believe you by the syllable of what you shall deliver, yet give
me leave, how came you in these parts? where were you bred?

MARINA

The King my Father did in *Tharsus* leave me,
Till cruel Cleon with his wicked wife,
Did seek to murder me: and having wooed a villain
To attempt it, who having drawn to do't,
A crew of Pirates came and rescued me,
Brought me to *Myteline*.
But, good sir, whither will you have me? why do you weep? It may
be you think me an imposter, no good faith. I am the daughter to
King *Pericles*, if good King *Pericles* be.

The Winter's Tale

ACT I, SCENE 2—
LEONTES, CAMILLO

LEONTES

Camillo, this great Sir will yet stay longer.

CAMILLO

You had much ado to make his Anchor hold,
When you cast out, it still came home.

LEONTES

Didst note it?

CAMILLO

He would not stay at your Petitions, made
His Business more material.

LEONTES

Didst perceive it?
They're here with me already: whisp'ring, rounding:
Sicilia is a so-forth: 'tis far gone,
When I shall gust it last. How cam't (*Camillo*)
That he did stay?

CAMILLO

At the good Queen's entreaty.

LEONTES

At the Queen's be't: Good should be pertinent,
But so it is, it is not. Was this taken
By any understanding Pate but thine?
For thy Conceit is soaking, will draw in

More than the common Blocks. Not noted, is't,
But of the finer Natures? By some Severals
Of Head-piece extraordinary? Lower Messes
Perchance are to this Business purblind? say.

CAMILLO

Business, my Lord? I think most understand
Bohemia stays here longer.

LEONTES

Ha?

CAMILLO

Stays here longer.

LEONTES

I, but why?

CAMILLO

To satisfy your Highness, and the Entreaties
Of our most gracious Mistress.

LEONTES

Satisfy?
Th'entreaties of your Mistress? Satisfy?
Let that suffice. I have trusted thee (*Camillo*)
With all the nearest things to my heart, as well
My Chamber-Counsels, wherein (Priest-like) thou
Hast cleans'd my Bosom: I, from thee departed
Thy Penitent reform'd: but we have been
Deceiv'd in thy Integrity, deceiv'd
In that which seems so.

CAMILLO

Be it forbid (my Lord.)

LEONTES

To bide upon't: thou art not honest: or
If thou inclin'st that way, thou art a Coward,

Which hoxes honesty behind, restraining
From Course requir'd: or thou must be counted
A Servant, grafted in my serious Trust,
And therein negligent: or else a Fool,
That seest a Game play'd home, the rich Stake Drawn,
And tak'st it all for jest.

CAMILLO

My gracious Lord,
I may be negligent, foolish, and fearful,
In every one of these, no man is free,
But that his negligence, his folly, fear,
Among the infinite doings of the World,
Sometime puts forth in your affairs (my Lord.)
If ever I were wilful-negligent,
It was my folly: if industriously
I play'd the Fool, it was my negligence,
Not weighing well the end: if ever fearful
To do a thing, where I the issue doubted,
Whereof the execution did cry out
Against the non-performance, 'twas a fear
Which oft infects the wisest: these (my Lord)
Are such allow'd Infirmities, that honesty
Is never free of. But beseech your Grace
Be plainer with me, let me know my Trespass
By its own visage; if I then deny it,
'Tis none of mine.

LEONTES

Ha' not you seen *Camillo*?
(But that's past doubt: you have, or your eye-glass
Is thicker than a Cuckold's Horn) or heard?
(For to a Vision so apparent, Rumor
Cannot be mute) or thought? (for Cogitation
Resides not in that man, that does not think)
My Wife is slippery? If thou wilt confess,
Or else be impudently negative,
To have nor Eyes, nor Ears, nor Thought, then say

256

My Wife's a Hobby-Horse, deserves a Name
As rank as any Flax-Wench, that puts to
Before her troth-plight: say't, and justify't.

CAMILLO

I would not be a stander-by, to hear
My Sovereign Mistress clouded so, without
My present vengeance taken: 'shrew my heart,
You never spoke what did become you less
Than this; which to reiterate, were sin
As deep as that, though true.

LEONTES

Is whispering nothing?
Is leaning Cheek to Cheek? is meeting Noses?
Kissing with in-side Lip? stopping the Career
Of Laughter, with a sigh? (a Note infallible
Of breaking Honesty) horsing foot on foot?
Skulking in corners? wishing Clocks more swift?
Hours, Minutes? Noon, Mid-night? and all Eyes
Blind with the Pin and Web, but theirs; theirs only,
That would unseen be wicked? Is this nothing?
Why then the World, and all that's in't, is nothing,
The covering Sky is nothing, *Bohemia* nothing,
My Wife is nothing, nor Nothing have these Nothings,
If this be nothing.

CAMILLO

Good my Lord, be cur'd
Of this diseas'd Opinion, and betimes,
For 'tis most dangerous.

LEONTES

Say it be, 'tis true.

CAMILLO

No, no, my Lord.

LEONTES

It is: you lie, you lie:
I say thou liest *Camillo,* and I hate thee,
Pronounce thee a gross Lout, a mindless Slave,
Or else a hovering Temporizer, that
Canst with thine eyes at once see good and evil,
Inclining to them both: were my Wife's Liver
Infected (as her life) she would not live
The running of one Glass.

CAMILLO

Who does infect her?

LEONTES

Why he that wears her like her Medal, hanging
About his neck (*Bohemia*) who, if I
Had Servants true about me, that bare eyes
To see alike mine Honor, as their Profits,
(Their own particular Thrifts) they would not do that
Which should undo more doing: I, and thou
His Cup-bearer, whom I from meaner form
Have Bench'd, and rear'd to Worship, who may'st see
Plainly, as Heaven sees Earth, and Earth sees Heaven,
How I am gall'd, might'st be-spice a Cup,
To give mine Enemy a lasting Wink:
Which Draught to me, were cordial.

CAMILLO

Sir (my Lord)
I could do this, and that with no rash Potion,
But with a ling'ring Dram, that should not work
Maliciously, like Poison: But I cannot
Believe this Crack to be in my dread Mistress
(So sovereignly being Honorable.)
I have lov'd thee.

LEONTES

Make that thy question, and go rot:
Do'st think I am so muddy, so unsettled,

258

To appoint my self in this vexation?
Sully the purity and whiteness of my Sheets
(Which to preserve, is Sleep; which being spotted,
Is Goads, Thorns, Nettles, Tails of Wasps)
Give scandal to the blood o'th' Prince, my Son,
(Who I do think is mine, and love as mine)
Without ripe moving to't? Would I do this?
Could man so blench?

CAMILLO

I must believe you (Sir)
I do, and will fetch off *Bohemia* for't:
Provided, that when he's remov'd, your Highness
Will take again your Queen, as yours at first,
Even for your Son's sake, and thereby for sealing
The Injury of Tongues, in Courts and Kingdoms
Known, and allied to yours.

LEONTES

Thou do'st advise me,
Even so as I mine own course have set down:
Ile give no blemish to her Honor, none.

CAMILLO

My Lord,
Go then; and with a countenance as clear
As Friendship wears at Feasts, keep with *Bohemia,*
And with your Queen: I am his Cup-bearer,
If from me he have wholesome Beverage,
Account me not your Servant.

LEONTES

This is all:
Do't, and thou hast the one half of my heart;
Do't not, thou splitt'st thine own.

CAMILLO

Ile do't, my Lord.

LEONTES
I will seem friendly, as thou hast advis'd me.

(Exit)

CAMILLO
O miserable Lady. But for me,
What case stand I in? I must be the poisoner
Of good *Polixenes,* and my ground to do't,
Is the obedience to a Master; one,
Who in Rebellion with himself, will have
All that are his, so too. To do this deed,
Promotion follows: If I could find example
Of thousands that had struck anointed Kings,
And flourish'd after, I'ld not do't: But since
Nor Brass, nor Stone, nor Parchment bears not one,
Let Villainy it self forswear't. I must
Forsake the Court: to do't, or no, is certain
To me a break-neck. Happy Star reign now,
Here comes *Bohemia.*

The Tempest

ACT I, SCENE 2—
PROSPERO, MIRANDA, CALIBAN

PROSPERO
Awake, dear heart awake, thou hast slept well,
Awake.

MIRANDA
The strangeness of your story, put
Heaviness in me.

PROSPERO

Shake it off: Come on,
We'll visit *Caliban,* my slave, who never
Yields us kind answer.

MIRANDA

'Tis a villain Sir, I do not love to look on.

PROSPERO

But as 'tis
We cannot miss him: he does make our fire,
Fetch in our wood, and serves in Offices
That profit us: What hoa: slave: *Caliban:*
Thou Earth, thou: speak.

CALIBAN

(*Within*)
There's wood enough within.

PROSPERO

Come forth I say, there's other business for thee:
Come thou Tortoise, when?
Thou poisonous slave, got by the devil himself
Upon thy wicked Dam; come forth.

(*Enter* CALIBAN)

CALIBAN

As wicked dew, as ere my mother brush'd
With Raven's feather from unwholesome Fen
Drop on you both: A Southwest blow on ye,
And blister you all o'er.

PROSPERO

For this be sure, tonight thou shalt have cramps,
Side-stitches, that shall pen thy breath up, Urchins
Shall forth at vast of night, that they may work
All exercise on thee: thou shalt be pinch'd

As thick as honey-comb, each pinch more stinging
Than Bees that made 'em.

CALIBAN

I must eat my dinner:
This Island's mine by *Sycorax* my mother,
Which thou tak'st from me: when thou cam'st first
Thou strok'st me, and make much of me: would'st give me
Water with berries in't: and teach me how
To name the bigger Light, and how the less
That burn by day, and night: and then I lov'd thee
And show'd thee all the qualities o'th' Isle,
The fresh Springs, Bring-pits; barren place and fertile,
Curs'd be I that did so: All the Charms
Of *Sycorax:* Toads, Beetles, Bats light on you:
For I am all the Subjects that you have,
Which first was mine own King: and here you sty me
In this hard Rock, whiles you do keep from me
The rest o'th' Island.

PROSPERO

Thou most lying slave,
Whom stripes may move, not kindness: I have us'd thee
(Filth as thou art) with humane care, and lodg'd thee
In mine own Cell, till thou did'st seek to violate
The honor of my child.

CALIBAN

Oh ho, oh ho, would it had been done:
Thou did'st prevent me, I had people'd else
This Isle with *Calibans*.

PROSPERO

Abhorred Slave,
Which any print of goodness wilt not take,
Being capable of all ill: I pitied thee,
Took pains to make thee speak, taught thee each hour
One thing or other: when thou did'st not (Savage)

Know thine own meaning; but would'st gabble, like
A thing most brutish, I endow'd thy purposes
With words that made them known: But thy vile race
(Though thou did'st learn) had that in't, which good natures
Could not abide to be with; therefore wast thou
Deservedly confin'd into this Rock, who had'st
Deserv'd more than a prison.

CALIBAN

You taught me Language, and my profit on't
Is, I know how to curse: the red-plague rid you
For learning me your language.

PROSPERO

Hag-seed, hence:
Fetch us in Fuel, and be quick thou'rt best
To answer other business: shrug'st thou (Malice)
If thou neglect'st, or dost unwillingly
What I command, Ile rack thee with old Cramps,
Fill all thy bones with Aches, make thee roar,
That beasts shall tremble at thy din.

CALIBAN

No, pray thee.
I must obey, his Art is of such pow'r,
It would control my Dam's god *Setebos,*
And make a vassal of him.

PROSPERO

So slave, hence.

PART III

The Age of Shakespeare:

SCENES BY SHAKESPEARE'S CONTEMPORARIES

INTRODUCTION

These scenes by Elizabethan and Jacobean writers other than Shakespeare offer their own special worlds, worlds that may feel quite alien to anyone whose only experience of this drama is via Shakespeare's plays. What is important is to determine the rules of each world. What kind of people live in it and how do they talk? What is the hierarchy of power? Is the environment hostile or friendly? What is the audience's role in all this?

Morality Plays

Everyman is a late medieval work, and, by most sophisticated dramatic standards, a primitive play. And yet, by virtue of its very simplicity, it retains even to this day a special power. It is a Morality Play, meant to be performed by traveling players as a lesson in applied religion. The very immediate and frontal presence of the audience is matched by the also very present sense of God watching. The scale is massive and the style is intentionally reminiscent of church ritual. Think of opera and you won't be far wrong; set it to music, and you will definitely get the picture. Everyman represents literally everyone in the audience, and Death is, of course, a direct personification. Look for the little clues that suggest elements of personality, and play them to the hilt.

More sophisticated and full of human detail is Mephistophilis's appearance to Faustus in Christopher Marlowe's *Dr. Faustus*. Still the scale remains grand, and the degree to which Marlowe's play directly derives from the conventions of Morality Drama is evident. Literally, most of the same rules apply.

It is interesting that it is Marlowe himself who overturns so many of these rules or expectations in *The Jew of Malta,* a play that features an apparently vicious "heathen," Barabas the Jew, in a role that functions ultimately as an indictment of Christian society. The scene included here between Barabas and his daughter Abigail is a comic balcony scene that recalls Shakespeare's *Romeo and Juliet,* but in best comic fashion, everything is topsy-turvy as Barabas calls "O girl! O gold! O beauty! O my bliss," and ends the scene with a Spanish phrase meaning "beautiful pleasure of money."

Seductions

Thomas Dekker's *The Shoemaker's Holiday* is a play of great vitality and vividness of character. Hammon's approach to Jane sets him up as a truly reprehensible villain for whom you can also be sorry, and creates her as the perfect ingenue whom you may cheer without reservation. Cueing and intelligence are essential to making this scene work.

John Fletcher was a popular collaborator, presumably associated with Shakespeare late in the Bard's career, but the plays he wrote with Francis Beaumont, outrageously melodramatic and highly theatrical, became a staple for the popular taste of the early seventeenth century. Pharamond's two seduction scenes from *Philaster* (the second overheard by the Galatea who is featured in the first) are excellent examples of the authors' lighter tone, abuzz with arch slyness. In severe contrast is the scene from *The Maid's Tragedy,* worthy of one of the better episodes of "Dallas," in which Melantius attacks his sister Evadne for becoming the king's mistress. In all three instances, any commentary on the actor's part must be avoided, and the situation, light or heavy, must be treated with complete seriousness.

More passionate still is the scene from Thomas Heywood's *A Woman Killed With Kindness,* in which Wendoll seduces Mistress Anne, his friend Frankford's wife. The extent to which the two talk about Frankford himself makes him very much a character in the scene. Note that the last two or three lines, and the couple's exit to bed, are overheard by Nicholas, a servant.

More oblique and trickier to perform is Lady Politic Would-Be's seduction of the feigning-bedridden Volpone. The scene would play like a stand-up comedy routine, with its asides and Lady Politic's exaggerated behavior, except that Volpone is lying down. Lady Politic is typical of many of Ben Jonson's characters who are driven by their excesses, and the appropriate motivating passion, or "humour," needs to be chosen carefully.

Revenge Dramas

Favored by the Jacobean audience were the elaborate revenge dramas, called Italianate because they reflected the blood lust of a distant, foreign, southern culture, a culture steeped, for the English, in the sins of the Borgias and the dubious politics of Machiavelli. John Ford's *'Tis Pity She's A Whore* centers on an incestuous affair between Giovanni and Annabella, who are brother and sister. The scene I have included, in which the two first acknowledge their more than filial love, is a masterpiece of simplicity and must above all not be overplayed. It is important that each listen to the other carefully for signs of what each wants to hear.

Much more laden with social, religious, and political overtones is John Webster's *The Duchess of Malfi*. In *'Tis Pity*, at least, there is the pretense of innocence. Here, for both the Duchess and Antonio, there is experience only, and this almost jaded—with, as the Duchess states, "but half a blush in't." The life of the scene depends on the intricacy and suggestiveness of the subtext.

In Thomas Middleton's *The Changeling*, the relationship is even further complicated by Beatrice's apparent loathing for De Flores, who is at once the instrument of her revenge and her apparent victim. It is a kind of beauty-and-the-beast situation, in which De Flores makes her dependent on him by means of his viciously faithful service—in a later scene he presents her with the ringed finger of her suitor Alonzo. De Flores's asides add an extra dimension to the scene, placing him in a conspiratorial relationship with the audience, winning their complicity in his actions.

Finally, in the granddaddy of all revenge dramas, Cyril Tourneur's *The Revenger's Tragedy*, Vendice arrives in disguise to test his sister

Castiza's and their mother Gratiana's virtue by attempting to win the former to the lecherous Duke's hateful service. The scene must move with considerable speed, especially near the beginning, so that Vendice can insinuate his persuasions without time for serious reflection until Castiza finally rebels. Gratiana's arguments gain authority by really sounding like a mother's honest advice. The power shifts several times during the scene, so make sure you know who is driving it at any particular moment.

Everyman
Anonymous
DEATH, EVERYMAN

DEATH

Lord, I will in the world go run over all,
And cruelly out search both great and small.
(GOD *withdraws*)
Every man will I beset that liveth beastly
Out of God's laws, and dreadeth not folly.
He that loveth riches I will strike with my dart,
His sight to blind, and from heaven to depart,
Except that alms be his good friend,
In hell for to dwell, world without end.
Lo, yonder I see Everyman walking;
Full little he thinketh on my coming;
His mind is on fleshly lusts and his treasure;
And great pain it shall cause him to endure
Before the Lord, Heaven King.
Everyman, stand still! Whither art thou going
Thus gaily? Hast thou thy Maker forgot?

EVERYMAN

Why askest thou?
Would'st thou know?

DEATH

Yea, sir, I will show you;
In great haste I am sent to thee
From God out of his Majesty.

EVERYMAN

What, sent to me?

DEATH

Yeah, certainly.
Though thou have forgot him here,
He thinketh on thee in the heavenly sphere,
As, ere we depart, thou shalt know.

EVERYMAN

What desireth God of me?

DEATH

That shall I show thee;
A reckoning he will needs have
Without any long respite.

EVERYMAN

To give a reckoning longer leisure I crave;
This blind matter troubleth my wit.

DEATH

On thee thou must take a long journey;
Therefore thy book of count with thee thou bring;
For turn again thou can not by no way.
And look thou be sure of thy reckoning,
For before God thou shalt answer and show
Thy many bad deeds, and good but a few,
How thou hast spent thy life, and in what wise,
Before the Chief Lord of paradise.
Have ado that we were in that way,
For, know thou well, thou shalt make none attorney.

EVERYMAN

Full unready I am such reckoning to give.
I know thee not. What messenger art thou?

DEATH

I am Death, that no man dreadeth.
For every man I arrest, and no man spareth;
For it is God's commandment
That all to me should be obedient.

EVERYMAN

O Death! thou comest when I had thee least in mind!
In thy power it lieth me to save,
Yet of my goods will I give thee, if thou will be kind;
Yea, a thousand pound shalt thou have,
If thou defer this matter till another day.

DEATH

Everyman, it may not be, by no way!
I set not by gold, silver, nor riches,
Nor by pope, emperor, king, duke, nor princes.
For, and I would receive gifts great,
All the world I might get;
But my custom is clean contrary.
I give thee no respite. Come hence, and not tarry.

EVERYMAN

Alas! shall I have no longer respite?
I may say Death giveth no warning.
To think on thee, it maketh my heart sick,
For all unready is my book of reckoning.
But twelve year and I might have abiding,
My counting-book I would make so clear,
That my reckoning I should not need to fear.
Wherefore, Death, I pray thee, for God's mercy,
Spare me till I be provided of remedy.

DEATH

Thee availeth not to cry, weep, and pray;
But haste thee lightly that thou were gone that journey,
And prove thy friends if thou can.
For know thou well the tide abideth no man;
And in the world each living creature
For Adam's sin must die of nature.

EVERYMAN

Death, if I should this pilgrimage take,
And my reckoning surely make,

Show me, for saint charity,
Should I not come again shortly?

DEATH

No, Everyman; and thou be once there,
Thou mayst never more come here,
Trust me verily.

EVERYMAN

O gracious God, in the high seat celestial,
Have mercy on me in this most need!
Shall I have no company from this vale terrestrial
Of mine acquaintance that way me to lead?

DEATH

Yea, if any be so hardy,
That would go with thee and bear thee company.
Hie thee that thou were gone to God's magnificence,
Thy reckoning to give before his presence.
What! weenest thou thy life is given thee,
And thy worldly goods also?

EVERYMAN

I had ween'd so, verily.

DEATH

Nay, nay; it was but lent thee;
For, as soon as thou art gone,
Another a while shall have it, and then go therefrom
Even as thou hast done.
Everyman, thou art mad! Thou hast thy wits five,
And here on earth will not amend thy life;
For suddenly I do come.

EVERYMAN

O wretched caitiff! whither shall I flee,
That I might 'scape endless sorrow?
Now, gentle Death, spare me till tomorrow,

That I may amend me
With good advisement.

Nay, thereto I will not consent,
Nor no man will I respite,
But to the heart suddenly I shall smite
Without any advisement.
And now out of thy sight I will me hie;
See thou make thee ready shortly,
For thou mayst say this is the day
That no man living may 'scape away.

(*Exit* DEATH)

EVERYMAN

Alas! I may well weep with sighs deep.
Now I have no manner of company
To help me in my journey and me to keep;
And also my writing is full unready.
How shall I do now for to excuse me?
I would to God I had never been got!
To my soul a full great profit it had be;
For now I fear pains huge and great.
The time passeth; Lord, help, that all wrought.
For though I mourn it availeth naught.
The day passeth, and is almost a-go;
I know not well what for to do.
To whom were I best my complaint to make?
What if I to Fellowship thereof spake,
And showed him of this sudden chance?
For in him is all mine affiance,
We have in the world so many a day
Been good friends in sport and play.
I see him yonder, certainly;
I trust that he will bear me company;
Therefore to him will I speak to ease my sorrow.

Well met, good Fellowship, and good morrow!
How shall I do now for to excuse me?

The Tragical History of Doctor Faustus
by Christopher Marlowe

SCENE 3—FAUSTUS, MEPHISTOPHILIS

(*Enter* MEPHISTOPHILIS, *a Devil*)

FAUSTUS

I charge thee to return and change thy shape;
Thou art too ugly to attend on me.
Go, and return an old Franciscan friar;
That holy shape becomes a devil best.
(*Exit* DEVIL)
I see there's virtue in my heavenly words;
Who would not be proficient in this art?
How pliant is this Mephistophilis,
Full of obedience and humility!
Such is the force of magic and my spells.
Now, Faustus, thou art conjuror laureate,
Thou canst command great Mephistophilis:
Quin regis Mephistophilis fratris imagine.

(*Re-enter* MEPHISTOPHILIS [*like a Franciscan Friar*])

MEPHISTOPHILIS

Now, Faustus, what would'st thou have me do?

FAUSTUS

I charge thee wait upon me whilst I live,
To do whatever Faustus shall command,

Be it to make the moon drop from her sphere,
Or the Ocean to overwhelm the world.

MEPHISTOPHILIS

I am a servant to great Lucifer,
And may not follow thee without his leave;
No more than he commands must we perform.

FAUSTUS

Did he not charge thee to appear to me?

MEPHISTOPHILIS

No, I came hither of mine own accord.

FAUSTUS

Did not my conjuring speeches raise thee? Speak:

MEPHISTOPHILIS

That was the cause, but yet *per accidens*;
For when we hear one rack the name of God,
Abjure the Scriptures and his Saviour Christ,
We fly in hope to get his glorious soul;
Nor will we come, unless he use such means
Whereby he is in danger to be damn'd:
Therefore the shortest cut for conjuring
Is stoutly to abjure the Trinity,
And pray devoutly to the Prince of Hell.

FAUSTUS

So Faustus hath
Already done; and holds this principle,
There is no chief but only Belzebub,
To whom Faustus doth dedicate himself.
This word "damnation" terrifies not him,
For he confounds hell in Elysium;
His ghost be with the old philosophers!
But, leaving these vain trifles of men's souls,
Tell me what is that Lucifer thy lord?

MEPHISTOPHILIS

Arch-regent and commander of all spirits.

FAUSTUS

Was not that Lucifer an angel once?

MEPHISTOPHILIS

Yes, Faustus, and most dearly lov'd of God.

FAUSTUS

How comes it then that he is Prince of devils?

MEPHISTOPHILIS

O, by aspiring pride and insolence;
For which God threw him from the face of Heaven.

FAUSTUS

And what are you that you live with Lucifer?

MEPHISTOPHILIS

Unhappy spirits that fell with Lucifer,
Conspir'd against our God with Lucifer,
And are for ever damn'd with Lucifer.

FAUSTUS

Where are you damn'd?

MEPHISTOPHILIS

In hell.

FAUSTUS

How comes it then that thou art out of hell?

MEPHISTOPHILIS

Why this is hell, nor am I out of it.
Think'st thou that I who saw the face of God,
And tasted the eternal joys of Heaven,

Am not tormented with ten thousand hells,
In being depriv'd of everlasting bliss?
O Faustus! leave these frivolous demands,
Which strike a terror to my fainting soul.

FAUSTUS

What, is great Mephistophilis so passionate
For being depriv'd of the joys of Heaven?
Learn thou of Faustus manly fortitude,
And scorn those joys thou never shalt possess.
Go bear these tidings to great Lucifer:
Seeing Faustus hath incurr'd eternal death
By desperate thoughts against Jove's deity,
Say he surrenders up to him his soul,
So he will spare him four and twenty years,
Letting him live in all voluptuousness;
Having thee ever to attend on me;
To give me whatsoever I shall ask,
To tell me whatsoever I demand,
To slay mine enemies, and aid my friends,
And always be obedient to my will.
Go and return to mighty Lucifer,
And meet me in my study at midnight,
And then resolve me of thy master's mind.

MEPHISTOPHILIS

I will, Faustus.

(*Exit*)

FAUSTUS

Had I as many souls as there be stars,
I'd give them all for Mephistophilis.
By him I'll be great Emperor of the world,
And make a bridge through the moving air,
To pass the ocean with a band of men;
I'll join the hills that bind the Afric shore,

And make that country continent to Spain,
And both contributory to my crown.
The Emperor shall not live but by my leave,
Nor any potentate of Germany.
Now that I have obtain'd what I desire,
I'll live in speculation of this art
Till Mephistophilis return again.

The Jew of Malta
by Christopher Marlowe
ACT II, SCENE 2—BARABAS, ABIGAIL

(*Enter* BARABAS *with a light*)

BARABAS
Thus, like the sad presaging raven, that tolls
The sick man's passport in her hollow beak,
And in the shadow of the silent night
Doth shake contagion from her sable wings,
Vex'd and tormented runs poor Barabas
With fatal curses towards these Christians.
The incertain pleasures of swift-footed Time
Have ta'en their flight, and left me in despair;
And of my former riches rests no more
But bare remembrance, like a soldier's scar,
That has no further comfort for his maim.
O thou, that with a fiery pillar led'st
The sons of Israel through the dismal shades,
Light Abraham's offspring, and direct the hand
Of Abigail this night; or let the day
Turn to eternal darkness after this!
No sleep can fasten on my watchful eyes,

Nor quiet enter my distemper'd thoughts,
Till I have answer of my Abigail.

(*Enter* ABIGAIL *above*)

ABIGAIL

Now have I happily espi'd a time
To search the plank my father did appoint;
And here behold, unseen, where I have found
The gold, the pearls, and jewels, which he hid.

BARABAS

Now I remember those old women's words,
Who in my wealth would tell me winter's tales,
And speak of spirits and ghosts that glide by night
About the place where treasure hath been hid:
And now methinks that I am one of those;
For whilst I live, here lives my soul's sole hope,
And, when I die, here shall my spirit walk.

ABIGAIL

Now that my father's fortune were so good
As but to be about this happy place!
'Tis not so happy: yet when we parted last,
He said he would attend me in the morn.
Then, gentle sleep, where'er his body rests,
Give charge to Morpheus that he may dream
A golden dream, and of the sudden walk,
Come and receive the treasure I have found.

BARABAS

But stay, what star shines yonder in the east?
The loadstar of my life, if Abigail.
Who's there?

ABIGAIL

Who's that?

BARABAS

Peace, Abigail, 'tis I.

ABIGAIL

Then, father, here receive thy happiness.

BARABAS

Hast thou't?

(*She throws down bags*)

ABIGAIL

Here, hast thou't? There's more, and more, and more.

BARABAS

O my girl,
My gold, my fortune, my felicity!
Strength to my soul, death to mine enemy!
Welcome the first beginner of my bliss!
O Abigail, Abigail, that I had thee here too!
Then my desires were fully satisfied:
But I will practise thy enlargement thence.
O girl! O gold! O beauty! O my bliss!

(*Hugs his bags*)

ABIGAIL

Father, it draweth towards midnight now,
And 'bout this time the nuns begin to wake;
To shun suspicion, therefore, let us part.

BARABAS

Farewell, my joy, and by my fingers take
A kiss from him that sends it from his soul.

(*Exit* ABIGAIL *above*)
Now Phoebus ope the eyelids of the day,
And for the raven wake the morning lark,
That I may hover with her in the air;
Singing o'er these, as she does o'er her young,
Hermoso placer de los dineros.

The Shoemaker's Holiday
by Thomas Dekker

ACT IV, SCENE 1—HAMMON, JANE

(JANE *in a Seamster's shop, working; enter Master* HAMMON, *muffled:
he stands aloof*)

HAMMON

Yonder's the shop, and there my fair love sits.
She's fair and lovely, but she is not mine.
O, would she were! Thrice have I courted her,
Thrice hath my hand been moist'ned with her hand,
Whilst my poor famisht eyes do feed on that
Which made them famish. I am unfortunate:
I still love one, yet nobody loves me.
I muse in other men what women see
That I so want! Fine Mistress Rose was coy,
And this too curious! Oh, no, she is chaste,
And for she thinks me wanton, she denies
To cheer my cold heart with her sunny eyes.
How prettily she works! Oh pretty hand!
Oh happy work! It doth me good to stand
Unseen to see her. Thus I oft have stood
In frosty evenings, a light burning by her,
Enduring biting cold, only to eye her.
One only look hath seem'd as rich to me

As a king's crown; such is love's lunacy.
Muffled I'll pass along, and by that try
Whether she know me.

JANE

Sir, what is't you buy?
What is't you lack, sir, calico, or lawn,
Fine cambric shirts, or bands, what will you buy?

HAMMON

(*Aside*)
That which thou wilt not sell.
Faith, yet I'll try:—
How do you sell this handkerchief?

JANE

Good cheap.

HAMMON

And how these ruffs?

JANE

Cheap too.

HAMMON

And how this band?

JANE

Cheap too.

HAMMON

All cheap; how sell you then this hand?

JANE

My hands are not to be sold.

HAMMON

To be given then!
Nay, faith, I come to buy.

JANE

But none knows when.

HAMMON

Good sweet, leave work a little while; let's play.

JANE

I cannot live by keeping holiday.

HAMMON

I'll pay you for the time which shall be lost.

JANE

With me you shall not be at so much cost.

HAMMON

Look, how you wound this cloth, so you wound me.

JANE

It may be so.

HAMMON

'Tis so.

JANE

What remedy?

HAMMON

Nay, faith, you are too coy.

JANE

Let go my hand.

HAMMON

I will do any task at your command,
I would let go this beauty, were I not
In mind to disobey you by a power
That controls kings: I love you!

JANE

So, now part.

HAMMON

With hands I may, but never with my heart.
In faith, I love you.

JANE

I believe you do.

HAMMON

Shall a true love in me breed hate in you?

JANE

I hate you not.

HAMMON

Then you must love?

JANE

I do.
What are you better now? I love not you.

HAMMON

All this, I hope, is but a woman's fray,
That means, "Come to me," when she cries, "Away!"
In earnest, mistress, I do not jest,
A true chaste love hath ent'red in my breast.
I love you dearly, as I love my life,
I love you as a husband loves a wife;
That, and no other love, my love requires.
Thy wealth, I know, is little; my desires

Thirst not for gold. Sweet, beauteous Jane, what's mine
Shall, if thou make myself thine, all be thine.
Say, judge, what is thy sentence, life or death?
Mercy or cruelty lies in thy breath.

JANE

Good sir, I do believe you love me well;
For't is a silly conquest, silly pride
For one like you—I mean a gentleman—
To boast that by his love-tricks he hath brought
Such and such women to his amorous lure;
I think you do not so, yet many do,
And make it even a very trade to woo.
I could be coy, as many women be,
Feed you with sunshine smiles and wanton looks,
But I detest witchcraft; say that I
Do constantly believe, you constant have——

HAMMON

Why dost thou not believe me?

JANE

I believe you;
But yet, good sir, because I will not grieve you
With hopes to taste fruit which will never fall,
In simple truth this is the sum of all:
My husband lives, at least, I hope he lives.
Prest was he to these bitter wars in France;
Bitter they are to me by wanting him.
I have but one heart, and that heart's his due.
How can I then bestow the same on you?
Whilst he lives, his I live, be it ne'er so poor,
And rather be his wife than a king's whore.

HAMMON

Chaste and dear woman, I will not abuse thee,
Although it cost my life, if thou refuse me.
Thy husband, prest for France, what was his name?

JANE

Ralph Damport.

HAMMON

Damport?—Here's a letter sent
From France to me, from a dear friend of mine,
A gentleman of place; here he doth write
Their names that have been slain in every fight.

JANE

I hope death's scroll contains not my love's name.

HAMMON

Cannot you read?

JANE

I can.

HAMMON

Peruse the same.
To my remembrance such a name I read
Amongst the rest. See here.

JANE

Ay me, he's dead!
He's dead! If this be true, my dear heart's slain!

HAMMON

Have patience, dear love.

JANE

Hence, hence!

HAMMON

Nay, sweet Jane,
Make not poor sorrow proud with these rich tears.
I mourn thy husband's death, because thou mourn'st.

JANE

That bill is forg'd; 'tis sign'd by forgery.

HAMMON

I'll bring thee letters sent besides to many,
Carrying the like report: Jane, 'tis too true.
Come, weep not: mourning, though it rise from love,
Helps not the mourned, yet hurts them that mourn.

JANE

For God's sake, leave me.

HAMMON

Whither dost thou turn?
Forget the dead, love them that are alive;
His love is faded, try how mine will thrive.

JANE

'Tis now no time for me to think on love.

HAMMON

'Tis now best time for you to think on love,
Because your love lives not.

JANE

Though he be dead,
My love to him shall not be buried;
For God's sake, leave me to myself alone.

HAMMON

'Twould kill my soul, to leave thee drown'd in moan.
Answer me to my suit, and I am gone;
Say to me yea or no.

JANE

No.

HAMMON

Then farewell!
One farewell will not serve, I come again;

Come, dry these wet cheeks; tell me, faith, sweet Jane,
Yea or no, once more.

JANE

Once more I say no;
Once more be gone, I pray; else will I go.

HAMMON

Nay, then I will grow rude, by this white hand.
Until you change that cold "no"; here I'll stand
Till by your hard heart——

JANE

Nay, for God's love, peace!
My sorrows by your presence more increase.
Not that you thus are present, but all grief
Desires to be alone; therefore in brief
Thus much I say, and saying bid adieu:
If ever I wed man, it shall be you.

HAMMON

O blessed voice! Dear Jane, I'll urge no more,
Thy breath hath made me rich.

JANE

Death makes me poor.

Philaster or Love Lies A-Bleeding
by Francis Beaumont and John Fletcher
ACT II, SCENE 2—PHARAMOND, GALATEA

PHARAMOND

Why should these ladies stay so long? They must come this way.
I know the queen employs 'em not; for the reverend mother sent

me word, they would all be for the garden. If they should all prove honest now, I were in a fair taking; I was never so long without sport in my life, and, in my conscience, 'tis not my fault. Oh, for our country ladies!

(*Enter* GALATEA)

Here's one bolted; I'll hound at her.—Madam!

GALATEA

Your grace!

PHARAMOND

Shall I not be a trouble?

GALATEA

Not to me, sir.

PHARAMOND

Nay, nay, you are too quick. By this sweet hand——

GALATEA

You'll be forsworn, sir; 'tis but an old glove.
If you will talk at distance, I am for you:
But, good prince, be not bawdy, nor do not brag;
These two I bar;
And then, I think, I shall have sense enough
To answer all the weighty apophthegms
Your royal blood shall manage.

PHARAMOND

Dear lady, can you love?

GALATEA

Dear prince! how dear? I ne'er cost you a coach yet, nor put you to the dear repentance of a banquet. Here's no scarlet, sir, to blush the sin out it was given for. This wire mine own hair covers; and this face has been so far from being dear to any, that it ne'er cost penny painting; and, for the rest of my poor wardrobe, such as you see, it leaves no hand behind it, to make the jealous mercer's wife curse our good doings.

PHARAMOND

You mistake me, lady.

GALATEA

Lord, I do so; would you or I could help it!

(PHARAMOND

You're very dangerous bitter, like a potion.

GALATEA

No, sir, I do not mean to purge you, though
I mean to purge a little time on you.)

PHARAMOND

Do ladies of this country use to give
No more respect to men of my full being?

GALATEA

Full being! I understand you not, unless your grace means growing to fatness; and then your only remedy (upon my knowledge, prince) is, in a morning, a cup of neat white wine brewed with carduus, then fast till supper; about eight you may eat; use exercise, and keep a sparrow-hawk; you can shoot in a tiller: but, of all, your grace must fly phlebotomy, fresh pork, conger, and clarified whey; they are all duller of the vital spirits.

PHARAMOND

Lady, you talk of nothing all this while.

GALATEA

'Tis very true, sir; I talk of you.

PHARAMOND

(*Aside*)
This is a crafty wench; I like her wit well; 't will be rare to stir up a leaden appetite. She's a Danaë, and must be courted in a shower of gold.—Madam, look here; all these, and more than——

GALATEA

What have you there, my lord? Gold! now, as I live, 'tis fair gold! You would have silver for it, to play with the pages. You could not have taken me in a worse time; but, if you have present use, my lord, I'll send my man with silver and keep your gold for you.

PHARAMOND

Lady, lady!

GALATEA

She's coming, sir, behind, will take white money.—
(*Aside*)
Yet for all this I'll match ye.
(*Exit behind the hangings*)

PHARAMOND

If there be but two such more in this kingdom, and near the court, we may even hang up our harps. Ten such camphire constitutions as this would call the golden age again in question, and teach the old way for every ill-fac'd husband to get his own children; and what a mischief that would breed, let all consider!

Philaster or Love Lies A-Bleeding
by Francis Beaumont and John Fletcher
ACT II, SCENE 2—PHARAMOND, MEGRA, GALATEA

(*Enter* MEGRA)

PHARAMOND

Here's another: if she be of the same last, the devil shall pluck her
on.—Many fair mornings, lady!

MEGRA

As many mornings bring as many days,
Fair, sweet and hopeful to your grace!

PHARAMOND

(*Aside*)
She gives good words yet; sure this wench is free.—
If your more serious business do not call you,
Let me hold quarter with you; we will talk
An hour out quickly.

MEGRA

What would your grace talk of?

PHARAMOND

Of some such pretty subject as yourself:
I'll go no further than your eye, or lip;
There's theme enough for one man for an age.

MEGRA

Sir, they stand right, and my lips are yet even,
Smooth, young enough, ripe enough, and red enough,
Or my glass wrongs me.

PHARAMOND

Oh, they are two twinn'd cherries dy'd in blushes
Which those fair suns above with their bright beams
Reflect upon and ripen. Sweetest beauty,
Bow down those branches, that the longing taste
Of the faint looker-on may meet those blessings,
And taste and live.

(*They kiss*)

MEGRA

(*Aside*)
Oh, delicate sweet prince!
She that hath snow enough about her heart
To take the wanton spring of ten such lines off,
May be a nun without probation.—Sir,
You have in such neat poetry gathered a kiss,
That if I had but five lines of that number,
Such pretty begging blanks, I should commend
Your forehead or your cheeks, and kiss you too.

PHARAMOND

Do it in prose; you cannot miss it, madam.

MEGRA

I shall, I shall.

PHARAMOND

By my life, but you shall not;
I'll prompt you first.
(*Kisses her*)
Can you do it now?

MEGRA

Methinks 'tis easy, now you ha' done 't before me;
But yet I should stick at it.

(*Kisses him*)

PHARAMOND

Stick till to-morrow;
I'll ne'er part you, sweetest. But we lose time:
Can you love me?

MEGRA

Love you, my lord! How would you have me love you?

PHARAMOND

I'll teach you in a short sentence, 'cause I will not load your memory;
this is all: love me, and lie with me.

MEGRA

Was it "lie with you" that you said? 'Tis impossible.

PHARAMOND

Not to a willing mind, that will endeavour. If I do not teach you
to do it as easily in one night as you'll go to bed, I'll lose my royal
blood for't.

MEGRA

Why, prince, you have a lady of your own
That yet wants teaching.

PHARAMOND

I'll sooner teach a mare the old measures than teach her anything
belonging to the function. She's afraid to lie with herself if she have
but any masculine imaginations about her. I know, when we are
married, I must ravish her.

MEGRA

By mine honour, that's a foul fault, indeed;
But time and your good help will wear it out, sir.

PHARAMOND

And for any other I see, excepting your dear self, dearest lady, I had rather be Sir Tim the schoolmaster, and leap a dairy-maid, madam.

MEGRA

Has your grace seen the court-star, Galatea?

PHARAMOND

Out upon her! She's as cold of her favour as an apoplex; she sail'd by but now.

MEGRA

And how do you hold her wit, sir?

PHRAMOND

I hold her wit? The strength of all the guard cannot hold it, if they were tied to it; she would blow 'em out of the kingdom. They talk of Jupiter; he's but a squib-cracker to her: look well about you, and you may find a tongue-bolt. But speak, sweet lady, shall I be freely welcome.

MEGRA

Whither?

PHARAMOND

To your bed. If you mistrust my faith, you do me the unnoblest wrong.

MEGRA

I dare not, prince, I dare not.

PHARAMOND

Make your own conditions, my purse shall seal 'em, and what you dare imagine you can want, I'll furnish you withal. Give two hours to your thoughts every morning about it.
Come I know you are bashful;
Speak in my ear, will you be mine? Keep this,
And with it, me: soon I will visit you.

MEGRA

My lord, my chamber's most unsafe; but when 'tis night,
I'll find some means to slip into your lodging;
Till when——

PHARAMOND

Till when, this and my heart go with thee!

(*Exeunt several ways*)
(*Re-enter* GALATEA *from behind the hangings*)

GALATEA

Oh, thou pernicious petticoat prince! are these your virtues? Well,
if I do not lay a train to blow your sport up, I am no woman: and,
Lady Towsabel, I'll fit you for 't.

(*Exit*)

The Maid's Tragedy
by Francis Beaumont and John Fletcher
ACT IV, SCENE 1—EVADNE, MELANTIUS

EVADNE

Now speak.

MELANTIUS

I'll lock the door first.

EVADNE

Why?

MELANTIUS

I will not have your gilded things, that dance
In visitation with their Milan skins,
Choke up my business.

EVADNE

You are strangely dispos'd, sir.

MELANTIUS

Good madam, not to make you merry.

EVADNE

No; if you praise me, it will make me sad.

MELANTIUS

Such a sad commendation I have for you.

EVADNE

Brother,
The court hath made you witty, and learn to riddle.

MELANTIUS

I praise the court for't: has it learn'd you nothing?

EVADNE

Me!

MELANTIUS

Ay, Evadne; thou art young and handsome,
A lady of a sweet complexion,
And such a flowing carriage, that it cannot
Choose but inflame a kingdom.

EVADNE

Gentle brother!

MELANTIUS

'Tis yet in thy repentance, foolish woman,
To make me gentle.

EVADNE

How is this?

MELANTIUS

'Tis base;
And I could blush, at these years, through all
My honour'd scars, to come to such a parley.

EVADNE

I understand you not.

MELANTIUS

You dare not, fool!
They that commit thy faults fly the remembrance.

EVADNE

My faults, sir! I would have you know, I care not
If they were written here, here in my forehead.

MELANTIUS

Thy body is too little for the story;
The lusts of which would fill another woman,
Though she had twins within her.

EVADNE

This is saucy:
Look you intrude no more! There's your way.

MELANTIUS

Thou art my way, and I will tread upon thee,
Till I find truth out.

EVADNE

What truth is that you look for?

MELANTIUS

Thy long-lost honour. Would the gods had set me
Rather to grapple with the plague, or stand

One of their loudest bolts! Come, tell me quickly,
Do it without enforcement, and take heed
You swell me not above my temper.

EVADNE

How, sir!
Where got you this report?

MELANTIUS

Where there was people,
In every place.

EVADNE

They and the seconds of it
Are base people: believe them not, they lied.

MELANTIUS

Do not play with mine anger; do not wretch!
(*Seizes her*)
I come to know that desperate fool that drew thee
From thy fair life. Be wise, and lay him open.

EVADNE

Unhand me, and learn manners! Such another
Forgetfulness forfeits your life.

MELANTIUS

Quench me this mighty humour, and then tell me
Whose whore you are; for you are one, I know it.
Let all mine honours perish but I'll find him
Though he lie lock'd up in thy blood! Be sudden;
There is no facing it; and be not flattered.
The burnt air, when the Dog reigns, is not fouler
Than thy contagious name, till thy repentance
(If the gods grant thee any) purge thy sickness.

EVADNE

Begone! you are my brother; that's your safety.

MELANTIUS

I'll be a wolf first. 'Tis, to be thy brother.
An infamy below the sin of coward.
I am as far from being part of thee
As thou art from thy virtue. Seek a kindred
'Mongst sensual beasts, and make a goat thy brother;
A goat is cooler. Will you tell me yet?

EVADNE

If you stay here and rail thus, I shall tell you
I'll ha' you whipt! Get you to your command,
And there preach to your sentinels, and tell them
What a brave man you are: I shall laugh at you.

MELANTIUS

You're grown a glorious whore! Where be your fighters?
What mortal fool durst raise thee to this daring,
And I alive! By my just sword, he'd safer
Bestrid a billow when the angry North
Ploughs up the sea, or made Heaven's fire his foe!
Work me no higher. Will you discover yet?

EVADNE

The fellow's mad. Sleep, and speak sense.

MELANTIUS

Force my swol'n heart no further; I would save thee.
Your great maintainers are not here, they dare not.
Would they were all, and armed! I would speak loud;
Here's one should thunder to 'em! Will you tell me?—
Thou hast no hope to scape. He that dares most,
And damns away his soul to do thee service,
Will sooner snatch meat from a hungry lion
Than come to rescue thee. Thou hast death about thee;—
Has undone thine honour, poison'd thy virtue,
And, of a lovely rose, left thee a canker.

EVADNE

Let me consider.

MELANTIUS

Do, whose child thou wert,
Whose honour thou hast murdered, whose grave opened,
And so pull'd on the gods that in their justice
They must restore him flesh again and life,
And raise his dry bones to revenge this scandal.

EVADNE

The gods are not of my mind; they had better
Let 'em lie sweet still in the earth; they'll stink here.

MELANTIUS

Do you raise mirth out of my easiness?
Forsake me, then, all weaknesses of nature,
(*Draws his sword*)
That make men women! Speak, you whore, speak truth,
Or, by the dear soul of thy sleeping father,
This sword shall be thy lover! Tell, or I'll kill thee;
And, when thou hast told all, thou wilt deserve it.

EVADNE

You will not murder me?

MELANTIUS

No: 'tis a justice, and a noble one,
To put the light out of such base offenders.

EVADNE

Help!

MELANTIUS

By thy foul self, no human help shall help thee,
If thou criest! When I have kill'd thee, as I
Have vow'd to do, if thou confess not, naked
As thou hast left thine honour will I leave thee,

That on thy branded flesh the world may read
Thy black shame and my justice. Wilt thou bend yet?

EVADNE

Yes.

MELANTIUS

Up, and begin your story.

EVADNE

Oh, I am miserable!

MELANTIUS

'Tis true, thou art. Speak truth still.

EVADNE

I have offended: noble sir, forgive me!

MELANTIUS

With what secure slave?

EVADNE

Do not ask me, sir;
Mine own remembrance is a misery
Too mighty for me.

MELANTIUS

Do not fall back again;
My sword's unsheathed yet.

EVADNE

What shall I do?

MELANTIUS

Be true, and make your fault less.

EVADNE

I dare not tell.

MELANTIUS

Tell, or I'll be this day a-killing thee.

EVADNE

Will you forgive me, then?

MELANTIUS

Stay; I must ask mine honour first.
I have too much foolish nature in me: speak.

EVADNE

Is there none else here?

MELANTIUS

None but a fearful conscience; that's too many.
Who is't?

EVADNE

Oh, hear me gently! It was the King.

MELANTIUS

No more. My worthy father's and my services
Are liberally rewarded! King, I thank thee!
For all my dangers and my wounds thou hast paid me
In my own metal: these are soldiers' thanks!—
How long have you liv'd thus, Evadne?

EVADNE

Too long.

MELANTIUS

Too late you find it. Can you be sorry?

EVADNE

Would I were half as blameless!

MELANTIUS

Evadne, thou wilt to thy trade again.

EVADNE

First to my grave.

MELANTIUS

Would gods thou hadst been so blest!
Dost thou not hate this King now? Prithee, hate him:
Couldst thou not curse him? I command thee, curse him;
Curse till the gods hear, and deliver him
To thy just wishes. Yet I fear, Evadne,
You had rather play your game out.

EVADNE

No; I feel
Too many sad confusions here, to let in
Any loose flame hereafter.

MELANTIUS

Dost thou not feel, 'mongst all those, one brave anger.
That breaks out nobly, and directs thine arm
To kill this base King?

EVADNE

All the gods forbid it!

MELANTIUS

No, all the gods require it;
They are dishonoured in him.

EVADNE

'Tis too fearful.

MELANTIUS

You're valiant in his bed, and bold enough
To be a stale whore, and have your madam's name
Discourse for grooms and pages; and hereafter,
When his cool majesty hath laid you by,
To be at pension with some needy sir

For meat and coarser clothes; thus far you know
No fear. Come, you shall kill him.

Good sir!

An't were to kiss him dead, thou'dst smother him:
Be wise, and kill him. Canst thou live, and know
What noble minds shall make thee, see thyself
Found out with every finger, made the shame
Of all successions, and in this great ruin
Thy brother and thy noble husband broken?
Thou shalt not live thus. Kneel, and swear to help me,
When I shall call thee to it; or, by all
Holy in Heaven and earth, thou shalt not live
To breathe a full hour longer; not a thought!
Come 'tis a righteous oath. Give me thy hands,
And, both to Heaven held up, swear, by that wealth
This lustful thief stole from thee, when I say it,
To let his foul soul out.

Here I swear it;
(*Kneels*)
And, all you spirits of abused ladies,
Help me in this performance!

(*Raising her*)
Enough. This must be known to none
But you and I, Evadne; not to your lord,
Though he be wise and noble, and a fellow
Dares step as far into a worthy action

As the most daring, ay, as far as justice.
Ask me not why. Farewell.
(*Exit*)

EVADNE

Would I could say so to my black disgrace!
Oh, where have I been all this time? How friended,
That I should lose myself thus desperately,
And none for pity show me how I wand'red?
There is not in the compass of the light
A more unhappy creature: sure, I am monstrous;
For I have done those follies, those mad mischiefs.
Would dare a woman. Oh, my loaden soul,
Be not so cruel to me; choke not up
The way to my repentance!

A Woman Killed with Kindness
by Thomas Heywood

ACT II, SCENE 3—MISTRESS FRANKFORD,
WENDOLL, NICHOLAS

MRS. FRANKFORD

You are well met, sir; now, in troth, my husband
Before he took horse, had a great desire
To speak with you; we sought about the house,
Halloo'd into the fields, sent every way,
But could not meet you. Therefore, he enjoin'd me
To do unto you his most kind commends,—
Nay, more: he wills you, as you prize his love,
Or hold in estimation his kind friendship,
To make bold in his absence, and command
Even as himself were present in the house;
For you must keep his table, use his servants,
And be a present Frankford in his absence.

WENDOLL

I thank him for his love.—
(*Aside*)
Give me a name, you, whose infectious tongues
Are tipt with gall and poison: as you would
Think on a man that had your father slain,
Murd'red your children, made your wives base strumpets,
So call me, call me so; print in my face
The most stigmatic title of a villain,
For hatching treason to so true a friend!

MRS. FRANKFORD

Sir, you are much beholding to my husband;
You are a man most dear in his regard.

WENDOLL

I am bound unto your husband, and you too.
(*Aside*)
I will not speak to wrong a gentleman
Of that good estimation, my kind friend.
I will not; zounds! I will not. I may choose,
And I will choose. Shall I be so misled,
Or shall I purchase to my father's crest
The motto of a villain? If I say
I will not do it, what thing can enforce me?
What can compel me? What sad destiny
Hath such command upon my yielding thoughts?
I will not;—ha! Some fury pricks me on;
The swift fates drag me at their chariot wheel,
And hurry me to mischief. Speak I must:
Injure myself, wrong her, deceive his trust!

MRS. FRANKFORD

Are you not well, sir, that you seem thus troubled?
There is sedition in your countenance.

WENDOLL

And in my heart, fair angel, chaste and wise.
I love you! Start not, speak not, answer not;

I love you,—nay, let me speak the rest;
Bid me to swear, and I will call to record
The host of Heaven.

MRS. FRANKFORD

The host of Heaven forbid
Wendoll should hatch such a disloyal thought?

WENDOLL

Such is my fate; to this suit was I born.
To wear rich pleasure's crown, or fortune's scorn.

MRS. FRANKFORD

My husband loves you.

WENDOLL

I know it.

MRS. FRANKFORD

He esteems you,
Even as his brain, his eye-ball, or his heart.

WENDOLL

I have tried it.

MRS. FRANKFORD

His purse is your exchequer, and his table
Doth freely serve you.

WENDOLL

So I have found it.

MRS. FRANKFORD

Oh! With what face of brass, what brow of steel,
Can you, unblushing, speak this to the face
Of the espous'd wife of so dear a friend?

It is my husband that maintains your state.—
Will you dishonour him that in your power
Hath left his whole affairs? I am his wife,
It is to me you speak.

WENDOLL

O speak no more;
For more than this I know, and have recorded
Within the red-leav'd table of my heart.
Fair, and of all belov'd, I was not fearful
Bluntly to give my life into your hand,
And at one hazard all my earthly means.
Go, tell your husband; he will turn me off,
And I am then undone. I care not, I;
'Twas for your sake. Perchance, in rage he'll kill me;
I care not, 'twas for you. Say I incur
The general name of villain through the world,
Of traitor to my friend; I care not, I.
Beggary, shame, death, scandal, and reproach,—
For you I'll hazard all. Why, what care I?
For you I'll live, and in your love I'll die.

MRS. FRANKFORD

You move me, sir, to passion and to pity.
The love I bear my husband is as precious
As my soul's health.

WENDOLL

I love your husband too,
And for his love I will engage my life.
Mistake me not; the augmentation
Of my sincere affection borne to you
Doth no whit lessen my regard to him.
I will be secret, lady, close as night;
And not the light of one small glorious star
Shall shine here in my forehead, to bewray
That act of night.

MRS. FRANKFORD

What shall I say?
My soul is wandering, hath lost her way.
Oh, Master Wendoll! Oh!

WENDOLL

Sigh not, sweet saint;
For every sigh you breathe draws from my heart
A drop of blood.

MRS. FRANKFORD

I ne'er offended yet:
My fault, I fear, will in my brow be writ.
Women that fall, not quite bereft of grace,
Have their offences noted in their face.
I blush, and am asham'd. Oh, Master Wendoll,
Pray God I be not born to curse your tongue,
That hath enchanted me! This maze I am in
I fear will prove the labyrinth of sin.

(*Enter* NICHOLAS [*behind*])

WENDOLL

The path of pleasure and the gate to bliss,
Which on your lips I knock at with a kiss!

NICHOLAS

I'll kill the rogue.

WENDOLL

Your husband is from home, your bed's no blab.
Nay, look not down and blush!

(*Exeunt* WENDOLL *and* MISTRESS FRANKFORD)

NICHOLAS

Zounds! I'll stab.
Ay, Nick, was it thy chance to come just in the nick?
I love my master, and I hate that slave;

I love my mistress, but these tricks I like not.
My master shall not pocket up this wrong;
I'll eat my fingers first. What say'st thou, metal?
Does not that rascal Wendoll go on legs
That thou must cut off? Hath he not hamstrings
That thou must hough? Nay, metal, thou shalt stand
To all I say. I'll henceforth turn a spy,
And watch them in their close conveyances
I never look'd for better of that rascal,
Since he came miching first into our house.
It is that Satan hath corrupted her;
For she was fair and chaste. I'll have an eye
In all their gestures. Thus I think of them:
If they proceed as they have done before,
Wendoll's a knave, my mistress is a——

(*Exit*)

Volpone or The Fox
by Ben Jonson
ACT III, SCENE 4—
VOLPONE, LADY POLITIC WOULD-BE

VOLPONE
The storm comes toward me.

LADY POLITIC
(*Goes to the couch*)
How does my Volpone?

VOLPONE
Troubl'd with noise, I cannot sleep; I dreamt
That a strange fury ent'red now my house,

And, with the dreadful tempest of her breath,
Did cleave my roof asunder.

LADY POLITIC

Believe me, and I
Had the most fearful dream, could I remember 't——

VOLPONE

(*Aside*)
Out on my fate! I have given her the occasion
How to torment me: she will tell me hers.

LADY POLITIC

Methought the golden mediocrity,
Polite, and delicate——

VOLPONE

O, if you do love me,
No more: I sweat, and suffer, at the mention
Of any dream; feel how I tremble yet.

LADY POLITIC

Alas, good soul! the passion of the heart.
Seed-pearl were good now, boil'd with syrup of apples,
Tincture of gold, and coral, citron-pills,
Your elecampane root, myrobalanes——

VOLPONE

Ay me, I have ta'en a grasshopper by the wing!

LADY POLITIC

Burnt silk and amber. You have muscadel
Good i' the house——

VOLPONE

You will not drink, and part?

LADY POLITIC

No, fear not that. I doubt we shall not get
Some English saffron, half a dram would serve;
Your sixteen cloves, a little musk, dried mints;
Bugloss, and barley-meal——

VOLPONE

(*Aside*)
She's in again!
Before I feign'd diseases, now I have one.

LADY POLITIC

And these appli'd with a right scarlet cloth.

VOLPONE

(*Aside*)
Another flood of words! a very torrent!

LADY POLITIC

Shall I, sir, make you a poultice?

VOLPONE

No, no, no.
I'm very well, you need prescribe no more.

LADY POLITIC

I have a little studied physic; but now
I'm all for music, save, i' the forenoons,
An hour or two for painting. I would have
A lady, indeed, to have all letters and arts,
Be able to discourse, to write, to paint,
But principal; as Plato holds, your music,
And so does wise Pythagoras, I take it,
Is your true rapture: when there is concent
In face, in voice, and clothes: and is, indeed,
Our sex's chiefest ornament.

VOLPONE

The poet
As old in time as Plato, and as knowing,
Says that your highest female grace is silence.

LADY POLITIC

Which of your poets? Petrarch, or Tasso, or Dante?
Guarini? Ariosto? Aretine?
Cieco di Hadria? I have read them all.

VOLPONE

(*Aside*)
Is everything a cause to my destruction?

LADY POLITIC

I think I have two or three of 'em about me.

VOLPONE

(*Aside*)
The sun, the sea, will sooner both stand still
Than her eternal tongue! nothing can scape it.

LADY POLITIC

Here's Pastor Fido——

VOLPONE

(*Aside*)
Profess obstinate silence;
That's now my safest.

LADY POLITIC

All our English writers,
I mean such as are happy in th' Italian,
Will deign to steal out of this author, mainly;
Almost as much as from Montagnié:
He has so modern and facile a vein,
Fitting the time, and catching the court-ear!
Your Petrarch is more passionate, yet he,
In days of sonnetting, trusted 'em with much:

316

Dante is hard, and few can understand him.
But for a desperate wit, there's Aretine;
Only his pictures are a little obscene——
You mark me not.

VOLPONE

Alas, my mind's perturb'd.

LADY POLITIC

Why, in such cases, we must cure ourselves,
Make use of our philosophy——

VOLPONE

Oh me!

LADY POLITIC

And as we find our passions do rebel,
Encounter them with reason, or divert 'em,
By giving scope unto some other humour
Of lesser danger: as, in politic bodies,
There's nothing more doth overwhelm the judgment,
And cloud the understanding, than too much
Settling and fixing, and, as 'twere, subsiding
Upon one object. For the incorporating
Of these same outward things, into that part
Which we call mental, leaves some certain faeces
That stop the organs, and, as Plato says,
Assassinate our knowledge.

VOLPONE

(Aside)
Now, the spirit
Of patience help me!

LADY POLITIC

Come, in faith, I must
Visit you more a days; and make you well:
Laugh and be lusty.

(*Aside*)
My good angel save me!

LADY POLITIC

There was but one sole man in all the world
With whom I e'er could sympathise; and he
Would lie you, often, three, four hours together
To hear me speak; and be sometime so rapt,
As he would answer me quite from the purpose,
Like you, and you are like him, just. I'll discourse,
An't be but only, sir, to bring you asleep,
How we did spend our time and loves together,
For some six years.

VOLPONE

Oh, oh, oh, oh, oh, oh!

LADY POLITIC

For we were coaetanei, and brought up——

VOLPONE

Some power, some fate, some fortune rescue me!

'Tis Pity She's a Whore
by John Ford

ACT I, SCENE 2—GIOVANNI, ANNABELLA, PUTANA

GIOVANNI

Lost! I am lost! My fates have doom'd my death.
The more I strive, I love; the more I love,
The less I hope: I see my ruin certain.

What judgment or endeavors could apply
To my incurable and restless wounds,
I throughly have examin'd, but in vain.
Oh, that it were not in religion sin
To make our love a god, and worship it!
I have even wearied Heaven with prayers, dried up
The spring of my continual tears, even starv'd
My veins with daily fasts; what wit or art
Could counsel, I have practic'd; but, alas,
I find all these but dreams, and old men's tales,
To fright unsteady youth; I'm still the same;
Or I must speak, or burst. 'Tis not, I know,
My lust, but 'tis my fate that leads me on.
Keep fear and low faint-hearted shame with slaves!
I'll tell her that I love her, though my heart
Were rated at the price of that attempt.
Oh me! She comes.

(*Enter* ANNABELLA *and* PUTANA)

ANNABELLA

Brother!

GIOVANNI

(*Aside*)
If such a thing
As courage dwell in men, ye heavenly powers,
Now double all that virtue in my tongue!

ANNABELLA

Why, brother, will you not speak to me?

GIOVANNI

Yes; how d'ye, sister?

ANNABELLA

Howsoever I am, methinks you are not well.

PUTANA

Bless us! Why are you so sad, sir?

GIOVANNI

Let me entreat you, leave us a while, Putana.
Sister, I would be private with you.

ANNABELLA

Withdraw, Putana.

PUTANA

I will.
(*Aside*)
If this were any other company for her, I should think my absence
an office of some credit; but I will leave them together.

(*Exit* PUTANA)

GIOVANNI

Come, sister, lend your hand; let's walk together. I hope you need
not blush to walk with me. Here's none but you and I.

ANNABELLA

How's this?

GIOVANNI

'Faith,
I mean no harm.

ANNABELLA

Harm?

GIOVANNI

No, good faith.
How is't with ye?

ANNABELLA

(*Aside*)
I trust he be not frantic.—
I am very well, brother.

GIOVANNI

Trust me, but I am sick; I fear so sick
'Twill cost my life.

ANNABELLA

Mercy forbid it! 'Tis not so, I hope.

GIOVANNI

I think you love me, sister.

ANNABELLA

Yes, you know
I do.

GIOVANNI

I know't, indeed. You're very fair.

ANNABELLA

Nay, then I see you have a merry sickness.

GIOVANNI

That's as it proves. The poets feign, I read,
That Juno for her forehead did exceed
All other goddesses; but I durst swear
Your forehead exceeds hers, as hers did theirs.

ANNABELLA

'Troth, this is pretty!

GIOVANNI

Such a pair of stars
As are thine eyes would, like Promethean fire,
If gently glanc'd, give life to senseless stones.

ANNABELLA

Fie upon ye!

GIOVANNI

The lily and the rose, most sweetly strange,
Upon your dimple cheeks do strive for change.
Such lips would tempt a saint; such hands as those
Would make an anchorite lascivious.

ANNABELLA

D'ye mock me or flatter me?

GIOVANNI

If you would see a beauty more exact
Than art can counterfeit or nature frame,
Look in your glass, and there behold your own.

ANNABELLA

Oh, you are a trim youth!

GIOVANNI

Here!

(*Offers his dagger to her*)

ANNABELLA

What to do?

GIOVANNI

And here's my breast; strike home!
Rip up my bosom; there thou shalt behold
A heart in which is writ the truth I speak.
Why stand ye?

ANNABELLA

Are you earnest?

GIOVANNI

Yes, most earnest.
You cannot love?

ANNABELLA

Whom?

GIOVANNI

Me. My tortur'd soul
Hath felt affliction in the heat of death.
Oh, Annabella, I am quite undone!
The love of thee, my sister, and the view
Of thy immortal beauty have untun'd
All harmony both of my rest and life.
Why d'ye not strike?

ANNABELLA

Forbid it, my just fears!
If this be true, 'twere fitter I were dead.

GIOVANNI

True, Annabella! 'Tis no time to jest.
I have too long suppress'd the hidden flames
That almost have consum'd me; I have spent
Many a silent night in sighs and groans,
Ran over all my thoughts, despis'd my fate,
Reason'd against the reasons of my love,
Done all that smooth'd-cheek virtue could advise,
But found all bootless; 'tis my destiny
That you must either love, or I must die.

ANNABELLA

Comes this in sadness from you?

GIOVANNI

Let some mischief
Befall me soon, if I dissemble aught.

323

ANNABELLA

You are my brother Giovanni.

GIOVANNI

You
My sister Annabella; I know this,
And could afford you instance why to love
So much the more for this; to which intent
Wise nature first in your creation meant
To make you mine, else't had been sin and foul
To share one beauty to a double soul.
Nearness in birth or blood doth but persuade
A nearer nearness in affection.
I have ask'd counsel of the holy church,
Who tells me I may love you; and 'tis just
That, since I may, I should; and will, yes, will.
Must I now live or die?

ANNABELLA

Live; thou hast won
The field, and never fought; what thou hast urg'd
My captive heart had long ago resolv'd.
I blush to tell thee,—but I'll tell thee now—
For every sigh that thou hast spent for me
I have sigh'd ten; for every tear shed twenty;
And not so much for that I lov'd, as that
I durst not say I lov'd, nor scarcely think it.

GIOVANNI

Let not this music be a dream, ye gods,
For pity's sake, I beg ye!

ANNABELLA

On my knees,
(*She kneels*)
Brother, even by our mother's dust, I charge you,
Do not betray me to your mirth or hate;
Love me or kill me, brother.

GIOVANNI

On my knees,
(*He kneels*)
Sister, even by my mother's dust, I charge you,
Do not betray me to your mirth or hate;
Love me or kill me, sister.

ANNABELLA

You mean good sooth, then?

GIOVANNI

In good troth, I do;
And so do you, I hope; say, I'm in earnest.

ANNABELLA

I'll swear it, I.

GIOVANNI

And I; and by this kiss,—
(*Kisses her*)
Once more! Yet once more—! Now let's rise by this;
I would not change this minute for Elysium.
What must we now do?

ANNABELLA

What you will.

GIOVANNI

Come, then;
After so many tears as we have wept,
Let's learn to court in smiles, to kiss, and sleep.

(*Exeunt*)

The Duchess of Malfi
by John Webster
ACT I, SCENE 3—
DUCHESS, ANTONIO

DUCHESS

I sent for you: sit down;
Take pen and ink, and write: are you ready?

ANTONIO

Yes.

DUCHESS

What did I say?

ANTONIO

That I should write somewhat.

DUCHESS

O, I remember.
After these triumphs and this large expense,
It's fit, like thrifty husbands, we inquire
What's laid up for to-morrow.

ANTONIO

So please your beauteous excellence.

DUCHESS

Beauteous!
Indeed, I thank you: I look young for your sake;
You have ta'en my cares upon you.

ANTONIO

I'll fetch your grace
The particulars of your revenue and expense.

DUCHESS

O, you are
An upright treasurer: but you mistook;
For when I said I meant to make inquiry
What's laid up for to-morrow, I did mean
What's laid up yonder for me.

ANTONIO

Where?

DUCHESS

In Heaven.
I am making my will (as 'tis fit princes should,
In perfect memory), and I pray, sir, tell me,
Were not one better make it smiling, thus,
Than in deep groans and terrible ghastly looks,
As if the gifts we parted with procur'd
That violent distraction?

ANTONIO

O, much better.

DUCHESS

If I had a husband now, this care were quit:
But I intend to make you overseer.
What good deed shall we first remember? say.

ANTONIO

Begin with that first good deed began i' the world
After man's creation, the sacrament of marriage:
I'd have you first provide for a good husband;
Give him all.

DUCHESS

All!

ANTONIO

Yes, your excellent self.

DUCHESS

In a winding-sheet?

ANTONIO

In a couple.

DUCHESS

Saint Winifred, that were a strange will!

ANTONIO

'Twere stranger if there were no will in you
To marry again.

DUCHESS

What do you think of marriage?

ANTONIO

I take't, as those that deny purgatory,
It locally contains or Heaven or hell;
There's no third place in't.

DUCHESS

How do you affect it?

ANTONIO

My banishment, feeding my melancholy,
Would often reason thus.

DUCHESS

Pray, let's hear it.

ANTONIO

Say a man never marry, nor have children,
What takes that from him? only the bare name
Of being a father, or the weak delight

To see the little wanton ride a-cock-horse
Upon a painted stick, or hear him chatter
Like a taught starling.

DUCHESS

Fie, fie, what's all this?
One of your eyes is blood-shot; use my ring to't,
They say 'tis very sovereign: 'twas my wedding-ring,
And I did vow never to part with it
But to my second husband.

ANTONIO

You have parted with it now.

DUCHESS

Yes, to help your eye-sight.

ANTONIO

You have made me stark blind.

DUCHESS

How?

ANTONIO

There is a saucy and ambitious devil
Is dancing in this circle.

DUCHESS

Remove him.

ANTONIO

How?

DUCHESS

There needs small conjuration, when your finger
May do it: thus; is it fit?

(She puts the ring upon his finger: he kneels)

ANTONIO

What said you?

DUCHESS

Sir,
This goodly roof of yours is too low built;
I cannot stand upright in't nor discourse,
Without I raise it higher: raise yourself;
Or, if you please, my hand to help you: so.

(Raises him)

ANTONIO

Ambition, madam, is a great man's madness,
That is not kept in chains and close-pent rooms,
But in fair lightsome lodgings, and is girt
With the wild noise of prattling visitants,
Which makes it lunatic beyond all cure.
Conceive not I am so stupid but I aim
Whereto your favours tend: but he's a fool
That, being a-cold, would thrust his hands i' the fire
To warm them.

DUCHESS

So, now the ground's broke,
You may discover what a wealthy mine
I make you lord of.

ANTONIO

O my unworthiness!

DUCHESS

You were ill to sell yourself:
This darkening of your worth is not like that

Which tradesmen use i' the city; their false lights
Are to rid bad wares off: and I must tell you,
If you will know where breathes a complete man
(I speak it without flattery), turn your eyes,
And progress through yourself.

ANTONIO

Were there nor Heaven nor hell,
I should be honest: I have long serv'd virtue,
And ne'er ta'en wages of her.

DUCHESS

Now she pays it.
The misery of us that are born great!
We are forced to woo, because none dare woo us;
And as a tyrant doubles with his words,
And fearfully equivocates, so we
Are forced to express our violent passions
In riddles and in dreams, and leave the path
Of simple virtue, which was never made
To seem the thing it is not. Go, go brag
You have left me heartless; mine is in your bosom:
I hope 'twill multiply love there. You do tremble:
Make not your heart so dead a piece of flesh,
To fear more than to love me. Sir, be confident:
What is't distracts you? This is flesh and blood, sir;
'Tis not the figure cut in alabaster
Kneels at my husband's tomb. Awake, awake, man!
I do here put off all vain ceremony,
And only do appear to you a young widow
That claims you for her husband, and, like a widow,
I use but half a blush in't.

ANTONIO

Truth speak for me;
I will remain the constant sanctuary
Of your good name.

DUCHESS

I thank you, gentle love:
And 'cause you shall not come to me in debt,
Being now my steward, here upon your lips
I sign your *Quietus est.* This you should have begg'd now:
I have seen children oft eat sweetmeats thus,
As fearful to devour them too soon.

ANTONIO

But for your brothers?

DUCHESS

Do not think of them:
All discord without this circumference
Is only to be pitied, and not fear'd:
Yet, should they know it, time will easily
Scatter the tempest.

ANTONIO

These words should be mine,
And all the parts you have spoke, if some part of it
Would not have savour'd flattery.

DUCHESS

Kneel.

(CARIOLA *comes from behind the arras*)

ANTONIO

Ha!

DUCHESS

Be not amaz'd; this woman's of my counsel:
I have heard lawyers say, a contract in a chamber
Per verba presenti is absolute marriage.
(*She and* ANTONIO *kneel*)
Bless, Heaven, this sacred gordian, which let violence
Never untwine!

ANTONIO

And may our sweet affections, like the spheres,
Be still in motion!

DUCHESS

Quickening, and make
The like soft music!

ANTONIO

That we may imitate the loving palms,
Best emblem of a peaceful marriage,
That never bore fruit, divided!

DUCHESS

What can the church force more?

ANTONIO

That fortune may not know an accident,
Either of joy or sorrow, to divide
Our fixed wishes!

DUCHESS

How can the church build faster?
We now are man and wife, and 'tis the church
That must but echo this.—Maid, stand apart:
I now am blind.

ANTONIO

What's your conceit in this?

DUCHESS

I would have you lead your fortune by the hand
Unto your marriage bed:
(You speak in me this, for we now are one:)
We'll only lie, and talk together, and plot
To appease my humorous kindred; and if you please,
Like the old tale in Alexander and Lodowick,
Lay a naked sword between us, keep us chaste.

O, let me shrowd my blushes in your bosom,
Since 'tis the treasury of all my secrets!

(*Exeunt* DUCHESS *and* ANTONIO)

The Changeling
by Thomas Middleton

ACT II, SCENE 2—
BEATRICE, DE FLORES

BEATRICE

(*Aside*)
Why, put case I loath'd him
As much as youth and beauty hates a sepulchre,
Must I needs show it? Cannot I keep that secret,
And serve my turn upon him?—See, he's here.
—De Flores!

DE FLORES

(*Aside*)
Ha, I shall run mad with joy!
She call'd me fairly by my name, De Flores,
And neither rogue nor rascal.

BEATRICE

What ha' you done
To your face a-late? Y'have met with some good physician;
Y'have prun'd yourself, methinks; you were not wont
To look so amorously.

DE FLORES

(*Aside*)
Not I;
'Tis the same physnomy, to a hair and pimple,
Which she call'd scurvy scarce an hour ago;
How is this?

BEATRICE

Come hither; nearer, man.

DE FLORES

(*Aside*)
I'm up to the chin in heaven!

BEATRICE

Turn, let me see;
Faugh, 'tis but the heat of the liver, I perceiv't;
I thought it had been worse.

DE FLORES

(*Aside*)
Her fingers touch'd me!
She smells all amber.

BEATRICE

I'll make a water for you shall cleanse this
Within a fortnight.

DE FLORES

With your own hands, lady?

BEATRICE

Yes, mine own, sir; in a work of cure
I'll trust no other.

DE FLORES

(*Aside*)
'Tis half an act of pleasure
To hear her talk thus to me.

BEATRICE

When we're us'd
To a hard face, 'tis not so unpleasing;
It mends still in opinion, hourly mends,
I see it by experience.

DE FLORES

(*Aside*)
I was blest
To light upon this minute; I'll make use on't.

BEATRICE

Hardness becomes the visage of a man well,
It argues service, resolution, manhood,
If cause were of employment.

DE FLORES

'Twould be soon seen,
If e'er your ladyship had cause to use it.
I would but wish the honour of a service
So happy as that mounts to.

BEATRICE

We shall try you—
Oh my De Flores!

DE FLORES

(*Aside*)
How's that? She calls me hers
Already, *my* De Flores!—You were about
To sigh out somewhat, madam?

BEATRICE

No, was I?
I forgot—Oh!—

DE FLORES

There 'tis again, the very fellow on't.

BEATRICE

You are too quick, sir.

DE FLORES

There's no excuse for't now; I heard it twice, madam;
That sigh would fain have utterance, take pity on't,
And lend it a free word; 'las, how it labours
For liberty! I hear the murmur yet
Beat at your bosom.

BEATRICE

Would creation—

DE FLORES

Ay, well said, that's it.

BEATRICE

Had form'd me man!

DE FLORES

Nay, that's not it.

BEATRICE

Oh, 'tis the soul of freedom!
I should not then be forc'd to marry one
I hate beyond all depths; I should have power
Then to oppose my loathings, nay, remove 'em
For ever from my sight.

DE FLORES

(*Aside*)
O blest occasion!—
Without change to your sex, you have your wishes.
Claim so much man in me.

BEATRICE

In thee, De Flores?
There's small cause for that.

DE FLORES

Put it not from me;
It's a service that I kneel for to you.

(*Kneels*)

BEATRICE

You are too violent to mean faithfully;
There's horror in my service, blood and danger;
Can those be things to sue for?

DE FLORES

. If you knew
How sweet it were to me to be employ'd
In any act of yours, you would say then
I fail'd, and us'd not reverence enough
When I receive the charge on't.

BEATRICE

(*Aside*)
This is much, methinks;
Belike his wants are greedy, and to such
Gold tastes like angel's food.—Rise.

DE FLORES

I'll have the work first.

BEATRICE

(*Aside*)
Possible his need
Is strong upon him.—There's to encourage thee;
(*Gives him money*)
As thou art forward and thy service dangerous,
Thy reward shall be precious.

DE FLORES

That I have thought on;
I have assur'd myself of that beforehand,
And know it will be precious; the thought ravishes.

BEATRICE

Then take him to thy fury!

DE FLORES

I thirst for him.

BEATRICE

Alonzo de Piracquo!

DE FLORES

His end's upon him;
He shall be seen no more.

BEATRICE

How lovely now
Dost thou appear to me! Never was man
Dearlier rewarded.

DE FLORES

I do think of that.

BEATRICE

Be wondrous careful in the execution.

DE FLORES

Why, are not both our lives upon the cast?

BEATRICE

Then I throw all my fears upon thy service.

DE FLORES

They ne'er shall rise to hurt you.

BEATRICE

When the deed's done,
I'll furnish thee with all things for thy flight;
Thou may'st live bravely in another country.

DE FLORES

Ay, ay, we'll talk of that hereafter.

BEATRICE

(*Aside*)
I shall rid myself
Of two inveterate loathings at one time,
Piracquo, and his dog-face.

(*Exit*)

DE FLORES

Oh my blood!
Methinks I feel her in mine arms already,
Her wanton fingers combing out this beard,
And, being pleased, praising this bad face.
Hunger and pleasure, they'll commend sometimes
Slovenly dishes, and feed heartily on 'em,
Nay, which is stranger, refuse daintier for 'em.
Some women are odd feeders.—I'm too loud.
Here comes the man goes supperless to bed,
Yet shall not rise tomorrow to his dinner.

The Revenger's Tragedy
by Cyril Tourneur

ACT II, SCENE 1—
CASTIZA, VENDICE, GRATIANA

CASTIZA

I hope some happy tidings from my brother,
That lately travelled, whom my soul affects.
Here he comes.

(*Enter* VENDICE, *disguised*)

VENDICE

Lady, the best of wishes to your sex—
Fair skins and new gowns,

CASTIZA

O, they shall thank you, sir.
Whence this?

VENDICE

O, from a dear and worthy mighty friend.

CASTIZA

From whom?

VENDICE

The duke's son!

CASTIZA

Receive that.
(*Boxes his ear*)
I swore I would put anger in my hand,
And pass the virgin limits of my sex,

To him that next appear'd in that base office,
To be his sin's attorney. Bear to him.
That figure of my hate upon thy cheek,
Whilst 'tis yet hot, and I'll reward thee for't;
Tell him my honour shall have a rich name,
When several harlots shall share his with shame.
Farewell; commend me to him in my hate.

(*Exit*)

VENDICE

It is the sweetest box that e'er my nose came nigh;
The finest drawn-work cuff that e'er was worn;
I'll love this blow for ever, and this cheek
Shall still henceforward take the wall of this.
O, I'm above my tongue: most constant sister,
In this thou hast right honourable shown;
Many are called by their honour, that have none;
Thou art approv'd for ever in my thoughts.
It is not in the power of words to taint thee.
And yet for the salvation of my oath,
As my resolve in that point, I will lay
Hard siege unto my mother, though I know
A syren's tongue could not bewitch her so.
Mass, fitly here she comes! thanks, my disguise—
Madam, good afternoon.

(*Enter* GRATIANA)

GRATIANA

Y'are welcome, sir.

VENDICE

The next of Italy commends him to you,
Our mighty expectation, the duke's son.

GRATIANA

I think myself much honour'd that he pleases
To rank me in his thoughts.

342

VENDICE

So may you, lady:
One that is like to be our sudden duke;
The crown gapes for him every tide, and then
Commander o'er us all; do but think on him,
How bless'd were they, now that could pleasure him—
E'en with anything almost!

GRATIANA

Ay, save their honour.

VENDICE

Tut, one would let a little of that go too,
And ne'er be seen in't—ne'er be seen in't, mark you;
I'd wink, and let it go.

GRATIANA

Marry, but I would not.

VENDICE

Marry but I would, I hope; I know you would too,
If you'd that blood now, which you gave your daughter.
To her indeed 'tis this wheel comes about;
That man that must be all this, perhaps ere morning
(For his white father does but mould away),
Has long desir'd your daughter.

GRATIANA

Desir'd?

VENDICE

Nay, but hear me;
He desires now, that will command hereafter:
Therefore be wise. I speak as more a friend
To you than him: madam, I know you're poor,
And, 'lack the day!

There are too many poor ladies already;
Why should you wax the number? 'Tis despis'd.
Live wealthy, rightly understand the world,
And chide away that foolish country girl
Keeps company with your daughter—Chastity.

GRATIANA

O fie, fie! the riches of the world cannot hire
A mother to such a most unnatural task.

VENDICE

No, but a thousand angels can.
Men have no power, angels must work you to't:
The world descends into such baseborn evils,
That forty angels can make fourscore devils.
There will be fools still, I perceive—still fools.
Would I be poor, dejected, scorn'd of greatness,
Swept from the palace, and see others' daughters
Spring with the dew o' the court, having mine own
So much desir'd and lov'd by the duke's son?
No, I would raise my state upon her breast;
And call her eyes my tenants; I would count
My yearly maintenance upon her cheeks;
Take coach upon her lip; and all her parts
Should keep men after men, and I would ride
In pleasure upon pleasure.
You took great pains for her, once when it was;
Let her requite it now, though it be but some.
You brought her forth: she may well bring you home.

GRATIANA

O Heavens! this o'ercomes me!

VENDICE

Not, I hope, already?
(*Aside*)

GRATIANA

It is too strong for me; men know that know us,
We are so weak their words can overthrow us;
He touched me nearly, made my virtues bate,
When his tongue struck upon my poor estate.
(*Aside*)

VENDICE

I e'en quake to proceed, my spirit turns edge.
I fear me she's unmothered; yet I'll venture.
"That woman is all male, whom none can enter."
(*Aside*)
What think you now, lady? Speak, are you wiser?
What said advancement to you? Thus it said:
The daughter's fall lifts up the mother's head.
Did it not, madam? But I'll swear it does
In many places: tut, this age fears no man.
" 'Tis no shame to be bad, because 'tis common."

GRATIANA

Ay, that's the comfort on't.

VENDICE

The comfort on't!
I keep the best for last—can these persuade you
To forget Heaven—and—

(*Gives her money*)

GRATIANA

Ay, these are they—

VENDICE

O!

GRATIANA

That enchant our sex. These are
The means that govern our affections—that woman
Will not be troubled with the mother long,
That sees the comfortable shine of you:
I blush to think what for your sakes I'll do.

VENDICE

O suffering Heaven, with thy invisible finger,
E'en at this instant turn the precious side
Of both mine eyeballs inward, not to see myself.
(*Aside*)

GRATIANA

Look you, sir.

VENDICE

Hollo.

GRATIANA

Let this thank your pains.

VENDICE

O, you're kind, madam.

GRATIANA

I'll see how I can move.

VENDICE

Your words will sting.

GRATIANA

If she be still chaste, I'll ne'er call her mine.

VENDICE

Spoke truer than you meant it.

GRATIANA

Daughter Castiza.

(*Re-enter* CASTIZA)

CASTIZA

Madam.

VENDICE

O, she's yonder;
Meet her: troops of celestial soldiers guard her heart.
Yon dam has devils enough to take her part.

CASTIZA

Madam, what makes yon evil-offic'd man
In presence of you?

GRATIANA

Why?

CASTIZA

He lately brought
Immodest writing sent from the duke's son,
To tempt me to dishonourable act.

GRATIANA

Dishonourable act!—good honourable fool,
That wouldst be honest, 'cause thou wouldst be so,
Producing no one reason but thy will.
And't has a good report, prettily commended,
But pray, by whom? Poor people, ignorant people;
The better sort, I'm sure, cannot abide it.
And by what rule should we square out our lives,
But by our betters' actions? O, if thou knew'st
What 'twere to lose it, thou would never keep it!
But there's a cold curse laid upon all maids,
Whilst others clip the sun, they clasp the shades.
Virginity is paradise locked up.

You cannot come by yourselves without fee;
And 'twas decreed that man should keep the key!
Deny advancement! treasure! the duke's son!

CASTIZA

I cry you mercy! lady! I mistook you!
Pray did you see my mother? which way went you?
Pray God, I have not lost her.

VENDICE

Prettily put by!
(*Aside*)

GRATIANA

Are you as proud to me, as coy to him?
Do you not know me now?

CASTIZA

Why, are you she?
The world's so changed one shape into another,
It is a wise child now that knows her mother.

VENDICE

Most right i' faith.
(*Aside*)

GRATIANA

I owe your cheek my hand
For that presumption now; but I'll forget it.
Come, you shall leave those childish 'haviours,
And understand your time. Fortunes flow to you;
What, will you be a girl?
If all fear'd drowning that spy waves ashore,
Gold would grow rich, and all the merchants poor.

CASTIZA

It is a pretty saying of a wicked one;
But methinks now it does not show so well
Out of your mouth—better in his!

VENDICE

Faith, bad enough in both,
Were I in earnest, as I'll seem no less.
(*Aside*)
I wonder, lady, your own mother's words
Cannot be taken, nor stand in full force.
'Tis honesty you urge; what's honesty?
'Tis but Heaven's beggar; and what woman is
So foolish to keep honesty,
And be not able to keep herself? No,
Times are grown wiser, and will keep less charge.
A maid that has small portion now intends
To break up house, and live upon her friends;
How blessed are you! you have happiness alone;
Others must fall to thousands, you to one,
Sufficient in himself to make your forehead
Dazzle the world with jewels, and petitionary people
Start at your presence.

GRATIANA

O, if I were young, I should be ravish'd.

CASTIZA

Ay, to lose your honour!

VENDICE

'Slid, how can you lose your honour
To deal with my lord's grace?
He'll add more honour to it by his title;
Your mother will tell you how.

GRATIANA

That I will.

VENDICE

O, think upon the pleasure of the palace!
Secured ease and state! the stirring meats,
Ready to move out of the dishes, that e'en now
Quicken when they are eaten!
Banquets abroad by torchlight! music! sports!
Bareheaded vassals, that had ne'er the fortune
To keep on their own hats, but let horns wear 'em!
Nine coaches waiting—hurry, hurry, hurry—

CASTIZA

Ay, to the devil.

VENDICE

(*Aside*)
Ay, to the devil!—
To the duke, by my faith.

GRATIANA

Ay, to the duke: daughter, you'd scorn to think o' the devil, an
you were there once.

VENDICE

True, for most there are as proud as he for his heart, i' faith.
(*Aside*)
Who'd sit at home in a neglected room,
Dealing her short-liv'd beauty to the pictures,
That are as useless as old men, when those
Poorer in face and fortune than herself
Walk with a hundred acres on their backs,
Fair meadows cut into green foreparts? O,
It was the greatest blessing ever happened to woman
When farmers' sons agreed and met again,
To wash their hands, and come up gentlemen!
The commonwealth has flourish'd ever since:
Lands that were mete by the rod, that labour's spar'd:
Tailors ride down, and measure 'em by the yard.

Fair trees, those comely foretops of the field,
Are cut to maintain head-tires—much untold.
All thrives but chastity; she lies a-cold.
Nay, shall I come nearer to you? mark but this:
Why are there so few honest women, but because 'tis the poorer
profession? that's accounted best that's best followed; least in trade,
least in fashion; and that's not honesty, believe it; and do but note
the love and dejected price of it—
Lose but a pearl, we search, and cannot brook it:
But that once gone, who is so mad to look it?

GRATIANA

Troth, he says true.

CASTIZA

False! I defy you both:
I have endur'd you with an ear of fire;
Your tongues have struck hot irons on my face.
Mother, come from that poisonous woman there.

GRATIANA

Where?

CASTIZA

Do you not see her? she's too inward, then!
Slave, perish in thy office! you Heavens, please
Henceforth to make the mother a disease,
Which first begins with me: yet I've outgone you.

(*Exit*)

VENDICE

O angels, clap your wings upon the skies,
And give this virgin crystal plaudites!
(*Aside*)

351

GRATIANA

Peevish, coy, foolish!—but return this answer,
My lord shall be most welcome, when his pleasure
Conducts him this way. I will sway mine own.
Women with women can work best alone.

(*Exit*)

VENDICE

Indeed, I'll tell him so.
O, more uncivil, more unnatural,
Than those base-titled creatures that look downward;
Why does not Heaven turn black, or with a frown
Undo the world? Why does not earth start up,
And strike the sins that tread upon't? O,
Were't not for gold and women, there would be no damnation.
Hell would look like a lord's great kitchen without fire in't.
But 'twas decreed, before the world began,
That they should be the hooks to catch at man.

PART IV

The Age of Style:

RESTORATION AND
EIGHTEENTH-CENTURY
SCENES

INTRODUCTION

To say that the scenes in this section deal with style at the expense of substance would be an oversimplification, but it is true that issues of style and appearance dominate with some regularity, and it would seem that under these conditions only those persons most gifted at artifice can truly succeed. The Restoration world in particular is divided into two categories of people: the true wits, and those would-be wits who merely ape the behavior of their betters.

Innocence and Education

In William Wycherly's *The Country Wife,* the rural innocent Margery Pinchwife would seem to be an untutored victim of her husband's odius restrictions, but it turns out that she has in fact more true wit and can turn his stratagems to her advantage with relative ease. If the repeated words and phrases are particularly emphasized, a great deal of comic color comes through. Note, for example, the repetition of "So," a word initiated by Pinchwife and then appropriated by Margery.

John Vanbrugh's *The Relapse* is also about the education of a relative innocent, in this case Amanda, who, although possessed of a certain sophistication, is rarely a match even for her husband, Loveless, with whom she compares the language of men and women, as each tests the other's fidelity. And later, when Amanda meets Berinthia, who has her own designs on Loveless, she falls prey to the other's calculated advice. It is important not to confuse innocence, a typical ingenue characteristic, with a lack of style or intelligence. Our sympathies stay with Amanda no matter what she has to put up with from others.

More evenly matched are Dorinda and Mrs. Sullen in George Farquhar's *The Beaux' Stratagem,* as they compare lovers in magniloquent terms. This scene cannot begin to work unless it is rapidly and fully cued.

The Feminist Viewpoint

I have included three scenes from Aphra Behn's *The Rover* because this elusive and historically much-maligned playwright has created scenes that seem to breathe with life in a way that very little material of this period manages. The women's roles especially, although emotionally very complete, do not suffer from even a suggestion of weakness. For example, when Angellica and Willmore, the rover himself out for a bargain, first meet, she is clearly swayed by him, but she is at the same time completely aware of what is happening to her. The scene is a model of sudden passion and love at first sight, written in a manner that makes sense even today.

The trio scene that brings Hellena's influence to bear on the already complex behavior of Willmore and Angellica is operatic, in one sense because its dynamics are orchestrated to play in a musical fashion, and also because it needs to be played almost completely forward, toward the audience, to work. When directing this play several years ago, I encountered resistance from actors who felt that they needed to stare into each other's eyes to draw sufficient emotional material to work with, and the scene never completely got off the ground. With Hellena in disguise anyway, the scene is hardly about the eyes as the principal medium of communication; hearing, touch, and smell can work much more fully.

Finally, Hellena's last scene with Willmore is exemplary of the woman who can acknowledge an attraction without giving up her freedom. It should be played with stillness and control, allowing the words their full, witty due.

Restoration Tragedy

Even more operatic than *The Rover* are those few examples of Restoration tragedy still considered dramatically acceptable. When working on the Belvidera and Jaffeir scene from *Venice Preserved,* I found myself trying to apply language techniques derived from my work with Shakespeare with little success, even though those same techniques had proved useful with other Restoration and, in fact, later drama. I soon realized that the language itself did not have the kind of variety and punch that I had come to expect from most classical English dramatic writing. Otway seemed to be relying instead on a smooth, fairly uninterrupted flow of words, allowing the melody, as it were, to carry the drama, rather than the details of story and relationship. Once I understood this, I was able to work with the actors on creating a simple, balletic kind of choreography that would support the melody of the writing, and the scene began to take on some real life.

The Jaffeir and Pierre scene requires a similar approach, and I would recommend working with music in rehearsal—any music at all that has scale: ballet, opera, a John Williams film score, a Rick Wakeman epic, or almost any heavy metal band. The last few lines scream for a musical finale, ". . . Vengeance shall have room—Revenge! . . . And liberty! . . . Revenge! Revenge—"

The scene from *All for Love,* John Dryden's adaptation of Shakespeare's *Antony and Cleopatra,* is a cat fight only slightly dignified by its public formality. I suggest that Cleopatra be very much in her element and seated until "Yet she who loves him best is Cleopatra," leaving Antony's wife, Octavia, to walk, explore, and attempt to dominate by height and action.

Ballad Opera

John Gay's *The Beggar's Opera* was, of course, intended to be played with frequent musical interludes (sixty-nine airs, in fact), some of them forwarding the action and others providing commentary or emotional support. I refer those actors wishing to explore the musical dimension to any of the inexpensive paperback editions of the play which include the melodies, popular tunes of the time, in the body of the text. Complete arrangements are also available at almost any public library. Another approach, though, that can be a great deal of fun is to improvise music of any chosen period or style to suit the lyrics in the text. And if the actors are not musically inclined, I recommend speaking the lyrics in rhythm, as a verse trope to a prose scene. The effect in any case will not differ dramatically in any substantial way. The songs, as well as the asides, demand direct audience address, and an interesting problem to work out is what the other actor or actors do while one is singing. My feeling is, the more variety the better.

The Country Wife
by William Wycherly

ACT IV, SCENE 2—
PINCHWIFE, MARGERY PINCHWIFE

PINCHWIFE

Come, tell me, I say.

MRS. PINCHWIFE

Lord! hadn't I told it an hundred times over?

PINCHWIFE

(*Aside*)
I would try, if in the repetition of the ungrateful tale, I could find her altering it in the least circumstance; for if her story be false, she is so too.——Come, how was't, baggage?

MRS. PINCHWIFE

Lord, what pleasure you take to hear it, sure!

PINCHWIFE

No, you take more in telling it, I find; but speak, how was't?

MRS. PINCHWIFE

He carried me up into the house next to the Exchange.

PINCHWIFE

So, and you two were only in the room!

MRS. PINCHWIFE

Yes, for he sent away a youth that was there, for some dried fruit, and China oranges.

PINCHWIFE

Did he so? Damn him for it—and for——

MRS. PINCHWIFE

But presently came up the gentlewoman of the house.

PINCHWIFE

Oh, 'twas well she did; but what did he do whilst the fruit came?

MRS. PINCHWIFE

He kissed me an hundred times, and told me he fancied he kissed my fine sister, meaning me, you know, whom he said he loved with all his soul, and bid me be sure to tell her so, and to desire her to be at her window, by eleven of the clock this morning, and he would walk under it at that time.

PINCHWIFE

(*Aside*)
And he was as good as his word, very punctual; a pox reward him for't.

MRS. PINCHWIFE

Well, and he said if you were not within, he would come up to her, meaning me, you know, bud, still.

PINCHWIFE

(*Aside*)
So—he knew her certainly; but for this confession, I am obliged to her simplicity.——But what, you stood very still when he kissed you?

MRS. PINCHWIFE

Yes, I warrant you; would you have had me discover myself?

PINCHWIFE

But you told me he did some beastliness to you, as you call it; what was't?

MRS. PINCHWIFE

Why, he put——

PINCHWIFE

What?

MRS. PINCHWIFE

Why, he put the tip of his tongue between my lips, and so mousled me—and I said, I'd bite it.

PINCHWIFE

An eternal canker seize it, for a dog!

MRS. PINCHWIFE

Nay, you need not be so angry with him neither, for to say truth, he has the sweetest breath I ever knew.

PINCHWIFE

The devil! you were satisfied with it then, and would do it again?

MRS. PINCHWIFE

Not unless he should force me.

PINCHWIFE

Force you, changeling! I tell you, no woman can be forced.

MRS. PINCHWIFE

Yes, but she may sure, by such a one as he, for he's a proper, goodly, strong man; 'tis hard, let me tell you, to resist him.

PINCHWIFE

(*Aside*)

So, 'tis plain she loves him, yet she has not love enough to make her conceal it from me; but the sight of him will increase her aversion for me and love for him; and that love instruct her how to deceive me and satisfy him, all idiot that she is. Love! 'twas he gave women first their craft, their art of deluding. Out of Nature's hands they came plain, open, silly, and fit for slaves, as she and

Heaven intended 'em; but damned Love—well—I must strangle that little monster whilst I can deal with him.——Go fetch pen, ink, and paper out of the next room.

MRS. PINCHWIFE

Yes, bud.

(*Exit*)

PINCHWIFE

Why should women have more invention in love than men? It can only be because they have more desires, more soliciting passions, more lust, and more of the devil.
(MRS. PINCHWIFE *returns*)
Come, minx, sit down and write.

MRS. PINCHWIFE

Ay, dear bud, but I can't do't very well.

PINCHWIFE

I wish you could not at all.

MRS. PINCHWIFE

But what should I write for?

PINCHWIFE

I'll have you write a letter to your lover.

MRS. PINCHWIFE

O Lord, to the fine gentleman a letter!

PINCHWIFE

Yes, to the fine gentleman.

MRS. PINCHWIFE

Lord, you do but jeer: sure you jest.

362

PINCHWIFE

I am not so merry: come, write as I bid you.

MRS. PINCHWIFE

What, do you think I am a fool?

PINCHWIFE

(*Aside*)
She's afraid I would not dictate any love to him, therefore she's
unwilling.——But you had best begin.

MRS. PINCHWIFE

Indeed, and indeed, but I won't, so I won't.

PINCHWIFE

Why?

MRS. PINCHWIFE

Because he's in town; you may send for him if you will.

PINCHWIFE

Very well, you would have him brought to you; is it come to this?
I say, take the pen and write, or you'll provoke me.

MRS. PINCHWIFE

Lord, what d'ye make a fool of me for? Don't I know that letters
are never writ but from the country to London, and from London
into the country? Now he's in town, and I am in town too; therefore
I can't write to him, you know.

PINCHWIFE

(*Aside*)
So, I am glad it is no worse; she is innocent enough yet.——Yes,
you may, when your husband bids you, write letters to people that
are in town.

MRS. PINCHWIFE

Oh, may I so? then I'm satisfied.

PINCHWIFE

Come, begin
(*Dictates*)
—"Sir"——

MRS. PINCHWIFE

Shan't I say, "Dear Sir"? You know one says always something more than bare "Sir."

PINCHWIFE

Write as I bid you, or I will write whore with this penknife in your face.

MRS. PINCHWIFE

Nay, good bud
(*She writes*)
—"Sir"——

PINCHWIFE

"Though I suffered last night your nauseous, loathed kisses and embraces"——Write!

MRS. PINCHWIFE

Nay, why should I say so? You know I told you he had a sweet breath.

PINCHWIFE

Write!

MRS. PINCHWIFE

Let me but put out "loathed."

PINCHWIFE

Write, I say!

MRS. PINCHWIFE

Well then.

(Writes)

PINCHWIFE

Let's see, what have you writ?—
(Takes the paper and reads)
"Though I suffered last night your kisses and embraces"——Thou
impudent creature! where is "nauseous" and "loathed"?

MRS. PINCHWIFE

I can't abide to write such filthy words.

PINCHWIFE

Once more write as I'd have you, and question it not, or I will spoil
thy writing with this. I will stab out those eyes that cause my
mischief.

(Holds up the penknife)

MRS. PINCHWIFE

O Lord! I will.

PINCHWIFE

So—so—let's see now.—
(Reads)
"Though I suffered last night your nauseous, loathed kisses and
embraces"—go on— "yet I would not have you presume that you
shall ever repeat them"—so——

(She writes)

MRS. PINCHWIFE

I have writ it.

PINCHWIFE

On, then— "I then concealed myself from your knowledge, to
avoid your insolencies."——

(*She writes*)

MRS. PINCHWIFE

So——

PINCHWIFE

"The same reason, now I am out of your hands"——

(*She writes*)

MRS. PINCHWIFE

So——

PINCHWIFE

"Makes me own to you my unfortunate, though innocent frolic, of being in man's clothes"——

(*She writes*)

MRS. PINCHWIFE

So——

PINCHWIFE

"That you may for evermore cease to pursue her, who hates and detests you"——

(*She writes on*)

MRS. PINCHWIFE

So—h——

(*Sighs*)

PINCHWIFE

What, do you sigh?—"detests you—as much as she loves her husband and her honour."

MRS. PINCHWIFE

I vow, husband, he'll ne'er believe I should write such a letter.

PINCHWIFE

What, he'd expect a kinder from you? Come, now your name only.

MRS. PINCHWIFE

What, shan't I say "Your most faithful humble servant till death"?

PINCHWIFE

No, tormenting fiend!—
(*Aside*)
Her style, I find, would be very soft.——Come, wrap it up now, whilst I go fetch wax and a candle; and write on the backside, "For Mr. Horner."

(*Exit* PINCHWIFE)

MRS. PINCHWIFE

"For Mr. Horner."——So, I am glad he has told me his name. Dear Mr. Horner! But why should I send thee such a letter that will vex thee, and make thee angry with me?——Well, I will not send it.——Ay, but then my husband will kill me—for I see plainly he won't let me love Mr. Horner—but what care I for my husband? I won't, so I won't, send poor Mr. Horner such a letter——But then my husband—but oh, what if I writ at bottom my husband made me write it?——Ay, but then my husband would see't—Can one have no shift? Ah, a London woman would have had a hundred presently. Stay—what if I should write a letter, and wrap it up like this, and write upon't too? Ay, but then my husband would see't— I don't know what to do.—But yet evads I'll try, so I will—for I will not send this letter to poor Mr. Horner, come what will on't.
    "Dear, sweet Mr. Horner"—
(*She writes and repeats what she hath writ*)
—so—"my husband would have me send you a base, rude, unmannerly letter; but I won't"—so—"and would have me forbid you loving me; but I won't"—so—"and would have me say to you, I

367

hate you, poor Mr. Horner; but I won't tell a lie for him"—there—
"for I'm sure if you and I were in the country at cards together"—
so—"I could not help treading on your toe under the table"—so—
"or rubbing knees with you, and staring in your face, till you saw
me"—very well—"and then looking down, and blushing for an hour
together"—so—"but I must make haste before my husband come:
and now he has taught me to write letters, you shall have longer
ones from me, who am, dear, dear, poor, dear Mr. Horner, your
most humble friend, and servant to command till death,—Margery
Pinchwife."

Stay, I must give him a hint at bottom—so—now wrap it up just
like t'other—so—now write "For Mr. Horner"—But oh now, what
shall I do with it? for here comes my husband.

(*Enter* PINCHWIFE)

PINCHWIFE

(*Aside*)
I have been detained by a sparkish coxcomb, who pretended a visit
to me; but I fear 'twas to my wife——What, have you done?

MRS. PINCHWIFE

Ay, ay, bud, just now.

PINCHWIFE

Let's see't: what d'ye tremble for? what, you would not have it go?

MRS. PINCHWIFE

Here—
(*Aside*)
No, I must not give him that: so I had been served if I had given
him this.

(*He opens and reads the first letter*)

PINCHWIFE

Come, where's the wax and seal?

(*Aside*)

"Lord, what shall I do now? Nay, then I have it——Pray let me see't. Lord, you think me so arrant a fool I cannot seal a letter; I will do't, so I will.

(*Snatches the letter from him, changes it for the other, seals it, and delivers it to him*)

PINCHWIFE

Nay, I believe you will learn that, and other things too, which I would not have you.

MRS. PINCHWIFE

So, han't I done it curiously?——
(*Aside*)
I think I have; there's my letter going to Mr. Horner, since he'll needs have me send letters to folks.

PINCHWIFE

'Tis very well; but I warrant you would not have it go now?

MRS. PINCHWIFE

Yes, indeed, but I would, bud, now.

PINCHWIFE

Well, you are a good girl then. Come, let me lock you up in your chamber till I come back; and be sure you come not within three strides of the window when I am gone, for I have a spy in the street.——
(*Exit* MRS. PINCHWIFE, PINCHWIFE *locks the door*)
At least, 'tis fit she think so. If we do not cheat women, they'll cheat us, and fraud may be justly used with secret enemies, of which a wife is the most dangerous; and he that has a handsome one to keep, and a frontier town, must provide against treachery, rather than open force. Now I have secured all within, I'll deal with the foe without, with false intelligence.

(*Holds up the letter. Exit* PINCHWIFE)

The Relapse
by Sir John Vanbrugh
ACT II—LOVELESS, AMANDA

LOVELESS

How do you like these lodgings, my dear? For my part, I am so well pleased with 'em, I shall hardly remove whilst we stay in town, if you are satisfied.

AMANDA

I am satisfied with everything that pleases you; else I had not come to town at all.

LOVELESS

Oh, a little of the noise and bustle of the world sweetens the pleasures of retreat: we shall find the charms of our retirement doubled when we return to it.

AMANDA

That pleasing prospect will be my chiefest entertainment, whilst (much against my will) I am obliged to stand surrounded with these empty pleasures which 'tis so much the fashion to be fond of.

LOVELESS

I own most of 'em are indeed but empty; nay, so empty, that one would wonder by what magic power they act, when they induce us to be vicious for their sakes. Yet some there are we may speak kindlier of: there are delights (of which a private life is destitute) which may divert an honest man, and be a harmless entertainment to a virtuous woman. The conversation of the town is one; and truly (with some small allowances) the plays, I think, may be esteemed another.

AMANDA

The plays, I must confess, have some small charms, and would have more would they restrain that loose, obscene encouragement to vice which shocks, if not the virtue of some women, at least the modesty of all.

LOVELESS

But till that reformation can be made I would not leave the whole-some corn for some intruding tares that grow amongst it. Doubtless the moral of a well-wrought scene is of prevailing force. Last night there happened one that moved me strangely.

AMANDA

Pray, what was that?

LOVELESS

Why, 'twas about—but 'tis not worth repeating.

AMANDA

Yes, pray let me know it.

LOVELESS

No, I think 'tis as well let alone.

AMANDA

Nay, now you make me have a mind to know.

LOVELESS

'Twas a foolish thing: you'd perhaps grow jealous should I tell it you, though without cause, heaven knows.

AMANDA

I shall begin to think I have cause, if you persist in making it a secret.

LOVELESS

I'll then convince you you have none, by making it no longer so. Know then, I happened in the play to find my very character, only with the addition of a relapse, which struck me so I put a sudden stop to a most harmless entertainment which till then diverted me between the acts. 'Twas to admire the workmanship of Nature in the face of a young lady that sate some distance from me, she was so exquisitely handsome.

AMANDA

"So exquisitely handsome!"

LOVELESS

Why do you repeat my words, my dear?

AMANDA

Because you seemed to speak 'em with such pleasure I thought I might oblige you with their echo.

LOVELESS

Then you are alarmed, Amanda?

AMANDA

It is my duty to be so, when you are in danger.

LOVELESS

You are too quick in apprehending for me; all will be well when you have heard me out. I do confess I gazed upon her, nay, eagerly I gazed upon her.

AMANDA

Eagerly? That's with desire.

LOVELESS

No, I desired her not: I viewed her with a world of admiration, but not one glance of love.

AMANDA

Take heed of trusting to such nice distinctions.

LOVELESS

I did take heed; for, observing in the play that he who seemed to represent me there was, by an accident like this unwarily surprised into a net in which he lay a poor entangled slave, and brought a train of mischiefs on his head, I snatched my eyes away; they pleaded hard for leave to look again, but I grew absolute, and they obeyed.

AMANDA

Were they the only things that were inquisitive? Had I been in your place, my tongue, I fancy, had been curious, too: I should have asked her name, and where she lived (yet still without design). Who was she, pray?

LOVELESS

Indeed I cannot tell.

AMANDA

You will not tell.

LOVELESS

By all that's sacred, then, I did not ask.

AMANDA

Nor do you know what company was with her?

LOVELESS

I do not.

AMANDA

Then I am calm again.

LOVELESS

Why were you disturbed?

AMANDA

Had I then no cause?

373

LOVELESS

None, certainly.

AMANDA

I thought I had.

LOVELESS

But you thought wrong, Amanda; for turn the case, and let it be your story. Should you come home, and tell me you had seen a handsome man, should I grow jealous because you had eyes?

AMANDA

But should I tell you he were exquisitely so; that I had gazed on him with admiration; that I had looked with eager eyes upon him; should you not think 'twere possible I might go one step farther, and enquire his name?

LOVELESS

(Aside)
She has reason on her side: I have talked too much; but I must turn it off another way.
(To AMANDA)
Will you then make no difference, Amanda, between the language of our sex and yours? There is a modesty restrains your tongues which makes you speak by halves when you commend; but roving flattery gives a loose to ours, which makes us still speak double what we think: you should not therefore in so strict a sense take what I said to her advantage.

AMANDA

Those flights of flattery, Sir, are to our faces only: when women once are out of hearing, you are as modest in your commendations as we are. But I shan't put you to the trouble of farther excuses; if you please, this business shall rest here. Only give me leave to wish, both for your peace and mine, that you may never meet this miracle of beauty more.

LOVELESS

I am content.

The Relapse
by Sir John Vanbrugh

ACT III, SCENE 2—BERINTHIA, AMANDA, WOMAN

BERINTHIA

I begin to fancy there may be as much pleasure in carrying on another body's intrigue as one's own. This at least is certain, it exercises almost all the entertaining faculties of a woman: for there's employment for hypocrisy, invention, deceit, flattery, mischief, and lying.

(*Enter* AMANDA, *her* WOMAN *following her*)

WOMAN

If you please, Madam, only to say, whether you'll have me buy 'em or not.

AMANDA

Yes, no, go fiddle! I care not what you do. Prithee leave me.

WOMAN

I have done.

(*Exit* WOMAN)

BERINTHIA

What in the name of Jove's the matter with you?

AMANDA

The matter, Berinthia! I'm almost mad, I'm plagued to death.

BERINTHIA

Who is it that plagues you?

AMANDA

Who do you think should plague a wife but her husband?

BERINTHIA

O ho, is it come to that? We shall have you wish yourself a widow by and by.

AMANDA

Would I were anything but what I am! A base ungrateful man, after what I have done for him, to use me thus!

BERINTHIA

What! he has been ogling now, I'll warrant you?

AMANDA

Yes, he has been ogling.

BERINTHIA

And so you are jealous? Is that all?

AMANDA

That all! Is jealousy then nothing?

BERINTHIA

It should be nothing, if I were in your case.

AMANDA

Why, what would you do?

BERINTHIA

I'd cure myself.

AMANDA

How?

BERINTHIA

Let blood in the fond vein: care as little for my husband as he did for me.

AMANDA

That would not stop his course.

BERINTHIA

Nor nothing else, when the wind's in the warm corner. Look you, Amanda, you may build castles in the air, and fume, and fret, and grow thin and lean and pale and ugly, if you please. But I tell you, no man worth having is true to his wife, or can be true to his wife, or ever was, or ever will be so.

AMANDA

Do you then really think he's false to me? for I did but suspect him.

BERINTHIA

Think so? I know he's so.

AMANDA

Is it possible? Pray tell me what you know.

BERINTHIA

Don't press me then to name names, for that I have sworn I won't do.

AMANDA

Well, I won't; but let me know all you can without perjury.

BERINTHIA

I'll let you know enough to prevent any wise woman's dying of the pip; and I know you'll pluck up your spirits, and show, upon occasion, you can be as good a wife as the best of 'em.

AMANDA

Well, what a woman can do I'll endeavour.

BERINTHIA

Oh, a woman can do a great deal, if once she sets her mind to it. Therefore pray don't stand trifling any longer, and teasing yourself with this and that, and your love and virtue, and I know not what. But resolve to hold up your head, get a-tiptoe, and look over 'em all; for to my certain knowledge your husband is a-pickering else-where.

AMANDA

You are sure on't?

BERINTHIA

Positively; he fell in love at the play.

AMANDA

Right, the very same; do you know the ugly thing?

BERINTHIA

Yes, I know her well enough; but she's no such an ugly thing, neither.

AMANDA

Is she very handsome?

BERINTHIA

Truly, I think so.

AMANDA

Hey ho!

BERINTHIA

What do you sigh for now?

AMANDA

Oh, my heart!

BERINTHIA

(*Aside*) Only the pangs of nature! she's in labour of her love; heaven send her a quick delivery; I'm sure she has a good midwife.

AMANDA

I'm very ill, I must go to my chamber. Dear Berinthia, don't leave me a moment.

BERINTHIA

No, don't fear.

(*Aside*)

I'll see you safe brought to bed, I'll warrant you.

(*Exeunt,* AMANDA *leaning upon* BERINTHIA)

The Beaux' Stratagem
by George Farquhar

ACT IV, SCENE 1—MRS. SULLEN, DORINDA

(*Enter* MRS. SULLEN *and* DORINDA, *meeting*)

MRS. SULLEN

Well, Sister!

DORINDA

And well, Sister!

MRS. SULLEN

What's become of my lord?

DORINDA

What's become of his servant?

MRS. SULLEN

Servant! he's a prettier fellow, and a finer gentleman by fifty degrees than his master.

DORINDA

O' my conscience I fancy you could beg that fellow at the gallows-foot!

MRS. SULLEN

O' my conscience I could, provided I could put a friend of yours in his room.

DORINDA

You desired me, Sister, to leave you, when you transgressed the bounds of honour.

MRS. SULLEN

Thou dear censorious country girl! what dost mean? You can't think of the man without the bedfellow, I find.

DORINDA

I don't find anything unnatural in that thought; while the mind is conversant with flesh and blood, it must conform to the humours of the company.

MRS. SULLEN

How a little love and good company improves a woman! Why, child, you begin to live—you never spoke before.

DORINDA

Because I was never spoke to. My lord has told me that I have more wit and beauty than any of my sex; and truly I begin to think the man is sincere.

MRS. SULLEN

You're in the right, Dorinda; pride is the life of a woman, and flattery is our daily bread; and she's a fool that won't believe a man there, as much as she that believes him in anything else. But I'll lay you a guinea that I had finer things said to me than you had.

DORINDA

Done! What did your fellow say to ye?

MRS. SULLEN

My fellow took the picture of Venus for mine.

DORINDA

But my lover took me for Venus herself.

MRS. SULLEN

Common cant! Had my spark called me a Venus directly, I should have believed him a footman in good earnest.

DORINDA

But my lover was upon his knees to me.

MRS. SULLEN

And mine was upon his tiptoes to me.

DORINDA

Mine vowed to die for me.

MRS. SULLEN

Mine swore to die with me.

DORINDA

Mine spoke the softest moving things.

MRS. SULLEN

Mine had his moving things too.

DORINDA

Mine kissed my hand ten thousand times.

MRS. SULLEN

Mine has all that pleasure to come.

DORINDA

Mine offered marriage.

MRS. SULLEN

O Lard! D'ye call that a moving thing?

DORINDA

The sharpest arrow in his quiver, my dear Sister! Why, my ten thousand pounds may lie brooding here this seven years, and hatch nothing at last but some ill-natured clown like yours. Whereas, if I marry my Lord Aimwell, there will be title, place, and precedence, the Park, the play, and the drawing-room, splendour, equipage, noise, and flambeaux.—"Hey, my Lady Aimwell's servants there!—Lights, lights to the stairs!—My Lady Aimwell's coach put forward!—Stand by, make room for her Ladyship!"—Are not these things moving?——What! melancholy of a sudden?

MRS. SULLEN

Happy, happy Sister! your angel has been watchful for your happiness, whilst mine has slept regardless of his charge. Long smiling years of circling joys for you, but not one hour for me!

(*Weeps*)

DORINDA

Come my dear, we'll talk of something else.

MRS. SULLEN

O Dorinda! I own myself a woman, full of my sex, a gentle, generous soul—easy and yielding to soft desires; a spacious heart, where Love and all his train might lodge. And must the fair apartment of my breast be made a stable for a brute to lie in?

DORINDA

Meaning your husband, I suppose?

MRS. SULLEN

Husband! no—even husband is too soft a name for him.——But, come, I expect my brother here to-night or to-morrow; he was abroad when my father married me; perhaps he'll find a way to make me easy.

DORINDA

Will you promise not to make yourself easy in the meantime with my lord's friend?

MRS. SULLEN

You mistake me, Sister. It happens with us as among the men, the greatest talkers are the greatest cowards; and there's a reason for it; those spirits evaporate in prattle, which might do more mischief if they took another course. Though, to confess the truth, I do love that fellow; and if I met him dressed as he should be, and I undressed as I should be—look ye, Sister, I have no supernatural gifts—I can't swear I could resist the temptation; though I can safely promise to avoid it; and that's as much as the best of us can do.

(*Exeunt* MRS. SULLEN *and* DORINDA)

The Rover
by Aphra Behn

ACT II, SCENE 2—
ANGELLICA, WILLMORE, MORETTA

ANGELLICA

Insolent sir, how durst you pull down my picture?

WILLMORE

Rather, how durst you set it up to tempt poor am'rous mortals with so much excellence, which I find you have but too well consulted by the unmerciful price you set upon't. Is all this heaven of beauty shown to move despair in those that cannot buy? And can you think th'effects of that despair should be less extravagant than I have shown?

ANGELLICA

I sent for you to ask my pardon, sir, not to aggravate your crime. I thought I should have seen you at my feet imploring it.

WILLMORE

You are deceived. I came to rail at you, and rail such truths too,
as shall let you see the vanity of that pride which taught you how
to set such a price on sin.
For such it is whilst that which is love's due
Is meanly barter'd for.

ANGELLICA

Ha! Ha! Ha! Alas, good captain, what pity 'tis your edifying doctrine
will do no good upon me. Moretta, fetch the gentleman a glass,
and let him survey himself to see what charms he has.—
(*Aside, in a soft tone*)
And guess my business.

MORETTA

Good weatherbeaten corporal, will you march off? We have no
need of your doctrine, though you have of our charity. But at
present we have no scraps; we can afford no kindness for God's
sake. In fine, sirrah, the price is too high i'th'mouth for you, therefore troop, I say.

ANGELLICA

Nay, do not abuse the poor creature.

WILLMORE

Yes, I am poor. But I'm a gentleman,
And one that scorns this baseness which you practice.
Poor as I am I would not sell myself.
No, not to gain your charming high-priz'd person.
Though I admire you strangely for your beauty,
Yet I contemn your mind.
And yet I would at any rate enjoy you;
At your own rate; but cannot. See here
The only sum I can command on earth:
I know not where to eat when this is gone.
Yet such a slave I am to love and beauty
This last reserve I'll sacrifice to enjoy you.
Nay, do not frown, I know you're to be bought,
And would be bought by me. By me,

For a meaning trifling sum, if I could pay it down.
Which happy knowledge I will still repeat,
And lay it to my heart: it has a virtue in't,
And soon will cure those wounds your eyes have made.
And yet, there's something so divinely powerful there—
Nay, I will gaze, to let you see my strength.
(*Holds her, looks on her, and pauses and sighs*)
By heav'n, bright creature, I would not for the world
Thy fame were half so fair as is thy face.

(*Turns her away from him*)

ANGELLICA

(*Aside*)
His words go through me to the very soul—
If you have nothing else to say to me—

WILLMORE

Yes, you shall hear how infamous you are—
For which I do not hate thee—
But that secures my heart, and all the flames it feels
Are but so many lusts:
I know it by their sudden bold intrusion.
The fire's impatient and betrays; 'tis false.
For had it been the purer flame of love,
I should have pin'd and languish'd at your feet,
Ere found the impudence to have discover'd it.
I now dare stand your scorn and your denial.

MORETTA

(*Aside*)
Sure she's bewitched, that she can stand thus tamely and hear his
saucy railing—Sirrah, will you be gone?

ANGELLICA

(*to* MORETTA)
How dare you take this liberty! Withdraw! —Pray tell me, sir, are
not you guilty of the same mercenary crime? When a lady is pro-

posed to you for a wife, you never ask how fair, discreet, or virtuous she is, but what's her fortune; which, if but small, you cry "She will not do my business," and basely leave her, though she languish for you. Say, is not this as poor?

WILLMORE

It is a barbarous custom, which I will scorn to defend in our sex, and do despise in yours.

ANGELLICA

Thou'rt a brave fellow! Put up thy gold, and know,
That were thy fortune as large as is thy soul,
Thou shouldst not buy my love
Couldst thou forget those mean effects of vanity
Which set me out to sale,
And as a lover prize my yielding joys.
Canst thou believe they'll be entirely thine,
Without considering they were mercenary?

WILLMORE

I cannot tell, I must bethink me first.
(*Aside*)
Ha! Death, I'm going to believe her.

ANGELLICA

Prithee confirm that faith, or if thou canst not,
Flatter me a little: 'twill please me from thy mouth.

WILLMORE

(*Aside*)
Curse on thy charming tongue! Dost thou return
My feign'd contempt with so much subtlety?—
Thou'st found the easiest way into my heart,
Though I yet know that all thou say'st is false.

(Turning from her in rage)

ANGELLICA

By all that's good, 'tis real;
I never lov'd before, though oft a mistress.
Shall my first vows be slighted?

WILLMORE

(Aside)
What can she mean?

ANGELLICA

(In an angry tone)
I find you cannot credit me.

WILLMORE

I know you take me for an errant ass,
An ass that may be sooth'd into belief,
And then be us'd at pleasure;
But, madam, I have been so often cheated
By perjured, soft, deluding hypocrites,
That I've no faith left for the cozening sex,
Expecially for women of your trade.

ANGELLICA

The low esteem you have of me perhaps
May bring my heart again:
For I have pride that yet surmounts my love.

(She turns with pride; he holds her)

WILLMORE

Throw off this pride, this enemy to bliss,
And show the power of love: 'tis with those arms
I can be only vanquish'd, made a slave.

ANGELLICA

Is all thy mighty expectation vanish'd?
No, I will not hear thee talk; thou hast a charm

In every word that draws my heart away,
And all the thousand trophies I design'd
Thou hast undone. Why art thou soft?
Thy looks are bravely rough, and meant for war.
Couldst thou not storm on still?
I then perhaps had been as free as thou.

WILLMORE
(*Aside*)
Death, how she throws her fire about my soul!—
Take heed, fair creature, how you raise my hopes,
Which once assum'd pretends to all dominion:
There's not a joy thou has in store
I shall not then command.
For which I'll pay you back my soul, my life!
Come, let's begin th'account this happy minute!

ANGELLICA
And will you pay me then the price I ask?

WILLMORE
Oh, why dost thou draw me from an awful worship,
By showing thou are no divinity.
Conceal the fiend, and show me all the angel!
Keep me but ignorant, and I'll be devout
And pay my vows forever at this shrine.

(*Kneels and kisses her hand*)

ANGELLICA
The pay I mean is but thy love for mine.
Can you give that?

WILLMORE
Entirely. Come, let's withdraw where I'll renew my vows, and
breathe 'em with such ardor thou shalt not doubt my zeal.

ANGELLICA

Thou hast a power too strong to be resisted.

The Rover
by Aphra Behn

ACT IV, SCENE 2—
WILLMORE, ANGELLICA, HELLENA,
MORETTA, SEBASTIAN

WILLMORE

How now, turned shadow?
Fly when I pursue, and follow when I fly?
(*Sings*)

> *Stay, gentle shadow of my dove,*
> *And tell me ere I go,*
> *Whether the substance may not prove*
> *A fleeting thing like you.*

(*As she turns she looks on him*)

There's a soft kind look remaining yet.

ANGELLICA

Well, sir, you may be gay: all happiness, all joys pursue you still.
Fortune's your slave, and gives you every hour choice of new hearts
and beauties, till you are cloyed with the repeated bliss which others
vainly languish for. But know, false man, that I shall be revenged.

(*Turns away in rage*)

WILLMORE

So, gad, there are of those faint-hearted lovers, whom such a sharp
lesson next their hearts would make as impotent as fourscore. Pox

o' this whining; my business is to laugh and love. A pox on't, I hate your sullen lover: a man shall lose as much time to put you in humor now as would serve to gain a new woman.

ANGELLICA

I scorn to cool that fire I cannot raise,
Or do the drudgery of your virtuous mistress.

WILLMORE

A virtuous mistress? Death, what a thing thou hast found out for me! Why, what the devil should I do with a virtuous woman, a sort of ill-natured creatures that take a pride to torment a lover. Virtue is but an infirmity in woman, a disease that renders even the handsome ungrateful; whilst the ill-favored, for want of solicitations and address, only fancy themselves so. I have lain with a woman of quality who has all the while been railing at whores.

ANGELLICA

I will not answer for your mistress's virtue,
Though she be young enough to know no guilt;
And I could wish you would persuade my heart
'Twas the two hundred thousand crowns you courted.

WILLMORE

Two hundred thousand crowns! What story's this? What trick? What woman, ha?

ANGELLICA

How strange you make it. Have you forgot the creature you entertained on the Piazzo last night?

WILLMORE

(Aside)
Ha! My gipsy worth two hundred thousand crowns! Oh, how I long to be with her! Pox, I knew she was of quality.

ANGELLICA

False man! I see my ruin in thy face.
How many vows you breathed upon my bosom
Never to be unjust. Have you forgot so soon?

WILLMORE

Faith, no; I was just coming to repeat 'em. But here's a humor
indeed would make a man a saint.—
(*Aside*)
Would she would be angry enough to leave me, and command me
not to wait on her.

(*Enter* HELLENA *dressed in man's clothes*)

HELLENA

This must be Angellica: I know it by her mumping matron here.
Ay, ay, 'tis she. My mad captain's with her, too, for all his swearing.
How this unconstant humor makes me love him!—Pray, good grave
gentlewoman, is not this Angellica?

MORETTA

My too young sir, it is.—
(*Aside*)
I hope 'tis one from Don Antonio.

(*Goes to* ANGELLICA)

HELLENA

(*Aside*)
Well, something I'll do to vex him for this.

ANGELLICA

I will not speak with him. Am I in humor to receive a lover?

WILLMORE

Not speak with him? Why, I'll be gone, and wait your idler minutes.
Can I show less obedience to the thing I love so fondly?

(*Offers to go*)

ANGELLICA
A fine excuse this! Stay—

WILLMORE
And hinder your advantage? Should I repay your bounties so ungratefully?

ANGELLICA
(*to* HELLENA)
Come hither, boy.—
(*to* WILLMORE)
That I may let you see
How much above the advantages you name
I prize one minute's joy with you.

WILLMORE
(*Impatient to be gone*)
Oh, you destroy me with this endearment.—
(*Aside*)
Death, how shall I get away?—Madam, 'twill not be fit I should be seen with you. Besides, it will not be convenient. And I've a friend—that's dangerously sick.

ANGELLICA
I see you're impatient. Yet you shall stay.

WILLMORE
(*Aside*)
And miss my assignation with my gipsy.

(*Walks about impatiently;* MORETTA *brings* HELLENA, *who addresses herself to* ANGELLICA)

HELLENA
Madam,
You'll hardly pardon my instrusion

When you shall know my business,
And I'm too young to tell my tale with art;
But there must be a wondrous store of goodness
Where so much beauty dwells.

ANGELLICA

A pretty advocate, whoever sent thee.
Prithee proceed.
(*To* WILLMORE, *who is stealing off*)
—Nay, sir, you shall not go.

WILLMORE

(*Aside*)
Then I shall lose my dear gipsy forever. Pox on't, she stays me out
of spite.

HELLENA

I am related to a lady, madam,
Young, rich, and nobly born, but has the fate
To be in love with a young English gentleman.
Strangely she loves him, at first sight she loved him,
But did adore him when she heard him speak;
For he, she said, had charms in every word
That failed not to surprise, to wound and conquer.

WILLMORE

(*Aside*)
Ha! Egad, I hope this concerns me.

ANGELLICA

(*Aside*)
'Tis my false man he means. Would he were gone:
This praise will raise his pride, and ruin me.
(*To* WILLMORE)
—Well, Since you are so impatient to be gone,
I will release you, sir.

WILLMORE

(*Aside*)

Nay, then I'm sure 'twas me he spoke of: this cannot be the effects
of kindness in her.—No, Madam, I've considered better on't, and
will not give you cause of jealousy.

ANGELLICA

But sir, I've business that—

WILLMORE

This shall not do; I know 'tis but to try me.

ANGELLICA

Well, to your story, boy.—
(*Aside*)
Though 'twill undo me.

HELLENA

With this addition to his other beauties,
He won her unresisting tender heart.
He vowed, and sighed, and swore he lov'd her dearly;
And she believ'd the cunning flatterer,
And thought herself the happiest maid alive.
Today was the appointed time by both
To consummate their bliss:
The virgin, altar, and the priest were dress'd;
And whilst she languished for th'expected bridegroom,
She heard he paid his broken vows to you.

WILLMORE

(*Aside*)

So, this is some dear rogue that's in love with me, and this way lets
me know it. Or, if it be not me, he means someone whose place I
may supply.

ANGELLICA

Now I perceive
The cause of thy impatience to be gone,
And all the business of this glorious dress.

WILLMORE

Damn the young prater; I know not what he means.

HELLENA

Madam,
In your fair eyes I read too much concern
To tell my farther business.

ANGELLICA

Prithee, sweet youth, talk on: thou mayst perhaps
Raise here a storm that may undo my passion,
And then I'll grant thee anything.

HELLENA

Madam, 'tis to entreat you (oh unreasonable)
You would not see this stranger.
For it you do, she vows you are undone;
Though nature never made a man so excellent,
And sure he'd been a god, but for inconstancy.

WILLMORE

(Aside)
Ah, rogue, how finely he's instructed! 'Tis plain, some woman that
has seen me *en passant.*

ANGELLICA

Oh, I shall burst with jealousy! Do you know the man you
speak of?

HELLENA

Yes, madam, he used to be in buff and scarlet.

ANGELLICA

(To WILLMORE)
Thou false as hell, what canst thou say to this?

WILLMORE

By heaven—

ANGELLICA

Hold, do not damn thyself—

HELLENA

Nor hope to be believed.

(*He walks about; they follow*)

. ANGELLICA

Oh perjured man!
Is't thus you pay my generous passion back?

HELLENA

Why would you, sir, abuse my lady's faith?

ANGELLICA

And use me so unhumanely.

HELLENA

A maid so young, so innocent—

WILLMORE

Ah, young devil!

ANGELLICA

Dost thou not know thy life is in my power?

HELLENA

Or think my lady cannot be revenged?

WILLMORE

(*Aside*)
So, so, the storm comes finely on.

ANGELLICA

Now thou art silent: guilt has struck thee dumb.
Oh, hadst thou still been so, I'd lived in safety.

(She turns away and weeps)

WILLMORE

(Aside to HELLENA)
Sweetheart, the lady's name and house—quickly! I'm impatient to
be with her.

*(Looks toward ANGELLICA to watch her turning, and as she comes
towards them he meets her)*

HELLENA

(Aside)
So, now is he for another woman.

WILLMORE

The impudent'st young thing in nature: I cannot persuade him out
of his error, madam.

ANGELLICA

I know he's in the right; yet thou'st a tongue
That would persuade him to deny his faith.

(In rage walks away)

WILLMORE

(Said softly to HELLENA)
Her name, her name, dear boy!

HELLENA

Have you forgot it, sir?

WILLMORE

(Aside)
Oh, I perceive he's not to know I am a stranger to his lady.
—Yes, yes, I do know, but I have forgot the—
(ANGELLICA *turns*)
—By heaven, such early confidence I never saw.

ANGELLICA

Did I not charge you with this mistress, sir?
Which you denied, though I beheld your perjury.
This little generosity of thine has rendered back my heart.

(*Walks away*)

WILLMORE

(*To* HELLENA)

So, you have made sweet work here, my little mischief. Look your
lady be kind and good-natured now, or I shall have but a cursed
bargain on't.
(ANGELLICA *turns toward them*)
—The rogue's bred up to mischief; art thou so great a fool to credit
him?

ANGELLICA

Yes, I do, and you in vain impose upon me. Come hither, boy. Is
not this he you spake of?

HELLENA

I think it is. I cannot swear, but I vow he has just such another
lying lover's look.

(HELLENA *looks in his face; he gazes on her*)

WILLMORE

(*Aside*)

Ha! Do I not know that face? By heaven, my little gipsy! What a
dull dog was I: had I but looked that way I'd known her. Are all
my hopes of a new woman banished?—Egad, if I do not fit thee
for this, hang me.—
(*To* ANGELLICA)
Madam, I have found out the plot.

HELLENA

(*Aside*)
Oh lord, what does he say? Am I discovered now?

WILLMORE

Do you see this young spark here?

HELLENA

(*Aside*)
He'll tell her who I am.

WILLMORE

Who do you think this is?

HELLENA

(*Aside*)
Ay, ay, he does know me.—Nay, dear captain, I am undone if you discover me.

WILLMORE

Nay, nay, no cogging; she shall know what a precious mistress I have.

HELLENA

Will you be such a devil?

WILLMORE

Nay, nay, I'll teach you to spoil sport you will not make.—This small ambassador comes not from a person of quality, as you imagine and he says, but from a very errant gipsy: the talking'st, prating'st, canting'st little animal thou ever saw'st.

ANGELLICA

What news you tell me, that's the thing I mean.

HELLENA

(*Aside*)
Would I were well off the place! If ever I go a-captain-hunting
again—

WILLMORE

Mean that thing? That gipsy thing? Thou mayst as well be jealous
of thy monkey or parrot as of her. A German motion were worth
a dozen of her, and a dream were a better enjoyment—a creature
of a constitution fitter for heaven than man.

HELLENA

(*Aside*)
Though I'm sure he lies, yet this vexes me.

ANGELLICA

You are mistaken: she's a Spanish woman made up of no such dull
materials.

WILLMORE

Materials? Egad, an she be made of any that will either dispense
or admit of love, I'll be bound to continence.

HELLENA

(*Aside to him*)
Unreasonable man, do you think so?

WILLMORE

You may return, my little brazen head, and tell your lady, that till
she be handsome enough to be beloved, or I dull enough to be
religious, there will be small hopes of me.

ANGELLICA

Did you not promise, then, to marry her?

WILLMORE

Not I, by heaven.

ANGELLICA

You cannot undeceive my fears and torments, till you have vowed you will not marry her.

HELLENA

(*Aside*)

If he swears that, he'll be revenged on me indeed for all my rogueries.

ANGELLICA

I know what arguments you'll bring against me: fortune and honor.

WILLMORE

Honor! I tell you, I hate it in your sex; and those that fancy themselves possessed of that foppery are the most impertinently troublesome of all womankind, and will transgress nine commandments to keep one. And to satisfy your jealousy, I swear—

HELLENA

(*Aside to him*)

Oh, no swearing, dear captain.

WILLMORE

If it were possible I should ever be inclined to marry, it should be some kind young sinner: one that has generosity enough to give a favor handsomely to one that can ask it discreetly, one that has wit enough to manage an intrigue of love. Oh, how civil such a wench is to a man that does her the honor to marry her.

ANGELLICA

By heaven, there's no faith in anything he says.

(*Enter* SEBASTIAN)

SEBASTIAN

Madam, Don Antonio—

ANGELLICA

Come hither.

HELLENA

(*Aside*)

Ha! Antonio! He may be coming hither, and he'll certainly discover me. I'll therefore retire without a ceremony.

(*Exit* HELLENA)

ANGELLICA

I'll see him. Get my coach ready.

SEBASTIAN

It waits you, madam.

WILLMORE

(*Aside*)

This is lucky.—What, madam, now I may be gone and leave you to the enjoyment of my rival?

ANGELLICA

Dull man, that canst not see how ill, how poor,
That false dissimulation looks. Be gone,
And never let me see thy cozening face again,
Lest I relapse and kill thee.

WILLMORE

Yes, you can spare me now. Farewell, till you're in better humor.—
(*Aside*)
I'm glad of this release. Now for my gipsy;
For though to worse we change, yet still we find
New joys, new charms, in a new miss that's kind.

(*Exit* WILLMORE)

ANGELLICA

He's gone, and in this ague of my soul
The shivering fit returns.
Oh, with what willing haste he took his leave,

As if the longed-for minute were arrived
Of some blest assignation.
In vain I have consulted all my charms,
In vain this beauty prized, in vain believed
My eyes could kindle any lasting fires;
I had forgot my name, my infamy,
And the reproach that honor lays on those
That dare pretend a sober passion here.
Nice reputation, though it leave behind
More virtues than inhabit where that dwells,
Yet that once gone, those virtues shine no more.
Then since I am not fit to be beloved,
I am resolved to think on a revenge
On him that soothed me thus to my undoing.

(Exeunt)

The Rover
by Aphra Behn
ACT V—WILLMORE, HELLENA

WILLMORE
Ha! My gipsy! Now a thousand blessings on thee for this kindness.
Egad, child, I was e'en in despair of ever seeing thee again; my
friends are all provided for within, each man his kind woman.

HELLENA
Ha! I thought they had served me some such trick!

WILLMORE
And I was e'en resolved to go aboard, and condemn myself to my
lone cabin, and the thoughts of thee.

HELLENA

And could you have left me behind? Would you have been so ill natured?

WILLMORE

Why, 'twould have broke my heart, child. But since we are met again, I defy foul weather to part us.

HELLENA

And would you be a faithful friend now, if a maid should trust you?

WILLMORE

For a friend I cannot promise: thou art of a form so excellent, a face and humor too good for cold dull friendship. I am parlously afraid of being in love, child; and you have not forgotten how severely you have used me?

HELLENA

That's all one; such usage you must still look for: to find out all your haunts, to rail at you to all that love you, till I have made you love only me in your own defense, because nobody else will love you.

WILLMORE

But hast thou no better quality to recommend thyself by?

HELLENA

Faith, none, captain. Why, 'twill be the greater charity to take me for thy mistress. I am a lone child, a kind of orphan lover; and why I should die a maid, and in a captain's hands too, I do not understand.

WILLMORE

Egad, I was never clawed away with broadsides from any female before. Thou hast one virtue I adore—good nature. I hate a coy demure mistress, she's as troublesome as a colt; I'll break none. No, give me a mad mistress when mewed, and in flying, one I dare trust upon the wing, that whilst she's kind will come to the lure.

HELLENA

Nay, as kind as you will, good captain, whilst it lasts. But let's lose no time.

WILLMORE

My time's as precious to me as thine can be. Therefore, dear creature, since we are so well agreed, let's retire to my chamber; and if ever thou wert treated with such savory love! Come, my bed's prepared for such a guest all clean and sweet as thy fair self. I love to steal a dish and a bottle with a friend, and hate long graces. Come, let's retire and fall to.

HELLENA

'Tis but getting my consent, and the business is soon done. Let but old gaffer Hymen and his priest say amen to't, and I dare lay my mother's daughter by as proper a fellow as your father's son, without fear or blushing.

WILLMORE

Hold, hold, no bug words, child. Priest and Hymen? Prithee add a hangman to 'em to make up the consort. No, no, we'll have no vows but love, child, nor witness but the lover: the kind deity enjoins naught but love and enjoy. Hymen and priest wait still upon portion and jointure; love and beauty have their own ceremonies. Marriage is as certain a bane to love as lending money is to friendship. I'll neither ask nor give a vow, though I could be content to turn gipsy and become a left-handed bridegroom to have the pleasure of working that great miracle of making a maid a mother, if you durst venture. 'Tis upse gipsy that, and if I miss I'll lose my labor.

HELLENA

And if you do not lose, what shall I get? A cradle full of noise and mischief, with a pack of repentance at my back? Can you teach me to weave incle to pass my time with? 'Tis upse gipsy that, too.

WILLMORE

I can teach thee to weave a true love's knot better.

HELLENA

So can my dog.

WILLMORE

Well, I see we are both upon our guards, and I see there's no way to conquer good nature but by yielding. Here, give me thy hand: one kiss, and I am thine.

HELLENA

One kiss! How like my page he speaks! I am resolved you shall have none, for asking such a sneaking sum. He that will be satisfied with one kiss will never die of that longing. Good friend single-kiss, is all your talking come to this? A kiss, a caudle! Farewell, captain single-kiss.

(*Going out; he stays her*)

WILLMORE

Nay, if we part so, let me die like a bird upon a bough, at the sheriff's charge. By heaven, both the Indies shall not buy thee from me. I adore thy humor and will marry thee, and we are so of one humor it must be a bargain. Give me thy hand.
(*Kisses her hand*)
And now let the blind ones, love and fortune, do their worst.

HELLENA

Why, god-a-mercy, captain!

WILLMORE

But hark'ee: the bargain is now made, but is it not fit we should know each other's names, that when we have reason to curse one another hereafter, and people ask me who 'tis I give to the devil, I may at least be able to tell what family you came of?

HELLENA

Good reason, captain; and where I have cause, as I doubt not but I shall have plentiful, that I may know at whom to throw my— blessings, I beseech ye your name.

WILLMORE

I am called Robert the Constant.

HELLENA

A very fine name! Pray was it your faulkner or butler that christened you? Do they not use to whistle when they call you?

WILLMORE

I hope you have a better, that a man may name without crossing himself—you are so merry with mine.

HELLENA

I am called Hellena the Inconstant.

Venice Preserved
by Thomas Otway

ACT II, SCENE 2—JAFFEIR, PIERRE

JAFFEIR

I am here; and thus, the shades of night around me,
I look as if all hell were in my heart,
And I in hell. Nay, surely, 'tis so with me;
For every step I tread methinks some fiend
Knocks at my breast and bids it not be quiet.
I've heard how desperate wretches like myself
Have wander'd out at this dead time of night
To meet the foe of mankind in his walk;
Sure, I'm so curst that, though of heav'n forsaken,
No minister of darkness cares to tempt me.
Hell! Hell! why sleepest thou?

(*Enter* PIERRE)

PIERRE

Sure, I have stay'd too long;
The clock has struck, and I may lose my proselyte.
——Speak, who goes there?

JAFFEIR

A dog that comes to howl
At yonder moon. What's he that asks the question?

PIERRE

A friend to dogs, for they are honest creatures,
And ne'er betray their masters; never fawn
On any that they love not. Well met, friend.
—Jaffeir!

JAFFEIR

The same. O Pierre! thou art come in season:
I was just going to pray.

PIERRE

Ah, that's mechanic:
Priests make a trade on't, and yet starve by't, too:
No praying; it spoils business, and time's precious.
Where's Belvidera?

JAFFEIR

For a day or two
I've lodg'd her privately, till I see farther
What fortune will do with me. Prithee, friend,
If thou wouldst have me fit to hear good counsel,
Speak not of Belvidera——

PIERRE

Speak not of her!

JAFFEIR

Oh, no!

PIERRE

Nor name her? Maybe I wish her well.

JAFFEIR

Who well?

PIERRE

Thy wife, thy lovely Belvidera;
I hope a man may wish his friend's wife well,
And no harm done!

JAFFEIR

Y'are merry, Pierre!

PIERRE

I am so.
Thou shalt smile too, and Belvidera smile;
We'll all rejoice.
(*Gives him a purse*)
Here's something to buy pins,
Marriage is chargeable.

JAFFEIR

I but half wished
To see the devil, and he's here already.
——Well!
What must this buy—rebellion, murder, treason?
Tell me which way I must be damn'd for this.

PIERRE

When last we parted, we had no qualms like these,
But entertain'd each other's thoughts like men
Whose souls were well acquainted. Is the world
Reform'd since our last meeting? What new miracles
Have happen'd? Has Priuli's heart relented?
Can he be honest?

JAFFEIR

Kind heav'n! let heavy curses
Gall his old age! cramps, aches, rack his bones,
And bitterest disquiet wring his heart!
Oh, let him live till life become his burden;
Let him groan under't long, linger an age
In the worst agonies and pangs of death,
And find its ease but late!

PIERRE

Nay, couldst thou not
As well, my friend, have stretch'd the curse to all
The Senate round, as to one single villain?

JAFFEIR

But curses stick not. Could I kill with cursing,
By heav'n, I know not thirty heads in Venice
Should not be blasted; senators should rot
Like dogs on dunghills, but their wives and daughters
Die of their own diseases. Oh for a curse
To kill with!

PIERRE

Daggers, daggers, are much better.

JAFFEIR

Ha!

PIERRE

Daggers.

JAFFEIR

But where are they?

PIERRE

Oh, a thousand
May be dispos'd in honest hands in Venice.

JAFFEIR

Thou talk'st in clouds.

PIERRE

But yet a heart half wrong'd
As thine has been, would find the meaning, Jaffeir.

JAFFEIR

A thousand daggers, all in honest hands,
And have not I a friend will stick one here?

PIERRE

Yes, if I thought thou were not to be cherish'd
To a nobler purpose, I'd be that friend.
But thou hast better friends, friends whom thy wrongs
Have made thy friends, friends worthy to be call'd so.
I'll trust thee with a secret: there are spirits
This hour at work. But as thou art a man
Whom I have pick'd and chosen from the world,
Swear that thou wilt be true to what I utter;
And when I have told thee that which only gods
And men like gods are privy to, then swear
No chance or change shall wrest it from thy bosom.

JAFFEIR

When thou wouldst bind me, is there need of oaths?
(Green-sickness girls lose maidenheads with such counters!)
For thou art so near my heart that thou mayst see
Its bottom, sound its strength and firmness to thee.
Is coward, fool, or villain in my face?
If I seem none of these, I dare believe
Thou wouldst not use me in a little cause,
For I am fit for honour's toughest task,
Nor ever yet found fooling was my province;
And for a villainous, inglorious enterprise,
I know thy heart so well, I dare lay mine
Before thee, set it to what point thou wilt.

PIERRE

Nay, it's a cause thou wilt be fond of, Jaffeir,
For it is founded on the noblest basis—
Our liberties, our natural inheritance.
There's no religion, no hypocrisy in't;
We'll do the business, and ne'er fast and pray for't;
Openly act a deed the world shall gaze
With wonder at, and envy when 'tis done.

JAFFEIR

For liberty!

PIERRE

For liberty, my friend!
Thou shalt be freed from base Priuli's tyranny,
And thy sequestred fortunes heal'd again.
I shall be freed from opprobrious wrongs
That press me now and bend my spirit downward:
All Venice free, and every growing merit
Succeed to its just right: fools shall be pull'd
From wisdom's seat—those baleful, unclean birds,
Those lazy owls, who (perch'd near fortune's top)
Sit only watchful with their heavy wings
To cuff down new fledg'd virtues, that would rise
To nobler heights and make the grove harmonious.

JAFFEIR

What can I do?

PIERRE

Canst thou not kill a senator?

JAFFEIR

Were there one wise or honest, I could kill him
For herding with that nest of fools and knaves.

By all my wrongs, thou talk'st as if revenge
Were to be had, and the brave story warms me.

PIERRE

Swear then!

JAFFEIR

I do, by all those glittering stars
And yond great ruling planet of the night!
By all good pow'rs above, and ill below,
By love and friendship, dearer than my life,
No pow'r or death shall make me false to thee!

PIERRE

Here we embrace, and I'll unlock my heart.
A council's held hard by, where the destruction
Of this great empire's hatching: there I'll lead thee!
But be a man, for thou art to mix with men
Fit to disturb the peace of all the world,
And rule it when it's wildest.

JAFFEIR

I give thee thanks
For this kind warning. Yes, I will be a man,
And charge thee, Pierre, whene'er thou see'st my fears
Betray me less, to rip this heart of mine
Out of my breast, and show it for a coward's.
Come, let's begone, for from this hour I chase
All little thoughts, all tender human follies
Out of my bosom. Vengeance shall have room—
Revenge!

PIERRE

And liberty!

JAFFEIR

Revenge! Revenge——

Venice Preserved
by Thomas Otway

ACT IV, SCENE 1—
JAFFEIR, BELVIDERA

JAFFEIR

Where dost thou lead me? Every step I move,
Methinks I tread upon some mangled limb
Of a rack'd friend. O my dear charming ruin!
Where are we wand'ring?

BELVIDERA

To eternal honour;
To do a deed shall chronicle thy name
Among the glorious legends of those few
That have sav'd sinking nations. Thy renown
Shall be the future song of all the virgins
Who by thy piety have been preserv'd
From horrid violation. Every street
Shall be adorn'd with statues to thy honour,
And at thy feet this great inscription written,
Remember him that propp'd the fall of Venice.

JAFFEIR

Rather, remember him who, after all
The sacred bonds of oaths and holier friendship,
In fond compassion to a woman's tears,
Forgot his manhood, virtue, truth and honour,
To sacrifice the bosom that reliev'd him.
Why wilt thou damn me?

BELVIDERA

O inconstant man!
How will you promise? how will you deceive?

414

Do, return back, replace me in my bondage,
Tell all thy friends how dangerously thou lov'st me,
And let thy dagger do its bloody office.
Oh, that kind dagger, Jaffeir, how 'twill look
Stuck through my heart, drench'd in my blood to th'hilts!
Whilst these poor dying eyes shall with their tears
No more torment thee, then thou wilt be free.
Or if thou think'st it nobler, let me live
Till I am a victim to the hateful lust
Of that infernal devil, that old fiend
That's damn'd himself and would undo mankind:
Last night, my love!

JAFFEIR

Name, name it not again.
It shows a beastly image to my fancy
Will wake me into madness. Oh, the villain!
That durst approach such purity as thine
On terms so vile! Destruction, swift destruction
Fall on my coward head, and make my name
The common scorn of fools if I forgive him!
If I forgive him, if I not revenge
With utmost rage, and most unstaying fury,
Thy sufferings, thou dear darling of my life, love!

BELVIDERA

Delay no longer then, but to the Senate;
And tell the dismal'st story e'er was utter'd:
Tell 'em what bloodshed, rapines, desolations,
Have been prepar'd, how near's the fatal hour!
Save thy poor country, save the reverend blood
Of all its nobles, which to-morrow's dawn
Must else see shed. Save the poor, tender lives
Of all those little infants which the swords
Of murderers are whetting for this moment.
Think thou already hear'st their dying screams,
Think that thou seest their sad, distracted mothers
Kneeling before thy feet, and begging pity,

With torn, dishevell'd hair and streaming eyes,
Their naked, mangled breasts besmear'd with blood,
And even the milk with which their fondled babes
Softly they hush'd, dropping in anguish from 'em.
Think thou seest this, and then consult thy heart.

JAFFEIR

Oh!

BELVIDERA

Think too, if thou lose this present minute,
What miseries the next day bring upon thee.
Imagine all the horrors of that night,
Murder and rapine, waste and desolation,
Confusedly ranging. Think what then may prove
My lot! The ravisher may then come safe,
And 'midst the terror of the public ruin
Do a damn'd deed—perhaps to lay a train
May catch thy life; then where will be revenge,
The dear revenge that's due to such a wrong?

JAFFEIR

By all heaven's powers, prophetic truth dwells in thee;
For every word thou speak'st strikes through my heart
Like a new light, and shows it how't has wander'd.
Just what th'hast made me, take me, Belvidera,
And lead me to the place where I'm to say
This bitter lesson, where I must betray
My truth, my virtue, constancy, and friends.
Must I betray my friends? Ah, take me quickly,
Secure me well before that thought's renew'd;
If I relapse once more, all's lost forever.

BELVIDERA

Hast thou a friend more dear than Belvidera?

JAFFEIR

No, th'art my soul itself; wealth, friendship, honour,
All present joys, and earnest of all future,

Are summ'd in thee: methinks when in thy arms
Thus leaning on thy breast, one minute's more
Than a long thousand years of vulgar hours.
Why was such happiness not given me pure?
Why dash'd with cruel wrongs, and bitter wantings?
Come, lead me forward now like a tame lamb
To sacrifice; thus in his fatal garlands,
Deck'd fine, and pleas'd, the wanton skips and plays,
   Trots by th'enticing, flatt'ring priestess' side,
   And much transported with his little pride,
   Forgets his dear companions of the plain
   Till by her, bound, he's on the altar lain;
   Yet then too hardly bleats, such pleasure's in the pain.

All for Love
by John Dryden
ACT III—OCTAVIA, CLEOPATRA

OCTAVIA

I need not ask if you are Cleopatra;
Your haughty carriage——

CLEOPATRA

Shows I am a queen:
Nor need I ask you who you are.

OCTAVIA

A Roman:
A name that makes and can unmake a queen.

CLEOPATRA

Your lord, the man who serves me, is a Roman.

OCTAVIA

He was a Roman, till he lost that name,
To be a slave in Egypt; but I come
To free him thence.

CLEOPATRA

Peace, peace, my lover's Juno.
When he grew weary of that household clog,
He chose my easier bonds.

OCTAVIA

I wonder not
Your bonds are easy; you have long been practis'd
In that lascivious art: he's not the first
For whom you spread your snares: let Caesar witness.

CLEOPATRA

I lov'd not Caesar; 'twas but gratitude
I paid his love. The worst your malice can;
Is but to say the greatest of mankind
Has been my slave. The next, but far above him
In my esteem, is he whom law calls yours,
But whom his love made mine.

OCTAVIA

(*Coming up close to her*)
I would view nearer
That face which has so long usurp'd my right,
To find th' inevitable charms that catch
Mankind so sure, that ruin'd my dear lord.

CLEOPATRA

Oh, you do well to search; for had you known
But half these charms, you had not lost his heart.

OCTAVIA

Far be their knowledge from a Roman Lady,
Far from a modest wife! Shame of our sex,

418

Dost thou not blush to own those black endearments
That make sin pleasing?

CLEOPATRA

You may blush, who want 'em.
If bounteous nature, if indulgent heav'n
Have giv'n me charms to please the bravest man,
Should I not thank 'em? Should I be asham'd,
And not be proud? I am, that he has lov'd me;
And, when I love not him, heav'n change this face
For one like that.

OCTAVIA

Thou lov'st him not so well.

CLEOPATRA

I love him better, and deserve him more.

OCTAVIA

You do not, cannot: you have been his ruin.
Who made him cheap at Rome, but Cleopatra?
Who made him scorn'd abroad, but Cleopatra?
At Actium, who betray'd him? Cleopatra.
Who made his children orphans, and poor me
A wretched widow? only Cleopatra.

CLEOPATRA

Yet she who loves him best is Cleopatra.
If you have suffer'd, I have suffer'd more.
You bear the specious title of a wife
To gild your cause, and draw the pitying world
To favour it: the world contemns poor me,
For I have lost my honour, lost my fame,
And stain'd the glory of my royal house,
And all to bear the branded name of mistress.
There wants but life, and that too I would lose
For him I love.

Be't so, then; take thy wish.

(*Exit cum suis*)

The Beggar's Opera
by John Gay

ACT I, SCENES 7–11—POLLY, PEACHUM, MRS. PEACHUM

SCENE 7

POLLY

I know as well as any of the fine ladies how to make the most of myself and of my man too. A woman knows how to be mercenary, though she hath never been in a court or at an assembly. We have it in our natures, Papa. If I allow Captain Macheath some trifling liberties, I have this watch and other visible marks of his favour to show for it. A girl who cannot grant some things, and refuse what is most material, will make but a poor hand of her beauty, and soon be thrown upon the common.

AIR VI.   *What shall I do to show how much I love her?*

> *Virgins are like the fair flower in its lustre,*
>   *Which in the garden enamels the ground;*
> *Near it the bees in play flutter and cluster,*
>   *And gaudy butterflies frolic around.*
> *But, when once pluck'd, 'tis no longer alluring,*
>   *To Covent Garden 'tis sent (as yet sweet),*
> *There fades, and shrinks, and grows past all enduring,*
>   *Rots, stinks, and dies, and is trod under feet.*

PEACHUM

You know, Polly, I am not against your toying and trifling with a customer in the way of business, or to get out a secret, or so. But if I find out that you have played the fool and are married, you jade you, I'll cut your throat, hussy. Now you know my mind.

SCENE 8

AIR VII. *Oh London is a fine town*

MRS. PEACHUM

(In a very great passion)

Our Polly is a sad slut! nor heeds what we have taught her.
I wonder any man alive will ever rear a daughter!
For she must have both hoods and gowns, and hoops to swell her
*   pride,*
With scarfs and stays, and gloves and lace; and she will have men
*   beside;*
And when she's dress'd with care and cost, all-tempting, fine and gay,
As men should serve a cowcumber, she flings herself away.
*   Our Polly is a sad slut, etc.*

You baggage! you hussy! you inconsiderate jade! had you been hanged, it would not have vexed me, for that might have been your misfortune; but to do such a mad thing by choice! The wench is married, husband.

PEACHUM

Married! The captain is a bold man, and will risk anything for money; to be sure he believes her a fortune. Do you think your mother and I should have lived comfortably so long together, if ever we had been married? Baggage!

MRS. PEACHUM

I knew she was always a proud slut; and now the wench hath played the fool and married, because forsooth she would do like the gentry.

421

Can you support the expense of a husband, hussy, in gaming, drinking and whoring? have you money enough to carry on the daily quarrels of man and wife about who shall squander most? There are not many husbands and wives who can bear the charges of plaguing one another in a handsome way. If you must be married, could you introduce nobody into our family but a highwayman? Why, thou foolish jade, thou wilt be as ill used, and as much neglected, as if thou hadst married a lord!

PEACHUM

Let not your anger, my dear, break through the rules of decency, for the captain looks upon himself in the military capacity, as a gentleman by his profession. Besides what he hath already, I know he is in a fair way of getting, or of dying; and both these ways, let me tell you, are most excellent chances for a wife—Tell me, hussy, are you ruined or no?

MRS. PEACHUM

With Polly's fortune, she might very well have gone off to a person of distinction. Yes, that you might, you pouting slut!

PEACHUM

What, is the wench dumb? Speak, or I'll make you plead by squeezing out an answer from you. Are you really bound wife to him or are you only upon liking?

(*Pinches her*)

POLLY

(*Screaming*)
Oh!

MRS. PEACHUM

How the mother is to be pitied who hath handsome daughters! Locks, bolts, bars, and lectures of morality are nothing to them: they break through them all. They have as much pleasure in cheating a father and mother as in cheating at cards.

PEACHUM

Why, Polly, I shall soon know if you are married, by Macheath's keeping from our house.

AIR VIII. *Grim king of the ghosts*

POLLY

Can love be controll'd by advice?
   Will Cupid our mothers obey?
Though my heart were as frozen as ice,
   At his flame 'twould have melted away.
When he kiss'd me so closely he press'd,
   'Twas so sweet that I must have comply'd:
    So I thought it both safest and best
   To marry, for fear you should chide.

MRS. PEACHUM

Then all the hopes of our family are gone for ever and ever!

PEACHUM

And Macheath may hang his father and mother-in-law, in hope to get into their daughter's fortune.

POLLY

I did not marry him (as 'tis the fashion) coolly and deliberately for honour or money. But, I love him.

MRS. PEACHUM

Love him! worse and worse! I thought the girl had been better bred. O husband, husband! her folly makes me mad! my head swims! I'm distracted! I can't support myself——oh!

(*Faints*)

PEACHUM

See, wench, to what a condition you have reduced your poor mother! a glass of cordial, this instant. How the poor woman takes it to heart!

(POLLY *goes out and returns with it*)
Ah, hussy, now this is the only comfort your mother has left!

POLLY

Give her another glass. Sir; my mama drinks double the quantity whenever she is out of order.—This, you see, fetches her.

MRS. PEACHUM

The girl shows such a readiness, and so much concern, that I could almost find in my heart to forgive her.

AIR IX. *O Jenny, O Jenny, where hast thou been?*

> *O Polly, you might have toy'd and kiss'd.*
> *By keeping men off, you keep them on.*

POLLY

> *But he so teas'd me,*
> *And he so pleas'd me,*
> *What I did, you must have done.*

MRS. PEACHUM

Not with a highwayman.—You sorry slut!

PEACHUM

A word with you, wife. 'Tis no new thing for a wench to take man without consent of parents. You know 'tis the frailty of woman, my dear.

MRS. PEACHUM

Yes, indeed, the sex is frail. But the first time a woman is frail, she should be somewhat nice, methinks, for then or never is the time to make her fortune. After that, she hath nothing to do but to guard herself from being found out, and she may do what she pleases.

PEACHUM

Make yourself a little easy; I have a thought shall soon set all matters again to rights. Why so melancholy, Polly? since what is done cannot be undone, we must all endeavour to make the best of it.

424

Well, Polly; as far as one woman can forgive another, I forgive
thee.——Your father is too fond of you, hussy.

POLLY

Then all my sorrows are at an end.

MRS. PEACHUM

A mighty likely speech, in troth, for a wench who is just married!

AIR X. *Thomas I cannot*

POLLY

I, like a ship in storms, was toss'd;
    Yet afraid to put in to land;
For seiz'd in the port the vessel's lost,
Whose treasure is contraband.
        The waves are laid,
        My duty's paid.
    Oh joy beyond expression!
        Thus, safe ashore,
        I ask no more,
    My all is in my possession.

PEACHUM

I hear customers in t'other room. Go, talk with 'em, Polly; but
come to us again, as soon as they are gone.—But, hark ye, child,
if 'tis the gentleman who was here yesterday about the repeating
watch, say, you believe we can't get intelligence of it till to-morrow.
For I lent it to Suky Straddle, to make a figure with it to-night at
a tavern in Drury Lane. If t'other gentleman calls for the silver-
hilted sword, you know Beetle-browed Jemmy hath it on, and he
doth not come from Tunbridge till Tuesday night so that it cannot
be had till then.

SCENE 9

PEACHUM

Dear wife, be a little pacified. Don't let your passion run away with your senses. Polly, I grant you, hath done a rash thing.

MRS. PEACHUM

If she had had only an intrigue with the fellow, why the very best families have excused and huddled up a frailty of that sort. 'Tis marriage, husband, that makes it a blemish.

PEACHUM

But money, wife, is the true fuller's earth for reputations: there is not a spot or a stain but what it can take out. A rich rogue now-a-days is fit company for any gentleman; and the world, my dear, hath not such a contempt for roguery as you imagine. I tell you, wife, I can make this match turn to our advantage.

MRS. PEACHUM

I am very sensible, husband, that Captain Macheath is worth money, but I am in doubt whether he hath not two or three wives already, and then if he should die in a session or two, Polly's dower would come into dispute.

PEACHUM

That, indeed, is a point which ought to be considered.

AIR XI. *A soldier and a sailor*

> *A fox may steal your hens, Sir,*
> *A whore your health and pence, Sir,*
> *Your daughter rob your chest, Sir,*
> *Your wife may steal your rest, Sir,*
>   *A thief your goods and plate.*
> *But this is all but picking;*
> *With rest, pence, chest, and chicken,*
> *It ever was decreed, Sir,*
> *If lawyer's hand is fee'd, Sir,*
>   *He steals your whole estate.*

The lawyers are bitter enemies to those in our way. They don't care that anybody should get a clandestine livelihood but themselves.

SCENE 10

POLLY

'Twas only Nimming Ned. He brought in a damask window-curtain, a hoop-petticoat, a pair of silver candlesticks, a periwig, and one silk stocking, from the fire that happened last night.

PEACHUM

There is not a fellow that is cleverer in his way, and saves more goods out of the fire than Ned. But now, Polly, to your affair; for matters must not be left as they are. You are married then, it seems?

POLLY

Yes, Sir.

PEACHUM

And how do you propose to live, child?

POLLY

Like other women, Sir, upon the industry of my husband.

MRS. PEACHUM

What, is the wench turned fool? A highwayman's wife, like a soldier's, hath as little of his pay as of his company.

PEACHUM

And had not you the common views of a gentlewoman in your marriage, Polly?

POLLY

I don't know what you mean, Sir.

427

PEACHUM

Of a jointure, and of being a widow.

POLLY

But I love him, Sir: how then could I have thoughts of parting with him?

PEACHUM

Parting with him! Why, that is the whole scheme and intention of all marriage articles. The comfortable estate of widowhood is the only hope that keeps up a wife's spirits. Where is the woman who would scruple to be a wife, if she had it in her power to be a widow whenever she pleased? If you have any views of this sort, Polly, I shall think the match not so very unreasonable.

POLLY

How I dread to hear your advice! Yet I must beg you to explain yourself.

PEACHUM

Secure what he hath got, have him peached the next sessions, and then at once you are made a rich widow.

POLLY

What, murder the man I love! The blood runs cold at my heart with the very thought of it.

PEACHUM

Fie, Polly! What hath murder to do in the affair? Since the thing sooner or later must happen, I dare say the captain himself would like that we should get the reward for his death sooner than a stranger. Why, Polly, the captain knows that as 'tis his employment to rob, so 'tis ours to take robbers; every man in his business. So that there is no malice in the case.

MRS. PEACHUM

Ay, husband, now you have nicked the matter. To have him peached is the only thing could ever make me forgive her.

AIR XII. *Now ponder well, ye parents dear*

POLLY

Oh, ponder well! be not severe;
So save a wretched wife!
For on the rope that hangs my dear
Depends poor Polly's life.

MRS. PEACHUM

But your duty to your parents, hussy, obliges you to hang him. What would many a wife give for such an opportunity!

POLLY

What is a jointure, what is widowhood to me? I know my heart. I cannot survive him.

AIR XIII. *Le printemps, rappelle aux armes*

The turtle thus with plaintive crying,
Her lover dying,
The turtle thus with plaintive crying,
Laments her dove.
Down she drops, quite spent with sighing,
Pair'd in death, as pair'd in love.

Thus, Sir, it will happen to your poor Polly.

MRS. PEACHUM

What, is the fool in love in earnest then? I hate thee for being particular. Why, wench, thou art a shame to thy very sex.

POLLY

But hear, me Mother.——If you ever loved——

MRS. PEACHUM

Those cursed play-books she reads have been her ruin. One word more, hussy, and I shall knock your brains out, if you have any.

PEACHUM

Keep out of the way, Polly, for fear of mischief, and consider of
what is proposed to you.

MRS. PEACHUM

Away, hussy. Hang your husband, and be dutiful.

SCENE 11

(POLLY *listening*)

MRS. PEACHUM

The thing, husband, must and shall be done. For the sake of intelligence we must take other measures, and have him peached the
next session without her consent. If she will not know her duty,
we know ours.

PEACHUM

But really, my dear, it grieves one's heart to take off a great man.
When I consider his personal bravery, his fine stratagem, how much
we have already got by him, and how much more we may get,
methinks I can't find in my heart to have a hand in his death. I
wish you could have made Polly undertake it.

MRS. PEACHUM

But in a case of necessity—our own lives are in danger.

PEACHUM

Then, indeed, we must comply with the customs of the world, and
make gratitude give way to interest. He shall be taken off.

MRS. PEACHUM

I'll undertake to manage Polly.

PEACHUM

And I'll prepare matters for the Old Bailey.

Now I'm a wretch, indeed.——Methinks I see him already in the cart, sweeter and more lovely than the nosegay in his hand!—I hear the crowd extolling his resolution and intrepidity!——What volleys of sighs are sent from the windows of Holborn, that so comely a youth should be brought to disgrace!——I see him at the tree! The whole circle are in tears!—even butchers weep!——Jack Ketch himself hesitates to perform his duty, and would be glad to lose his fee by a reprieve. What then will become of Polly?

The Beggar's Opera
by John Gay
ACT III, SCENES 7–11—LUCY, POLLY

SCENE 7

LUCY

Jealousy, rage, love and fear are at once tearing me to pieces. How I am weatherbeaten and shattered with distresses!

AIR XLVII.   *One evening, having lost my way*

> *I'm like a skiff on the ocean toss'd,*
> > *Now high, now low, with each billow borne,*
> *With her rudder broke, and her anchor lost,*
> > *Deserted and all forlorn.*
> *While thus I lie rolling and tossing all night,*
> *That Polly lies sporting on seas of delight!*
> > *Revenge, revenge, revenge,*
> *Shall appease my restless sprite.*

I have the ratsbane ready. I run no risk, for I can lay her death upon the gin, and so many die of that naturally that I shall never be called in question. But say I were to be hanged—I never could be hanged for anything that would give me greater comfort than the poisoning that slut.

SCENE 8

LUCY

Dear Madam, your servant. I hope you will pardon my passion, when I was so happy to see you last. I was so overrun with the spleen, that I was perfectly out of myself. And really, when one hath the spleen everything is to be excused by a friend.

AIR XLVIII. *Now Roger, I'll tell thee, because thou'rt my son*

> *When a wife's in her pout,*
> *(As she's sometimes, no doubt),*
> *The good husband, as meek as a lamb,*
> *Her vapours to still,*
> *First grants her her will,*
> *And the quieting draught is a dram.*
> *Poor man! And the quieting draught is a dram.*

—I wish all our quarrels might have so comfortable a reconciliation.

POLLY

I have no excuse for my own behaviour, Madam, but my misfortunes. And really, Madam, I suffer too upon your account.

LUCY

But, Miss Polly—in the way of friendship, will you give me leave to propose a glass of cordial to you?

POLLY

Strong waters are apt to give me the headache—I hope, Madam, you will excuse me.

LUCY

Not the greatest lady in the land could have better in her closet, for her own private drinking. You seem mighty low in spirits, my dear.

POLLY

I am sorry, Madam, my health will not allow me to accept of your offer. I should not have left you in the rude manner I did when we met last, Madam, had not my papa hauled me away so unexpectedly. I was indeed somewhat provoked, and perhaps might use some expressions that were disrespectful. But really, Madam, the captain treated me with so much contempt and cruelty that I deserved your pity, rather than your resentment.

LUCY

But since his escape no doubt all matters are made up again. Ah Polly! Polly! 'tis I am the unhappy wife, and he loves you as if you were only his mistress.

POLLY

Sure, Madam, you cannot think me so happy as to be the object of your jealousy. A man is always afraid of a woman who loves him too well—so that I must expect to be neglected and avoided.

LUCY

Then our cases, my dear Polly, are exactly alike. Both of us, indeed, have been too fond.

AIR XLIX.　*Oh, Bessy Bell*

POLLY

A curse attends that woman's love,
　Who always would be pleasing.

LUCY

The pertness of the billing dove,
　Like tickling, is but teasing.

POLLY

What then in love can woman do?

LUCY

If we grow fond they shun us.

And when we fly them, they pursue.

But leave us when they've won us.

Love is so very whimsical in both sexes, that it is impossible to be lasting. But my heart is particular, and contradicts my own observation.

But really, Mistress Lucy, by his last behaviour, I think I ought to envy you. When I was forced from him, he did not show the least tenderness. But perhaps he hath a heart not capable of it.

AIR L.   *Would fate to me Belinda give*

> *Among the men, coquets we find,*
> *Who court by turns all womankind;*
> *And we grant all their hearts desir'd,*
> *When they are flatter'd and admir'd.*

The coquets of both sexes are self-lovers, and that is a love no other whatever can disposses. I fear, my dear Lucy, our husband is one of those.

Away with these melancholy reflections; indeed, my dear Polly, we are both of us a cup too low. Let me prevail upon you to accept of my offer.

AIR LI.   *Come, sweet lass*

> *Come, sweet lass,*
> *Let's banish sorrow*
> *Till to-morrow;*
> *Come, sweet lass,*
> *Let's take a chirping glass.*
> *Wine can clear*
> *The vapours of despair;*
> *And make us light as air;*
> *Then drink, and banish care.*

I can't bear, child, to see you in such low spirits. And I must persuade you to what I know will do you good.

(*Aside*)

I shall now soon be even with the hypocritical strumpet.

(*Exit* LUCY)

SCENE 9

POLLY

All this wheedling of Lucy cannot be for nothing. At this time, too, when I know she hates me! The dissembling of a woman is always the forerunner of mischief. By pouring strong waters down my throat, she thinks to pump some secrets out of me. I'll be upon my guard, and won't taste a drop of her liquor, I'm resolved.

SCENE 10

LUCY

(*With strong waters*)

Come, Miss Polly.

POLLY

Indeed, child, you have given yourself trouble to no purpose. You must, my dear, excuse me.

LUCY

Really, Miss Polly, you are so squeamishly affected about taking a cup of strong waters as a lady before company. I vow, Polly, I shall take it monstrously ill if you refuse me. Brandy and men (though women love them never so well) are always taken by us with some reluctance—unless 'tis in private.

POLLY

I protest, Madam, it goes against me.—What do I see! Macheath again in custody! Now every glimmering of happiness is lost.

(*Drops the glass of liquor on the ground*)

LUCY
(*Aside*)

Since things are thus, I'm glad the wench hath escaped: for by this event 'tis plain she was not happy enough to deserve to be poisoned.

SCENE 11
AIR LII.   *The last time I went o'er the moor*

POLLY
Hither, dear husband, turn your eyes.

LUCY
Bestow one glance to cheer me.

POLLY
Think, with that look, thy Polly dies.

LUCY
Oh, shun me not—but hear me.

POLLY
'Tis Polly sues.

LUCY
——*'Tis Lucy speaks.*

POLLY
Is thus true love requited?

LUCY
My heart is bursting.

POLLY

——*Mine too breaks.*

LUCY

Must I

POLLY

——*Must I be slighted?*

A P P E N D I X

Scenes by Principal Cast Breakdown

Scenes for One Man and One Woman

Agamemnon (CLYTEMNESTRA, AGAMEMNON)

Electra (ORESTES, ELECTRA)

Antigone (CREON, ANTIGONE)

Medea (JASON, MEDEA)

Lysistrata (CINESIAS, MYRRHINE)

The First Part of King Henry the Sixth (SUFFOLK, MARGARET)

The Second Part of King Henry the Sixth (ELINOR, HUMPHREY)

The Life and Death of Richard the Third (LADY ANNE, RICHARD DUKE OF GLOUCESTER)

Romeo and Juliet (ROMEO, JULIET)

A Midsummer Night's Dream (OBERON, TITANIA, PUCK)

A Midsummer Night's Dream (DEMETRIUS, HELENA)

The Taming of the Shrew (PETRUCHIO, KATHERINE)

The First Part of King Henry the Fourth (HOTSPUR, LADY PERCY)

Much Ado About Nothing (BENEDICK, BEATRICE)

The Merry Wives of Windsor (MISTRESS QUICKLY, FALSTAFF)

Twelfth Night (VIOLA, CLOWN)

All's Well That Ends Well (HELENA, PAROLLES, PAGE)

Hamlet (HAMLET, OPHELIA)

Macbeth (LADY MACBETH, MACBETH)

Antony and Cleopatra (CLEOPATRA, ANTONY)

Pericles, Prince of Tyre (MARINA, PERICLES)

The Jew of Malta (BARABAS, ABIGAIL)

The Shoemaker's Holiday (HAMMON, JANE)

Philaster or Love Lies A-Bleeding (PHARAMOND, GALATEA)

Philaster or Love Lies A-Bleeding (PHARAMOND, MEGRA)

The Maid's Tragedy (EVADNE, MELANTIUS)

A Woman Killed With Kindness (MISTRESS FRANKFORD, WENDOLL, NICHOLAS)

Volpone (VOLPONE, LADY POLITIC WOULD-BE)

'Tis Pity She's a Whore (GIOVANNI, ANNABELLA)

The Duchess of Malfi (DUCHESS, ANTONIO)

The Changeling (BEATRICE, DE FLORES)

The Country Wife (PINCHWIFE, MARGERY PINCHWIFE)

The Relapse (LOVELESS, AMANDA)

The Rover (ANGELLICA, WILLMORE, MORETTA)

The Rover (WILLMORE, HELLENA)

Venice Preserved (JAFFEIR, BELVIDERA)

Scenes for Two Women

Electra (CLYTEMNESTRA, ELECTRA)

Electra (CHRYSOTHEMIS, ELECTRA)

Hippolytus (NURSE, PHAEDRA)

The Two Gentlemen of Verona (JULIA, SILVIA)

Romeo and Juliet (JULIET, NURSE)

Twelfth Night (VIOLA, OLIVIA, MARIA)

All's Well That Ends Well (COUNTESS, HELENA)

Othello (EMILIA, DESDEMONA)

The Relapse (BERINTHIA, AMANDA)

The Beaux' Stratagem (MRS. SULLEN, DORINDA)

All for Love (OCTAVIA, CLEOPATRA)

The Beggar's Opera (LUCY, POLLY)

Scenes for Two Men

Antigone (HAIMON, CREON)

The Bacchae (PENTHEUS, DIONYSUS)

The Bacchae (DIONYSUS, PENTHEUS)

Hippolytus (THESEUS, HIPPOLYTUS)

The Merchant of Venice (ANTONIO, BASSIANO)

The Merry Wives of Windsor (FORD, FALSTAFF)

Julius Caesar (CASSIUS, BRUTUS)

Othello (IAGO, OTHELLO)

King Lear (GLOUCESTER, EDGAR)

The Winter's Tale (LEONTES, CAMILLO)

Everyman (DEATH, EVERYMAN)

Doctor Faustus (FAUSTUS, MEPHISTOPHILIS)

Venice Preserved (JAFFEIR, PIERRE)

Scenes for More Than Two Principal Actors

The Two Gentlemen of Verona (SPEED, VALENTINE, SILVIA)

As You Like It (CLOWN, AUDREY, JAQUES)

Troilus and Cressida (PANDARUS, TROILUS, CRESSIDA)

Hamlet (HAMLET, HORATIO, ROSENKRANTZ, GUILDENSTERN, POLONIUS)

Hamlet (POLONIUS, HAMLET, QUEEN, GHOST)

The Tempest (PROSPERO, MIRANDA, CALIBAN)

The Revenger's Tragedy (CASTIZA, VENDICE, GRATIANA)

The Rover (WILLMORE, ANGELLICA, HELLENA, MORETTA, SEBASTIAN)

The Beggar's Opera (POLLY, PEACHUM, MRS.PEACHUM)

A BIBLIOGRAPHY
OF CLASSICAL
RESOURCES
FOR ACTORS

Auchincloss, Louis. *Motiveless Malignity*. Boston: Houghton Mifflin Company, 1969.

Baldry, H.C. *The Greek Tragic Theatre*. New York: W. W. Norton & Co. Inc., 1971

Beckerman, Bernard. *Shakespeare at the Globe, 1599–1609*. New York: Macmillan, 1962.

Brown, John Russell, and Bernard Harris, eds. *Jacobean Theatre*. New York: Capricorn Books, 1967.

——————*Restoration Theatre*. New York: Capricorn Books, 1967.

Brubaker, E. S. *Shakespeare Aloud*. Published by the author, and available by mail from Professor Brubaker, 645 N. President Avenue, Lancaster, PA 17603.

Burgess, Anthony. *Nothing Like the Sun*. New York: W. W. Norton, 1964.

——————*Shakespeare*. New York: Alfred A. Knopf, 1970.

Dean, Leonard F., ed. *Shakespeare: Modern Essays in Criticism*. New York: Oxford University Press, 1967.

Dyer, T. Thistleton. *Folk-Lore of Shakespeare*. New York: Dover Books.

Ellis-Fermor, Una. *The Jacobean Drama: An Interpretation*. New York: Random House, 1961.

Else, Gerald F. *The Origin and Early Form of Greek Tragedy*. New York: W. W. Norton, 1972.

Fiedler, Leslie A. *The Stranger in Shakespeare*. Granada, 1974.

Flatter, Richard. *Shakespeare's Producing Hand: A Study of His Marks of Expression to Be Found in the First Folio*. New York: W. W. Norton, 1948.

French, Marilyn. *Shakespeare's Division of Experience*. New York: Summit Books, 1981.

Frye, Northrop. *Fools of Time: Studies in Shakespearean Tragedy*. University of Toronto Press, 1967.

Hill, Errol. *Shakespeare in Sable: A History of Black Shakespearean Actors*. Amherst: University of Massachusetts Press, 1984.

Hinman, Charleton, preparer. *The Norton Facsimile: The First Folio of Shakespeare*. New York: W. W. Norton.

Knight, G. Wilson. *The Wheel of Fire*. New York: Oxford University Press, 1930.

Kott, Jan. *The Bottom Translation: Marlowe and Shakespeare and the Carnival Tradition*. Evanston, IL: Northwestern University Press, 1987.

——————*The Eating of the Gods: An Interpretation of Greek Tragedy*. New York: Random House, 1973.

——————*Shakespeare Our Contemporary*. Garden City, NY: Doubleday, 1964.

Lenz, Carolyn Ruth Swift, Gayle Greene, and Carol Thomas Neely, eds. *The Woman's Part: Feminist Criticism of Shakespeare*. Urbana: University of Illinois Press, 1980.

Onions, C. T. *A Shakespeare Glossary*. New York: Oxford University Press, 1953.

MacInnes, Colin. *Three Years to Play*. London: MacGibbon & Kee, 1970.

Morgan, Fidelis. *The Female Wits: Women Playwrights of the Restoration*. Virago Press, 1981.

Nicholl, Charles. *The Chemical Theatre*. Routledge & Kegan Paul, 1980.

Odell, George C. D. *Shakespeare from Betterton to Irving*. 2 vols. New York: Dover Books, 1966.

Redfield, William. *Letters from an Actor*. New York: Limelight Books, 1984.

Rowse, A. L. *What Shakespeare Read and Thought*. New York: Coward McCann & Geoghegan, 1981.

Schmidt, Alexander. *Shakespeare Lexicon*. 2 vols. New York: Benjamin Blom, 1968.

Terry, Ellen. *Four Lectures on Shakespeare*. New York: Benjamin Blom, 1969.

Wilson, John Dover, ed. *Life in Shakespeare's England*. New York: Penguin Books, 1968.

FOR THE BEST IN PAPERBACKS, LOOK FOR THE

In every corner of the world, on every subject under the sun, Penguin represents quality and variety—the very best in publishing today.

For complete information about books available from Penguin—including Pelicans, Puffins, Peregrines, and Penguin Classics—and how to order them, write to us at the appropriate address below. Please note that for copyright reasons the selection of books varies from country to country.

In the United Kingdom: For a complete list of books available from Penguin in the U.K., please write to *Dept E.P., Penguin Books Ltd, Harmondsworth, Middlesex, UB7 0DA*.

In the United States: For a complete list of books available from Penguin in the U.S., please write to *Dept BA, Penguin*, Box 120, Bergenfield, New Jersey 07621-0120.

In Canada: For a complete list of books available from Penguin in Canada, please write to *Penguin Books Canada Ltd, 10 Alcorn Avenue, Suite 300, Toronto, Ontario, Canada M4V 3B2*.

In Australia: For a complete list of books available from Penguin in Australia, please write to the *Marketing Department, Penguin Books Ltd, P.O. Box 257, Ringwood, Victoria 3134*.

In New Zealand: For a complete list of books available from Penguin in New Zealand, please write to the *Marketing Department, Penguin Books (NZ) Ltd, Private Bag, Takapuna, Auckland 9*.

In India: For a complete list of books available from Penguin, please write to *Penguin Overseas Ltd, 706 Eros Apartments, 56 Nehru Place, New Delhi, 110019*.

In Holland: For a complete list of books available from Penguin in Holland, please write to *Penguin Books Nederland B.V., Postbus 195, NL-1380AD Weesp, Netherlands*.

In Germany: For a complete list of books available from Penguin, please write to *Penguin Books Ltd, Friedrichstrasse 10-12, D-6000 Frankfurt Main I, Federal Republic of Germany*.

In Spain: For a complete list of books available from Penguin in Spain, please write to *Longman, Penguin España, Calle San Nicolas 15, E-28013 Madrid, Spain*.

In Japan: For a complete list of books available from Penguin in Japan, please write to *Longman Penguin Japan Co Ltd, Yamaguchi Building, 2-12-9 Kanda Jimbocho, Chiyoda-Ku, Tokyo 101, Japan*.

FOR THE BEST DRAMA, LOOK FOR THE

☐ **THE CRUCIBLE**
Arthur Miller

Arthur Miller's classic dramatization of the Salem witch hunt, *The Crucible* is a chilling tale of mass hysteria, fear, and the power of suggestion.

152 pages   ISBN: 0-14-048138-9

☐ **PYGMALION**
Bernard Shaw

Shaw's portrayal of a Cockney flower girl's metamorphosis into a lady is not only a delightful fantasy but also an intriguing commentary on social class, money, spiritual freedom, and women's independence.

152 pages   ISBN: 0-14-045022-X

☐ **EQUUS**
Peter Shaffer

A deranged youth blinds six horses with a spike. A psychiatrist tries to help him. But what is help? *Equus* is a brilliant examination of the decay of modern man.

112 pages   ISBN: 0-14-048185-0

☐ **THE ACTOR'S BOOK OF CONTEMPORARY STAGE MONOLOGUES**
Edited by Nina Shengold

This unique anthology provides a wealth of materials for actors and acting students, and a wonderful overview of the best of recent plays for anyone interested in the theater.

356 pages   ISBN: 0-14-009649-3